DEBRA'S LIFETIME STORY WITH AMAZING BLESSINGS

Personal Reflections in Praising GOD

UNLEASHING DIVINE POWER THROUGH SCRIPTURE

DEBRA ROBINSON

CITI OF
BOOKS

CITIOFBOOKS, INC.
3736 Eubank NE Suite A1
Albuquerque, NM 87111-3579
www.citiofbooks.com
Hotline: 1 (877) 389-2759
Fax: 1 (505) 930-7244

Ordering Information:
Quantity sales. Special discounts are available on quantity purchases by corporations, associations, and others. For details, contact the publisher at the address above.

Printed in the United States of America.

ISBN-13:	Softcover	979-1-96095-293-6
	Hardcover	979-8-89391-291-3
	eBook	979-1-96095-294-3

Library of Congress Control Number: 2023914691

If you would like to send Debra an email, you can write her at:

abcsforgod@gmail.com

You may also call her and leave a message:

1-402-573-LOVE   402-573-5683

Visit the author's website :

www.authordebrarobinson.com

Contents

Lord of the universe, how I wish I had words to fashion beautiful prayers to praise You! But, alas, I cannot find these words. So, listen to me, O God, as I recite the letters of the alphabet. You know what I think and how I feel. Take these letters of the alphabet and form the words that express the yearning and the love for You in my heart.

TRANSLATIONS

(KJ21) Twenty-First Century King James Version

(ASV) American Standard Version

(AMP) Amplified Bible

(AMPC) Amplified Bible, Classic Edition

(BRG) Blue, Red, and Gold Letter Edition

(CSB) Christian Standard Bible

(CEB) Common English Bible

(CEV) Contemporary English Version

(DLNT) Disciples' Literal New Testament

(ERV) Easy-to-Read Version

(EHV) Evangelical Heritage Version

(ESV) English Standard Version

(GW) God's Word Translation

(GNT) Good News Translation

(HCSB) Holman Christian Standard Bible

(ICB) International Children's Bible

(ISV) International Standard Version

(KJV) King James Version

(TLB) Living Bible

(MEV) Modern English Version

(NABRE) New American Bible

(Revised Edition) (NASB) New American Standard Bible

(NASB 1995) New American Standard Bible 1995

(NCB) New Catholic Bible

(NCV) New Century Version

(NET) New English Translation

(NIRV) New International Reader's Version

(NIV) New International Version

(NIVUK) New International Version (UK)

(NKJV) New King James Version

(NLV) New Life Version

(NLT) New Living Translation

(NRSVA) New Revised Standard Version, Anglicized

(RSV) Revised Standard Version

(TPT) The Passion Translation

(TLV) Tree of Life Version

(VOICE) The Voice

(WEB) World English Bible

ACKNOWLEDGEMENTS

First and foremost, I would like to thank my close friend Sandra Hillman, whom I call Sandy. Our close friendship has lasted almost fifty years. In 2005, we started doing Bible studies, and as time went on, we read books together over the phone. It has been seventeen years now, and God has blessed us so much. We have both grown in the Lord together. I give my heartfelt thanks to her for helping me put this book together. She has prayed and sent her insights throughout the book. She has been an encouragement to my heart. I love you, Sandy, and I thank God for your blessed friendship!

My Lord and Savior, Jesus Christ—the love and inspiration behind my words along with God, the Father, who has given me the motivation to pursue this book and the Holy Spirit who lives inside me and speaks to me daily. I want more of You and less of me.

My husband, Dennis, for putting up with me working on this book for countless hours.

Two friends from Crosspoint Bible Church have been there for me during this time for prayer and encouragement. I thank God for Marge Kirkpatrick and Kathy Isgro. They have led my Monday night women's Bible study group for years and have prayed faithfully for me in many things and for many years. Marge, thank you for telling me about John 3:16 and for putting my name in that verse:

> God so loved the world that He gave His only begotten
> Son that whosoever believeth in Him should not perish,
> but have everlasting life. (John 3:16 KJV)

God so loved [Debra] that He gave His only begotten
Son that whosoever believeth in Him should not perish,
but have everlasting life.

This has been such a blessing for me. I have used it for the prison
ministry many times.

Another amazing prayer warrior is Stella Boyd, a sister in Christ who
came into my life several years ago. She is involved in a ladies' Bible
study group and has asked all of them to pray for me as time has gone
on. She and I have blessed each other tremendously. She has helped my
little online Avon business thrive, and it has helped cover the expenses
of publishing this book. I praise God for all these wonderful people
who God has placed in my life at the time He wanted me to meet
them, including those listed in the introduction.

INTRODUCTION

Falling in love with God can miraculously transform your life in a million ways.

I have learned the first commandment:

> You shall love the Lord your God with all your heart, and with all your soul, and with all your mind, and with all your strength. This is the first commandment. (Mark 12:30 ESV)

Do you know that our obedience demonstrates our love?

> The person who has My commandments and obeys them is the one who loves Me. The one who loves Me will be loved by my Father, and I will love him and will reveal Myself to him. (John 14:21 TPT)

To love and obey God is to praise and worship Him daily on an ongoing basis.

My lifetime verse is Romans 8:28 (NET):

> And we know that all things work together for good to those who love God, and to those who are called according to His purpose.

You will find out how God has worked so many things out for my good, and He has given me a purpose in life. This is so amazing!

My friend Sandy and I started reading a book on worshipping God, and it was touching and convicting that God gave us an idea. We were asked to come up with a new way to worship God daily. We found another verse that really hit us:

> "I am the A and the Z, the Beginning and the Ending of all things," says God, who is the Lord, the All Powerful One who is, and was, and is coming again! (Revelation 1:8 TPT)

We thought about this and realized how neat it would be to take the alphabet and find verses to praise and worship God using the alphabet's letters. The alphabet has 26 letters, and we were thinking that months are around 30 days so this would be amazing to take one letter a day and reach the end of the alphabet every month. You can also read one full letter every two weeks, and it will take you a year to complete the alphabet. Twenty-six letters (in the full alphabet) times two weeks constitutes a whole year of 52 weeks. It is really perfect to find a plan where you can give God love and obedience in your life every day.

We took the Father, the Son, and the Holy Spirit and searched each one in the scriptures. We shared so much about how magnificent they are. As we started searching each letter for God's attributes, Jesus coming into the world to save us, and how the Holy Spirit lives inside us, we continued to receive more blessings from God. He began to reveal more and more to us than we could ever imagine.

God gave me a dream one night, and I really wanted to share this amazing story with the world. When you praise and worship God daily, you know that you are being obedient to God. He has commanded us to love Him and His Word. I found another verse that God gave me right away after this dream. God is absolutely amazing.

> Be enthusiastic to serve the Lord, keeping your passion toward Him boiling hot! Radiate with the glow of the Holy Spirit and let Him fill you with excitement as you serve Him. (Romans 12:11 TPT)

This is exactly how I felt, and this verse says it in a perfect way. I am very excited and enthusiastic about serving God through searching the scriptures, and I want to share this with the world. It is a glorious life to praise and worship God daily.

I hope everyone will want to be touched by God and learn to know Him better. You definitely will be blessed by God in a beautiful way by letting these scripture verses touch your heart daily. Jesus is right there with you. He will wrap His arms around you because He loves you. In following God daily, His Spirit will also touch us on the inside and guide us in the direction we should go:

> Shout praises to the Lord! The Lord blesses everyone who worships Him and gladly obeys his teachings. (Psalm 112:1 CEV)

TO MY LOVING AUNT JUNE

Tribute spoken at her funeral service on October 22, 2022

June Esther Wolfe Little, Memphis, Tennessee
June 2, 1930–October 14, 2022

Aunt June is my wonderful and special aunt. I thank God for her life so many times and in so many ways. As a little girl, in my growing up years, I really wasn't surrounded by love, and as I grew into my teens, I had many suicidal thoughts. Aunt June was really the only support I received from an adult relative while growing up. She led me to the Lord and prayed earnestly that I wouldn't commit suicide. We talked for hours, and she always listened to me and never turned me away.

Aunt June enjoyed our visits when we went there on summer vacations, and she welcomed us with open arms. She was such an understanding person. She told me that I was loved by God and was a person of value. I became a much more positive person because of her love and her prayers in my life. Last week, God revealed to me that my faith has increased, and I am now strong enough to handle life with her memories. God used her to keep me from committing suicide and to believe in Jesus. She was the one who showed me love. She shared many Bible passages with me. I have never grieved over losing a loved one, but this time will be different. I still feel her touch in my heart.

I would like to end by telling you of two miracles that happened as Aunt June left this earth. I have asked God many times why I was born into this family, and God revealed to me that it is because of Aunt June.

I wouldn't have known her or been related to her if I hadn't been born into this family. I am so thankful to God for this answer to my prayer after almost seventy years of wondering. God is truly amazing!

This book is on the verge of being published. Because of her death and the timing of everything, God told me to dedicate this book to her and include this tribute with our picture together. God has worked it all out for good; again, this is another example of how Romans 8:28 has worked in my life.

I love you, Aunt June, and you will be missed!

June 2021

CHAPTER 1

MY LIFETIME STORY

This story is about Debra who is the author of this book. This is a true story about her life. The family names have been changed.

God has totally helped me overcome this hypercritical and condemning life while growing up. I never thought it was possible to get past my insecurity, lack of confidence, and shame but with God all things are possible. I grew up in a world of very little love which was heartbreaking and sad and I don't really recall any good memories with my immediate family. Praise God that I have been transformed and my life isn't hopeless anymore. Let's begin ...

Gilbert and Willa are Debra's parents. They met one day at a Valentine's dance in Memphis, TN, and really enjoyed each other's company. As time went on, they were married June, 1950. Gilbert applied at an Architecture Engineer College in Kansas City, MO. He was accepted so they moved to Kansas City and rented an apartment. July, 1951, they gave birth to their first child, a daughter, and they named her Debra.

Gilbert continued his school for a year. During the summer of 1952, Willa and Debra moved back to Memphis, TN for five to six months and lived with Willa's folks, Teddy and Mae. These were Debra's grandparents. Gilbert looked for a job and landed one in

Barnwell, South Carolina working for Dupont Engineering at the Savannah River Project. This work involved the Atomic Energy and it was a very private position.

Gilbert found a place for the family to live in a trailer court in South Carolina. Willa and Debra left the home in Memphis, TN sometime in the fall and arrived at this new trailer. The baby, Debra, had epilepsy seizures while staying there. She would walk and then would stop in her tracks and just stare into space never blinking an eye. Willa took Debra to the doctor to have her checked out and fortunately, the problem grew out of this little girl.

On June 30, 1953, Gilbert and Willa had their second child which was another daughter. They named her Gwen. Debra and Gwen were sisters and they used to play together by crawling all over the floor. Gilbert and Willa moved back to Memphis, TN, when Willa became pregnant again due to another job change per Gilbert. They rented an unfurnished house in Memphis, TN and signed a 6-month lease. The family sat on the floor and ate their meals. They did have beds, but there were no tables, no chairs, and no couch. This went on for six months during Willa's pregnancy.

On July 12, 1954, Gilbert and Willa had their third child which was another daughter. They named her Lois. Now there were three little girls which were sisters. After Lois turned a month old, Gilbert landed a job in Russellville, Arkansas. He worked for Southwestern Bell Telephone Company in the Architecture Field of building the "Dial Telephone Buildings." They stayed in Russellville for a year and then the job ended at this location.

Gilbert was transferred to West Memphis, Arkansas, and then Debra was four years old. She had to go to kindergarten a year early because she had experienced different problems. One day she ran away from her mother on the street and she took off so fast as a streak of lightning. Willa ran down the street after her and could hardly keep up with this four-year-old. This little girl crossed streets as fast as she could and didn't even think about cars driving down the streets. Debra ran through red lights and Willa had to buy a dog leash to put on her when she would take her for a walk down the city streets. This little girl would just take off and run. Willa did not drive; she took many street cars to different places and even took her three daughters at times.

Debra started in kindergarten and Mrs. Massey was her teacher. Willa had a talk with this teacher and asked her if she thought her daughter was mentally retarded. Willa thought for sure this was possible because her daughter just wouldn't talk. When Debra turned five, she spent another year in the kindergarten class with the same teacher due to her speech problems.

Willa became pregnant again in the spring of 1956. During the summer, Gilbert and Willa moved back to Memphis, Tennessee, and stayed there for around a year.

On December 23, 1956, their fourth child was born. They were thrilled to death to have their first son. They named him Gilbert, Jr., after the father. This little boy was the apple of their eye and they could not take their eyes off of him. Now, Debra was six, Gwen was four and Lois was three.

During the summer of 1957, Gilbert and Willa moved to Rogers, Arkansas. September, 1957, Debra started first grade in Mrs. White's class. One day, Mrs. White called Willa and asked her a question, "Is your daughter, Debra, a genius? Every time I tell your daughter a new word in her reading class, she remembers it forever … I never have to repeat it over one time! You need to take her to the University of Arkansas to get tested." Willa thought hard about that and did not do anything about it.

Gilbert Sr. had gotten an infection in his finger and he became hospitalized and almost lost his whole finger. At the end of the school year, Debra was very sad and just cried and cried. Debra got the address to Mrs. White and they corresponded with each other every Christmas until Debra was eighteen years old and at that time, Mrs. White had died.

Late summer, 1958, this family of six moved to Newport, Arkansas, where the Southwestern Bell work continued. Debra started second grade and met a nice friend named Carmen. They were there for three months and Gilbert and Willa had to leave again during the winter of 1958. Carmen was a real sweetheart and told Debra, "Please don't leave, I will miss you a lot." They both cried hard on their last day in December, 1958.

The last half of second grade was spent at Glasgow Village which is a suburb of St. Louis, Missouri. The teacher there insisted on using "Debra Lee" as her name. Debra hated that middle name with a passion and kids would make fun of her. The students would tease her and make her feel really bad. Debra would come home and cry and her mother and father would just let it go on. She rode a bus and got bullied by a little boy. She did complete second grade there.

The summer of 1959, Debra was eight years old and ready to attend third grade. Gilbert and Willa now moved to Afton, Missouri, and lived on Winthrop Court. Debra still remembers her telephone number from back there. That summer Debra wanted a bicycle for her eighth birthday and she cried and cried but did not receive one. Many neighborhood kids had bikes. Her third-grade teacher was Mrs. Cordes. Debra met a friend in that class named Meredith whom she just loved and when the school year ended, they wanted to stay buddies. The family had to move again and Debra cried and cried. Debra thought at that point in her life, "if I would someday have a little girl, I would name her Meredith after this sweet friend." Now, Debra does live on Meredith Avenue which is very special and she thinks about that friend.

Sometime in the summer of 1960, this family of six, moved to Fenton, Missouri where Gilbert started a job for the Leo A Daly Company as an Architecture Engineer. He purchased a little house for his family out there in the country. Debra attended Meramec School in the fourth, fifth, and sixth grades. When she first went to the school, lots of kids already had good friendships and she cried many nights because she just knew nobody liked her. She went outside at recess to jump rope and the kids told her not to play with them because she didn't do very good. They would yell at her and make fun of her in softball because she struck out a lot. She would come in and put her head down on her desk and just cry. Debra remembers this continued to happen all through the rest of grade school.

Next, it was the summer of 1963, Debra turned twelve years old and was ready to start Junior High School. She had to walk about two blocks down a rocky road by herself and catch a bus to attend Fox Junior High in Arnold, Missouri. She remembers this was the year that President John F Kennedy was shot. Debra did not know any of the students at this school. Seventh grade was becoming more difficult as time went on due to the many cliques that were already formed. Debra didn't have any nice clothes to wear to school. All the clothes were handmade or were from second hand stores such as the Goodwill. She wore strange looking saddle oxford shoes. Many kids at school would laugh and make fun of her. At this house in Fenton, the neighbors next door wanted the girls to come over and play ball out in their yard. Gilbert and Willa told her, "Absolutely not, you will not go into anyone else's yard!" She remembers it was the Martin's and Reiger's who lived next door.

The summer of 1964, Gilbert was transferred to Omaha, Nebraska. Debra became a thirteen-year-old in July, 1964. Debra attended Nathan Hale Junior High starting in the eighth grade. She walked almost five miles to and from school every day. In those days, girls had to wear dresses and carry books in their arms. Gilbert and Willa bought a house on Mormon Bridge Road which is in the Raven Oaks area. Debra had to attend a new school in a new state and she looked very strange. She had very few clothes and they were not in style. Debra really thought nobody cared in her family.

Debra didn't like to bathe. She was accused of wasting too much water and she didn't like to fight over the tub. There was only one bathtub in the house. She was also afraid of what her family was going to say about her after she left the room. She became extremely paranoid during her teen years and as time went on, she carried this personality trait wherever she went. So, she kind of stuck around so they wouldn't have much of a chance to say mean things about her.

Sometimes the family sat down and watched television together. Debra was not accepted well in the family setting. The siblings told her to not sit by them because she was ugly and to get out of there. She was a recluse and went upstairs to her bedroom and spent many nights by herself reading fairy tales, and children's magazines. Debra had a Siamese cat who was there for her every night. We called this cat, Kitty, and she would sit with Debra on her bed continuously. Debra became closer to God during these times and would ask God why she was even born because nobody loved her. During the prayers, she shed lots of tears.

Debra's sisters, Gwen and Lois, stuck together and would upset Debra so much. They told her that her eyes looked sad all the time because they were "glassy." They took care of their little brother and told her to get out. Their dad, Gilbert, was working out of town and Willa was busy in the kitchen cooking meals and canning. She sewed many dresses alike for her daughters. She washed clothes in an old antique washing machine, putting them through the ringer and then hanging them out on a clothesline to dry. She stood over an ironing board and starched Gilbert's shirts and spent a lot of time pressing them. In those days, there was no such thing as "permanent press" shirts as we know of today.

Willa spent hours yelling at her children daily. When Gilbert came home from working, he told Debra that she was the big girl and she didn't need her birthday celebrated personally. The four girls in the family had birthdays that were only two weeks apart; therefore, Debra had very few "individual" birthday celebrations.

Willa became involved in the Methodist Church as a Sunday School Teacher and also became a Girl Scout leader. Debra was in her mother's Sunday School class and also in the Girl Scout troop where Willa was the leader. Debra would get yelled at in these places and this was very disruptive for those meeting together. Willa embarrassed Debra at these events. Debra stood in the corner of the room in front of everyone.

Willa told Debra to shut up and when they returned home Willa took her hand and smacked Debra across the face. Willa continued doing this many times clear up to the time Debra was a senior in high school.

When Debra got settled in the eighth grade, she wanted to have money for a hot lunch. Most of her life she ate peanut butter and jelly sandwiches because the family was poor and there weren't enough funds for the children to have hot lunches. Sometimes Debra would take change laying around to have money for lunches. The children did not receive any spending money or an allowance.

When eighth grade started at Nathan Hale, Debra had a math teacher named Mr. Knebel. One day, Mr. Knebel and Willa spoke on the telephone and they developed a plan to check out how Debra got along with other kids. The next day in math class, Mr. Knebel told his class to have everyone take out a sheet of paper with a pen and answer a question.

This is the question, "If you were going to plan a party next weekend and you could invite everyone in the class except for one girl and one boy, who wouldn't you invite? Write down two names." Gilbert and Willa invited Mr. Knebel over to their home for dinner one Sunday afternoon to discuss the responses to this question. Debra's name was on every sheet of paper. That made her feel terrible. This young teen's feeling of rejection grew even worse. She didn't even want to go to school. Debra continued to live a life of facing rejection everywhere she went and felt hated.

September, 1965, ninth grade began at Nathan Hale. The School Principal was Mr. Blue. He contacted Debra's mother, Willa, and told her, "Since your daughter, Debra, can't get along with other students, we are going to place her in all special education classes in the ninth grade so she can gain better social skills and not have to concentrate so hard on her studies. Debra started these classes and several teachers asked her, "Why are you in my class? You're too smart for this class." Debra knew what was going on and felt even worse.

Tenth grade came in September, 1966, and Debra thought she would go to Benson High School where all the Nathan Hale students went. This summer, the family moved again to Florence Blvd in a different part of the city. So, Debra started attending North High and went there through the remainder of her high school years. Debra felt depressed and scared of rejection and again, didn't know anyone.

The family went to a Methodist Church and Debra talked to a pastor at the church. She was sixteen and he told her to never drink or smoke because her nerves were shot and she would turn into a basket case. He didn't teach her about our Lord, Jesus, at the time so she had never heard the gospel of getting saved. Debra did pray to God many nights and continued crying herself to sleep.

One day while going to North High, I came home and my mother was having a bad day and screamed at me and said, "I wish I never had you. You are not worth the salt that goes into your bones. I wish you were a thousand miles away." Both Gilbert and Willa continued to call Debra "stupid" most of her life. Debra was told frequently that she couldn't do anything right the first time she tried.

Gilbert would put his high school daughters to bed and Debra shared a bedroom with her two sisters and there were two double beds in this large room. Her two sisters would always sleep together because they "liked each other better." There wasn't any support or encouragement to have the three girls treat each other with love and have the girls take turns to share beds with each other. Gilbert tied the girls down in their beds at night. The two younger girls were able to help each other untie the knots but Debra couldn't get the knots out and had a really hard time. She was scared to go to the bathroom because she didn't want her dad to catch her out of bed after he tied her down because he better not dare catch his girls up. Most of the time if there was something that someone did all would say, "Debra did it," because they could stand up for each other and lie their way out and they knew their big sister would get into trouble. Debra got beat with many belts across her back and rear end and sometimes on the legs. Many days and nights of constant yelling and rages went on for months and years.

One time the other five members of Debra's family all went to have a family picture taken and Debra was not included in the family picture. Debra felt unwanted in the family.

Debra spent countless nights crying hard and speaking to God about why He even created her. She suffered so much physical abuse when things were blamed on her. She became very bitter, angry, and negative.

Many counselors tried to help her and listen to her, but nothing really worked. She felt like she could never do anything right, and she could not please anyone—no matter how hard she tried.

Gilbert worked out of town for years, he came home on weekends and would leave again. Willa didn't drive so we all went to school the best way we could and mostly by walking for miles.

The hurts and rejection built up and nobody was ever told to say they were sorry because they never thought they had done anything wrong. When Debra was sixteen, she tried to commit suicide by plugging a cord into an electrical outlet and wanted to electrocute herself. In these days Debra would dream about dying and not wanting to go on living. She even looked into paying someone to kill her, but then she backed out because she knew that was against God. Debra begged God to intervene in her life and to help her die because there was no love in her world. She had no purpose in life to go on.

Willa told Debra when she was a little older that she was a "good child" because she didn't disobey her. Debra came home on time on the few dates she went out. Debra didn't lie about what she was out doing, she spoke the truth. Debra didn't date anyone till she was fifteen years and the boy would come in the house and meet the parents first before they would even go out. Debra showed her parents lots of respect.

Willa didn't want Debra to ever have her belly button showing at all in a swimsuit. She could not put on a bikini, and never owned one. Her swimsuits were all in one piece and even to this day, she has respected that.

Debra has never put a cigarette to her mouth, no taste of beer and doesn't know anything about marijuana, weed, etc. During this era in high school, many kids used heroin, acid, LSD, etc. and Debra never had any desire to try anything. Many kids called her weird and very different. Debra also never had sex outside of marriage at that time because she was taught that it was a sin against God.

Willa told Debra not to drive because she wasn't smart enough. So, Debra didn't learn to drive till she was twenty-eight years old after she was married for seven years.

As Debra became eighteen years old, she wanted out of the house as soon as possible. She up and left home and did the best she could to find a cheap place to live. She lived in a big house and rented a bedroom for $8.00 a week and would take buses to college and to work.

September, 1969, Debra attended Omaha University which is now called The University of Nebraska at Omaha. A nice girl at one of Debra's classes started talking to her and invited her to a youth conference at Grace University. Debra happily went because it was wonderful that someone asked her to do something with them. During that weekend, there was an altar call to go up to the front and receive Jesus as your Savior and they said that Jesus died for all and He paid the price for everyone's sins and how much He loved her. To be told that she was loved by someone was fantastic. She did ask Christ into her life. But, as life went on, Debra continued to struggle with the fact that God loved her and she never really believed it because she knew she wasn't worthy of love at all in her eyes.

As you can see, Debra's family moved eighteen times in sixteen years, which included five different states. She would make a friend, and then they would up and move again.

During that first year in college, Debra met a janitor whom she liked and they developed a friendship and dated awhile. Willa and Gilbert did not like him. This guy's name was Ron and he was a kind man and accepted Debra well. He didn't smoke or drink and didn't do much swearing. Those were the main features Debra looked for in a man. At twenty-one years old, Debra and Ron were married in May, 1973.

Another situation that was unique was that after Debra and Ron got married, she stayed a virgin for seventeen months! She was not a person who could relax, very frigid and afraid. She was never comfortable being close to a man in that respect; her parents showed very little love physically. They didn't kiss, hug or hardly touch each other in front of all of us kids.

Debra did get hired at Northwestern Bell in September, 1974. Ron and Debra attended the Salvation Army church after they were married. They didn't feel much support there and as time went on changed over to Pleasantview Berean Church.

They went to Chandler Acres Baptist church for a while and again, the same thing happened. They did not feel any close friendships and felt alone. So, they left the church.

Debra and Ron had three daughters, Angela in April, 1978; Michelle (who was named Rhonda at birth) in November, 1982; and Stephanie in January, 1986, during their life together. One day, Debra passed out and went to a specialist who tested her for many things. He couldn't find a lot wrong and he told her it's death or divorce because the stress was really bad in Debra's life with this man. He was not a responsible man and it wasn't a good marriage after all. Debra took care of her babies the best she knew how on her own. She continued to work full time and went from getting diaper bags ready to lunches, suppers, laundry, going to the store and the whole thing for years. It remained that way. There was no family member from either Debra's or Ron's immediate family who ever came over to help them or to be kind to them. What little the families saw them; there was only condemnation, trash talk with disparaging remarks.

As time went on, Debra decided on divorce because things did not get any better. The stress was more than she could handle. Debra went to an attorney and filed for divorce in June, 1988. We had a family friend whom everyone loved. His name was Dennis. He was jolly and got along with the girls well and they spoke of wanting a different daddy. I knew that I began having feelings for him and couldn't get him off my mind for months. Debra went to bed and couldn't sleep because she would fantasize about Dennis and couldn't quit thinking about him. Dennis and Debra hit it off really well and they took their time in a friendship and became closer and closer. They became married February, 1990. They felt that God put them together. Dennis was Catholic and they were faithful in taking the girls to mass at church.

One interesting point here is that Dennis never showed a sign of anger or getting upset about anything in all these years of friendship.

11

Debra just loved seeing a man "opposite" of her father with these qualities. Unfortunately, as time went on, Dennis would explode and blow up and he became a harsh father to the girls.

During the years between 1992 and 1999, Debra had no contact with her parents for seven years. Debra just couldn't tolerate the critical and judgmental remarks, or the mental and emotional abuse any longer. Debra had been a victim all of her life and had never fought back by standing up to her parents due to fear.

When Debra was 48 years old in June 1999, she had a colonoscopy done and the doctor discovered colon cancer. Debra had chemo therapy for twenty-eight weeks and she was off work for nine months and the telephone company held her job for her. The doctor said this was due to much stress in her life.

May of 2003, Debra was back at the doctor's and received a diagnosis that she had uterine cancer and had to have a hysterectomy. Debra was very thankful that the cancer had been discovered early and they were able to get rid of all of it both times.

Debra has continued to have annual physicals and has stayed cancer-free. Several times the doctors have asked Debra what changed in her life and she expressed turning to God and that is what has kept the cancer from reappearing and God has helped her to get rid of the stress.

Debra and Dennis are still married and most of the marriage has been good. We did struggle as parents at times when the girls grew up, but we have stayed together through thick and thin. God has touched our lives in so many different ways.

We have gone to see a psychologist and have taken several kinds of tests. The doctor said that we both were born with different degrees on the Autism Spectrum. We were also diagnosed with Asperger's Syndrome at different levels. When God revealed this truth to us, it has helped us understand ourselves and each other so much better. We have also seen the light that God created us and we learned that God doesn't make mistakes and we are all unique. Debra went to

Codependents Anonymous for about four years and that was also enlightening and helpful. She depends on God now more than any human being.

My parents are both deceased, and they had a house with lots of belongings. In their will, our brother received everything. Mom and Dad's three daughters didn't receive anything; we felt like our parents had disowned us. We were hurt, but again, Debra is thankful that God helped her to forgive and not obsess about this. She was finally able to overcome that and not allow it to wreck her life. God has given Debra retirement income, by working for a company which gave benefits and a good pension. Debra is grateful that God helped her with her skills.

Debra has often asked God how she could be born into such a mean and unloving family. It took her years to finally get over her past, and to move on with her life. God has succeeded in leading her to believe He loves her. The Holy Spirit lives in us and I thank God every day for His love and blessings.

Now I can't wait to share my fantastic blessings with you all . . . .

CHAPTER 2

AMAZING STORIES AND BLESSINGS FROM GOD

ROMANS 8:28

And we know that all things work together for good to those who love God, and to those who are called according to His purpose. (NET)

God's miracles have transformed my life. To start with, my dear friend and sister in Christ, Sandy, is reading books with me, and going through Study Guides that apply to the books. This is all on the phone and we are committed every week. God teaches us so much and He reveals many things to us. This has been going on for eighteen years! God knew how much I needed a guide to help my spiritual growth.

In 2020, God revealed a miraculous revelation. During the summer of 1964, I had just turned thirteen years old. That was the summer that we moved from Fenton, Missouri to Omaha, Nebraska. I walked to school by myself about four miles in dresses. In looking back, I realized that God had protected me every day. This was out in the country and the street was surrounded by a large forest. Thank You God for your protection!

That year, starting eighth grade, I had to sign up for classes. The principal asked if I would like to learn how to type. I decided to go ahead and try. Somehow, God guided me and told me that typing would be good to learn. Only by God's help, I was the top student in that class, and I received an honors certificate. Now I see God's hand in this because this is what I did for forty-three years in my data entry career, and I have always loved that kind of work. God has been with me in all my jobs, while using these wonderful skills. I have typed many bible studies, bible verses, and bible lessons.

Since retirement, I learned about serving in the Prison Ministry which is going on seven years now. This ministry has required me to study and learn various Bible passages and to be able to explain God's truth in the

best way possible that it could be understood. I have typed up the research which has continued to help the prisoners learn about Jesus and His love. God led me in this direction for years—without me even knowing it.

Hallelujah! Thank You, Father God!

In 1970, when I was nineteen years old, I went to a university and met Ann Schmadeke. She invited me to a weekend retreat at Grace College Institute. I went with her and learned that Jesus died for my sins and loved me. He gave me forgiveness, and they spoke about eternal life. The only way to go to heaven is to accept Christ in your heart as your personal Savior and to ask Jesus to forgive your sins. I went forward that night, repented of my sins, and asked Jesus to come live in my heart. I knew then that I was on my way to heaven.

Another blessing was that I used to bowl in leagues for years, that was how I met Dennis at Ames Bowl. I was the league secretary and typed up many bowling sheets with the rules and loved doing that kind of work. The manager of this bowling alley asked me one day if I would like to bowl on TV. "Sure, that would be fun." The bowling show was called "Strike it Lucky" and it was held at Leisure Lanes. During the fall of 1984, I showed up there to be on television. The crew asked me to do a couple trick shots. The first one was: "Throw one ball and leave the headpin by itself." Tom Kelley, Sr. owns a pro shop and he was standing right there. I asked him how this was done and he advised me to move a couple boards left of my target. I threw the ball and it happened; the headpin stood there by itself! I WON A CAR; it was a brand-new Ford Escort! That was God who through that ball. Such a memory for me from forty years ago!

The other shot was to hit one pin and you had to tell them what pin that was going to be. I said I would hit the ten-pin by itself. That also happened, I cut the ten-pin right off perfectly and won a pair of new bowling shoes. Unbelievable miracles that day.

I also learned several years later that I have a touch of Asperger's syndrome; but, because of God, I have been able to overcome the problems that it previously caused in my life. Once you realize that God created you and that everyone is unique, He can help you accept who you are. Everything becomes easier to deal with.

I was shown Psalm 139 and I have included a part of it. It has really touched my heart and I'm convicted that God knew what He was doing in His creation.

> For you created my inmost being; you knit me together in my mother's womb. I praise you because I am fearfully and wonderfully made, your works are wonderful. I know that full well. My frame was not hidden from you when I was made in the secret place, when I was woven together in the depths of the earth. Your eyes saw my unformed body; all the days ordained for me were written in your book before one of them came to be. How precious to me are your thoughts, God! How vast is the sum of them! Were I to count them they would outnumber the grains of sand when I awake, I am still with you. (Psalm 139:13–18 NIV)

Lying awake at night, I talked to God about this and realized that we are all fearfully and wonderfully made. The more you repeat these verses, the more you come to believe them. Then you can thank God over and over again. It shows that God did create me and He does love me. It took more than fifty-eight years for this to finally sink in.

I got married in 1973, and we went to Berean Fundamental church. I started to learn more about Jesus. In 1979, when I was in my early twenties, a friend, Ellen Thompson, went out of her way to disciple me and we spent a lot of time together. Ellen said many prayers to help me see the light, but I could not grasp how God could love me. I continued feeling hopeless and unworthy. Ellen invited me to her house to do Bible studies. My husband and I eventually left the church there because we felt little support. Ellen and I continued to keep in touch at Christmas by sending cards and letters, but we no longer saw each other.

Between 1991 and 1998, I didn't speak to my family. They were extremely mean to my husband and I. They continued to speak in a pessimistic and negative way about us to our children. I had to leave the family alone, and I had to handle all the holidays without them. I actually called them when I was hospitalized and diagnosed with cancer. My children were sent to foster care during those years, and it was a very difficult situation without any help.

At work, I met a fantastic Christian woman. Anne Christian helped me so much by daily listening to me and she continued to pray for me. She was another friend from God who tried to disciple me and kept telling me how much God loves me. She retired from the phone company in 1998, and we lost touch with each other. I was very thankful for her during those years.

Another beautiful miracle from God happened in 2014. A new coworker, Benita Greene, came to our department. As we were talking, the subject of God came up. She said she attended Salem Baptist Church, which was the church that Anne Christian had gone to. I told Benita about my sweet friend who went to that church.

Benita said, "She's one of my best friends!"

I was ecstatic and delighted. For several years, the three of us would get together and go out for dinner. Having Anne back in my life was a beautiful blessing. I told her how God had improved my life and brought me to a different church. Getting back in touch with Anne after sixteen years was an amazing blessing. Anne came over to our house many times for special occasions and she spent time with me on the phone; one of the most caring people I had ever known. Again, this is another close friend who recently died in the spring of 2023. God has helped me to deal with the losses of these significant people during my lifetime.

In the spring of 1998, at forty-seven years old, I came down with colon cancer. My job allowed me to take off nine months, and during that time, I received twenty-eight weeks of chemotherapy. I was hospitalized and they performed surgery on me by removing a large portion of my colon. God blessed me again because I was in a company that provided pay and benefits. It was wonderful that the Lord provided.

In the summer of 2002, I came down with cancer of the uterus. I was off work for six weeks and felt fortunate again that God provided our family with pay and benefits. I had to go to the hospital and have a hysterectomy.

Our oldest daughter, Angela, disowned us for about four years between 2003 - 2007. She had gotten angry, and we didn't even know where she was. She wrote us an ugly letter about how horrible we were. I was very angry and bitter for about five years.

While dealing with this cancer, God would speak to me during many nights about three o'clock in the morning. I prayed earnestly and learned that I would have to somehow forgive her. God revealed many scriptures to me about forgiveness. I wrote Angela a long letter, which God led me to do. God revealed many truths to me for days.

I shared the following verse with her:

> Admit your faults to one another and pray for each other so that you may be healed. The earnest prayer of a righteous man has great power and wonderful results. (James 5:16 TLB)

As God gave me spiritual eyes to see the truth, I wrote her many things that I realized were done wrong. God would speak to me during the night, then I would get out of bed, open the Bible, and write things down. It came together in a beautiful and miraculous way.

The Lord's Prayer says, "Forgive us our trespasses, as we forgive those who trespassed against us." I heard a sermon about how God will not forgive you if you don't forgive others. That was very convicting. I really believe that if I hadn't gotten cancer, this amazing forgiveness experience would have never happened. Again, such a miracle! My cancer turned into a major blessing.

I was speaking to my mother at this time and one day I went to my parents' house. Mom knew where Angela was and had her telephone #. Mom called Angela on her phone and she allowed me to leave a message for her. There was a cousin of Angela's that I heard was dying and wanted to let her know. Thankfully, mom allowed this and Angela told her grandma that she would contact me Sunday afternoon. So, Angela did call and we had a wonderful conversation.

This was the first time in my life that I learned what real forgiveness is all about. The two cancers were all about the stress in my life that I was living with. The amazing thing is that with God's help, our relationship is better now than it ever has been. We have had many long talks, and she is very close to the Lord. She married a wonderful man of God, and she is teaching her three children to believe in Jesus. She is living overseas, which is sometimes hard for me, but God has become my priority in life. I know that God has Angela and her family where He wants them. I know now that God meets all of our needs, and He takes care of us. This is phenomenal!

You won't believe what happened in September, 2009! Dennis and I bought a house and moved to northwest Omaha in March, 1995. One day at work at Qwest Communications, I became friends with a lady named Gwen. She listened quite well to my problems. She asked me, "Do you have a church family that you receive love and support from?" I said, No, not really." She said, "Deb, you really need a support group that will love on you." That never entered my mind while attending a Catholic church for almost 20 years. I started praying to God for direction in that area; because I felt that she was right. God had placed her in my department at work to speak this truth to me.

The next day I took a telephone directory and looked up churches in my area. I found three churches to contact, so I placed three calls.

Evangelical Bible Church (EBC) was only 5 blocks from our house and this was the only telephone number that someone answered the phone. I called them and they were very kind. They welcomed me to come visit with open arms and even offered to meet me at the door so I would be more comfortable. I went there the first Sunday in October, 2009! What beautiful miracles happened!

The only way to get to church was to drive our pickup truck, which was not easy to drive. This was my first time driving it in a long time. After church that day, I went out to the parking lot, and noticed that the truck was surrounded by other vehicles and I could hardly get out. While looking around, a couple whom I did not recognize came out of church. I went running out to them for some help. I told them that I would struggle to get my truck out of the parking space. The woman rolled down her window and offered to help. She said, "Give my husband your keys, and he can help you. He used to drive trucks." I handed him the keys. While he was moving the truck, the woman got out of her vehicle and came up to me and said, "I don't believe we have met before. My name is Ellen Thompson." I screamed, "Ellen Thompson!" It was the same Ellen I had met at Pleasant-view Berean back in the early 1970's! She did not really look familiar, but I recognized her voice, and we threw our arms around each other. God wanted us to get back together. What a miracle! I will never forget this wonderful story.

In 1973, I was blessed to land a job at Northwestern Bell Telephone Company. I was hired rather quickly because of my typing ability, which God gets all the credit for. It was His favor and blessing in my life. I worked there for forty-three years and didn't retire until I turned sixty-five years in July, 2016. When first getting hired at Northwestern

Bell, a kind lady named Linda Ewert befriended me and I knew that she loved Jesus. She would have nice and caring conversations with me at work.

Also, when going to EBC that first Sunday, I thought of Linda Ewert and had an inkling that this might be where she attended church. I was introduced to Pastor Don and I asked him right away if the Ewert's attended there. He said, "Yes, they are the greeters today, and they are right there." I hear a familiar voice and there was Linda with her nametag on. Linda said, "Do I know you?" I said, "Yes, but you may not remember me." I told her that I was Debbie Gladman that she had worked with back at the telephone company in the early 1970's. She smiled and said, "Oh, yes." It was really great seeing her, I felt like I was seeing an angel. We talked a little and then hugged. We have since had many wonderful talks and she has been a big help to me in several things and such a blessing.

It was wonderful to see Linda and Ellen that day, and I really believe God planned the whole day. This was one of the most dynamic miracles of my life. I still attend this church and they have now changed the name to Crosspoint Bible Church. Just a few months ago, Ellen passed away and I am so thankful for the memories that are in my heart. Thank you, Lord, that You have helped me to become stronger, and it's easier to deal with Ellen's death. I know she is with you God walking down those golden paths of glory.

I joined a woman's Sunday school class the next week. I have been a hoarder most of my life and have a hard time throwing anything away. The Sunday school teacher asked us to go around the room and share our prayer requests. Arla Vohnout shared that she was looking for houses to clean, and I was so touched. After class, I tracked her down and told her about my problems with housecleaning and holding onto everything. She said she would come over and help me.

In a couple months, she came over and talked to me, but she didn't want any money at that time. For ten years, she has come over several times when I've needed help. God bless her heart! Arla and I are in the Monday night women's Bible study, and we are good friends.

While in that Sunday School class, I met a lady by the name of Marge Kirkpatrick. She was good friends with Ellen and they offered to be my mentors, so we met for a private Sunday School with just the three of us. They did that with me for almost two years. There was such love shown and blessings experienced again while we grew closer to God in our faith journey. They both listened and said many prayers.

Kathy Isgro was another person who reached out to me. She is the leader of the First Place Group on Monday night. It is a women's Bible Study group; we read a book and learn about our health and losing weight. Kathy invited me and I started attending on Monday nights in 2014. There are three sessions a year; winter, summer, and fall. Each session is ten– twelve weeks long. We do prayer requests and people really show they care about you. Ever since I started going, I have never stopped. Many friendships have developed and people encourage each other. I am so happy to feel comfortable in that group and to honestly share my blessings and prayer requests.

During the spring of 2008, I needed to get a second job due to money issues. I began a job at PRC which is called Professional Research Consultants. I would make phone calls and type up patient surveys, healthcare surveys and other medical surveys over the phone. One day at work there, I "just happened" to sit next to Terri Christensen. I would get depressed at times, and she was a compassionate person and wanted to know if she could help me feel better. I learned that she was a believer in Jesus, and we got along very well. One night, she called out of the blue and told me about a class on "Rejection" that she had been invited to.

I screamed, "Rejection?"

"Yes", she said. That caught my attention in a major way and I wanted to know all about it. This was another "Godsend."

It was held at a church that wasn't far from our house. I started attending this class as soon as possible. I went there for the next five years! They taught all about the Bible and how Satan can attack you. There was lots of information on spiritual warfare and I learned so much about Satan that I had never known. So much of it is in your head and the way your thoughts work. God changed my heart tremendously, and I became a new person in Christ. Ever since, I have been filled with positive thoughts instead of negative thoughts; it has been such a miracle! Terri lives in Colorado now and we still keep in touch. Every Thanksgiving I send her a Thanksgiving card and thank her for that phone call one day that changed my life. God used her in an amazing way.

One night at PRC, our group was instructed to go work at another building, and I met another beautiful person. Carol Parrish and I "just happened" to sit next to each other. I know that it was God leading me in that direction. We became good friends. We would go out to eat together after work on Friday nights and sometimes on Saturdays we met for lunch. As time went on, we even did a Bible study over the phone. She was such a blessing. Our husbands met and they got along really well. We as two couples both own a camper and we have traditions now of going on weekend camping trips during the spring and summer. We have spent a day together over the Christmas holiday season for close to ten years. We have a nice meal together, share gifts and play cards which we love to do.

About three years ago, I met Lolita at our church. She was such a loving and compassionate person. We had some fun times together, and had lots of great talks. She was someone who we could both relate to each other on the many things we shared. She knew what rejection was all about and she knew all about the Lord and how much He loves us. Lolita told me one day that she had sold Avon for thirty-five years and felt she was getting too old to continue. I thought that might be fun to look into it. So, one day, she wrote out her list of customers and I rode along with her on her route and took notes. I love their products so I signed up to be an Avon representative. It has helped me to have a little extra income during retirement and I have purchased clothes, jewelry, and gifts at a discount. Lolita's health started to fail and she recently passed away in the summer of 2023.

One lady on our Avon route is Stella Boyd. The Lord brought Stella and I together in a divine appointment. We have shared tremendous things about the Lord together. Stella has helped me with my Avon business a lot. She has referred people to the products and also has encouraged me in many things. This book that I have written here was prayed for by Stella and her Bible Study group. She is extremely supportive and is one of the most devout Christian women I know.

I am so thankful to God for the people He has placed in my life. Thank You, Jesus!

A

Almighty

> Who is and who was and who is to come, the Almighty.
> (Revelation 1:8 CSB)

Alpha and the Omega

> I am the Alpha and the Omega, the First and the Last,
> the Beginning and the End. (Revelation 22:13 ASV)

Amen

> Saying, Amen: Blessing, and glory, and wisdom, and
> thanksgiving, and honor, and power, and might, be unto
> our God for ever and ever. Amen. (Revelation 7:12 ASV)

> Write the following to the messenger of the congregation
> in Laodicea, for these are the words of the Amen, the
> faithful and true witness, the ruler of God's creation.
> (Revelation 3:14 TPT)

Anybody Does Sin, An Advocate, Atoning Sacrifice

> My dear children, I write this to you so that you will not
> sin. But if Anybody Does Sin, we have An Advocate with
> the Father—Jesus Christ, the Righteous One. He is the
> Atoning Sacrifice for our sins, and not only for ours but
> also for the sins of the whole world. (1 John 2:1–2 NIV)

Author and Perfecter of Faith

> Fixing our eyes on Jesus, the Author and Perfecter of Faith, who for the joy set before Him endured the cross, despising the shame, and has sat down at the right hand of the throne of God. (Hebrews 12:2 NASB 1995)

All Authority

> Jesus said, "All Authority in heaven and on earth has been given to Me." (Matthew 28:18 NASB)

Agreeing

> Can two people walk together without Agreeing on the direction? (Amos 3:3 NLT)

Appreciate

> If you correct someone with constructive criticism, in the end he will Appreciate it more than flattery. (Proverbs 28:23 TPT)

Safe Anchor, All

> This hope is a Safe Anchor for our souls. It will never move. This hope goes into the Holiest Place of All behind the curtain (hope) of heaven. (Hebrews 6:19 NLV)

Great and Awesome God

> O Lord, God of heaven, the Great and Awesome God who keeps His covenant of unfailing love with those who love Him and obey His commands. (Nehemiah 1:5 NLT)

Alive for Evermore

> And the living one; I died, and behold I am Alive for Evermore, and I have the keys of Death and Hades. (Revelation 1:18 ESV)

Another King, Jesus

> And Jason has welcomed them, and they all act contrary to the decrees of Caesar, saying that there is Another King, Jesus. (Acts 17:7 NASB)

Angel of the Lord

> He suffered with them in all their troubles, and the Angel of The Lord saved them. In His loving-kindness He paid the price and made them free. He lifted them up and carried them all the days of long ago. (Isaiah 63:9 NLV)

God Has Set Apart

> Therefore, dear brothers whom God Has Set Apart for Himself—you who are chosen for heaven—I want you to think now about this Jesus who is God's Messenger and the High Priest of our faith. (Hebrews 3:1 TLB)

Strong Right Arm of the Lord

> Songs of joy and victory are sung in the camp of the godly. The Strong Right Arm of The Lord has done glorious things! (Psalm 118:15 NLT)

All Glory, Alone Is God, Authority, Amen

> All Glory to Him who Alone Is God, our Savior through Jesus Christ our Lord. All glory, majesty, power, and Authority are His before all time, and in the present, and beyond all time! Amen. (Jude 1:25 NLT)

Angels, Authorities, Accept His Authority

> Now Christ has gone to heaven. He is seated in the place of honor next to God, and all the Angels and Authorities and powers Accept His Authority. (1 Peter 3:22 NLT)

All-Knowing

> O Lord, you have examined my heart and know everything about me. You know when I sit down or stand up. You know my thoughts even when I'm far away. You see me when I travel and when I rest at home. You know everything I do. You know what I am going to say even before I say it, Lord. You go before me and follow me. You place your hand of blessing on my head. Such knowledge is too wonderful for me, too great for me to understand! (Psalm 139:1–6 NLT)

Whole Armor of God, Stand Against Devil

> Put on the Whole Armor of God, that ye may be able to Stand Against the wiles of the Devil. (Ephesians 6:11 KJ21)

Answers My Prayers

> The Lord has chosen everyone who is faithful to be His very own, and He Answers My Prayers. (Psalm 4:3 CEV)

Awe-Inspiring

> How Awe-Inspiring are your deeds, O God! How great your power! No wonder your enemies surrender! (Psalm 66:3 TLB)

All the People, Awe

> Then Samuel called on the Lord, and that same day the Lord sent thunder and rain. So, All the People stood in Awe of the Lord and of Samuel. (1 Samuel 12:18 NIVUK)

All Must Stand in Awe

> God is powerful; All Must Stand in Awe of Him; He keeps His heavenly kingdom in peace. (Job 25:2 GNT)

The whole world stands in Awe of the great things that You have done. Your deeds bring shouts of joy from one end of the earth to the other. (Psalm 65:8 GNT)

Works Are Awesome

Come and see God's deeds; His Works for human beings Are Awesome. (Psalm 66:5 CEB)

All Nations, Great and Awesome

Let All the Nations praise Your name. Your name is Great and Awesome. Your name is Holy. (Psalm 99:3 ERV)

Holy and Awesome

He sent redemption to His people; He has commanded His covenant forever. Holy And Awesome is His name! (Psalm 111:9 ESV)

All Things Are Possible

Jesus looked at them and said, "With man this is impossible, but with God All Things Are Possible." (Matthew 19:26 ESV)

Anointed by God, Went Around Doing Good, Healing All

And you no doubt know that Jesus of Nazareth was Anointed by God with the Holy Spirit and with power, and He Went Around Doing Good and Healing All who were possessed by demons, for God was with Him. (Acts 10:38 TLB)

Armor of Light

The night is far gone; the day of His return will soon be here. So quit the evil deeds of darkness and put on the Armor of Light, as we who live in the daylight should! (Romans 13:12 AMP)

Appointed Time

> Therefore, don't judge anything before the Appointed Time. Wait until the Lord comes. He will also bring to light what is hidden in the dark and reveal people's motives. Then each person will receive praise from God. (1 Corinthians 4:5 GW)

Anyone, an Advocate

> My dear children, I am writing this to you so that you will not sin. But if Anyone does sin, we have an Advocate who pleads our case before the Father. He is Jesus Christ, the one who is truly righteous. (1 John 2:1 NLT)

Christ Is All and Is in All

> Here there is no Gentile or Jew, circumcised or uncircumcised, barbarian, Scythian, slave or free, but Christ is All, and is in All. (Colossians 3:11 NIV)

Approached, Ancient One

> As my vision continued that night, I saw someone like a son of man coming with the clouds of heaven. He Approached the Ancient One and was led into His presence. (Daniel 7:13 NLT)

Ancient One, Arrived

> Until the Ancient One—the Most High—came and judged in favor of His holy people. Then the time Arrived for the holy people to take over the kingdom. (Daniel 7:22 NLT)

Abba, Father, Suffering Away

> "Abba, Father," He cried out, "everything is possible for You. Please take this cup of Suffering Away from me. Yet I want Your will to be done, not mine." (Mark 14:36 NLT)

Abba, Father

> And because we are His children, God has sent the Spirit of His Son into our hearts, prompting us to call out, "Abba, Father." (Galatians 4:6 NLT)

Adopted You, Abba, Father

> So, you have not received a spirit that makes you fearful slaves. Instead, you received God's Spirit when He Adopted You as His own children. Now we call Him, "Abba, Father." (Romans 8:15 NLT)

Abide in Me

> Abide In Me, and I in you. As the branch cannot bear fruit by itself, unless it Abides in the vine, neither can you, unless you Abide in Me. (John 15:4 ESV)

Above All, Loving One Another

> Above All, keep Loving One Another earnestly, since love covers a multitude of sins. (1 Peter 4:8 ESV)

Wisdom from Above, Always Pure, Any

> But the Wisdom from Above is Always Pure, filled with peace, considerate and teachable. It is filled with love and never displays prejudice or hypocrisy in Any form. (James 3:17 TPT)

Stay Alert, Around

> Stay Alert! Watch out for your great enemy, the devil. He prowls Around like a roaring lion, looking for someone to devour. (1 Peter 5:8 NLT)

Alert, Appointed Time

> Be on guard and stay constantly Alert [and pray]; for you do not know when the Appointed Time will come. (Mark 13:33 AMP)

31

At All Times, Stay Alert, All Believers

> Pray in the Spirit At All Times and on every occasion. Stay Alert and be persistent in your prayers for All Believers everywhere. (Ephesians 6:18 NLT)

An Alert Mind

> Devote yourselves to prayer with An Alert Mind and a thankful heart. (Colossians 4:2 NLT)

Am Alive Forever and Ever

> I Am the living one. I died, but look—I Am Alive Forever and Ever! And I hold the keys of death and the grave! (Revelation 1:18 NLT)

Angel, Now Alive

> Write this letter to the Angel of the church in Smyrna. This is the message from the one who is the First and the Last, who was dead but is Now Alive. (Revelation 2:8 NLT)

Word of God Alive and Powerful

> For the Word of God is Alive and Powerful. It is sharper than the sharpest two-edged sword, cutting between soul and spirit, between joint and marrow. It exposes our innermost thoughts and desires. (Hebrews 4:12 NLT)

Alive

> Christ died for us so that, whether we are dead or Alive when He returns, we can live with Him forever. (1 Thessalonians 5:10 NLT)

> But God is my helper. The Lord keeps me Alive! (Psalm 54:4 NLT)

Alive with Christ, Forgave All Sins

You were dead because of your sins and because your sinful nature was not yet cut away. Then God made you Alive with Christ, for He Forgave All our Sins. (Colossians 2:13 NLT)

And Alive to God through Christ Jesus

So, you also should consider yourselves to be dead to the power of sin And Alive to God through Christ Jesus. (Romans 6:11 NLT)

Alive, After Three Days

They told Him, "Sir, we remember what that deceiver once said while He was still Alive: 'After Three Days I will rise from the dead.'" (Matthew 27:63 NLT)

Armies of Angels

Yes, praise the Lord, you Armies of Angels who serve Him and do His will! (Psalm 103:21 NLT)

All His Angels, All the Armies

Praise Him, All His Angels! Praise Him, All the Armies of heaven! (Psalm 148:2 NLT)

Angel, Heaven's Armies

Then the Angel said to me, "Shout this message for all to hear: 'This is what the Lord of Heaven's Armies says: My love for Jerusalem and Mount Zion is passionate and strong.'" (Zechariah 1:14 NLT)

Await

And Await the mercy of our Lord Jesus Christ, who will bring you eternal life. In this way, you will keep yourselves safe in God's love. (Jude 1:21 NLT)

Awaits, All, His Appearing

> And now the prize Awaits me—the crown of righteousness, which the Lord, the righteous Judge, will give me on the day of His return. And the prize is not just for me but for All who eagerly look forward to His Appearing. (2 Timothy 4:8 NLT)

Are Honest and Good, Awaits

> Look At those who Are Honest and Good, for a wonderful future Awaits those who love peace. (Psalm 37:37 NLT)

Great Wonder and Awe, Amazing Things

> Everyone was gripped with Great Wonder and Awe, And they praised God, exclaiming, "We have seen Amazing things today!" (Luke 5:26 NLT)

All About You, Awe, Your Amazing Works

> I have heard All About You, Lord. I am filled with Awe by Your Amazing Works. (Habakkuk 3:2a NLT)

Among, About, Amazing, Above All

> Sing A new song to the Lord! Let the whole earth sing to the Lord! Sing to the Lord; praise His name. Each day proclaim the good news that He saves. Publish His glorious deeds Among the nations. Tell everyone About the Amazing things He does. Great is the Lord! He is most worthy of praise! He is to be feared Above All gods. (Psalm 96:1–4 NLT)

Amazing Deeds, All Who Delight

> How Amazing are the Deeds of the Lord! All Who Delight in Him should ponder them. (Psalm 111:2 NLT)

Amazing Things

> Yes, the Lord has done Amazing Things for us! What joy! (Psalm 126:3 NLT)

Assurance

> And He has given us His Spirit within us so that we can have the Assurance that He lives in us and that we live in Him. (1 John 4:13 TPT)

Assured

> I've written this letter to you who believe in the name of the Son of God so that you will be Assured and know without a doubt that you have eternal life. (1 John 5:13 TPT)

You Created All Things

> You are worthy, O Lord our God, to receive glory and honor and power. For You Created All Things, and they exist because You created what you pleased. (Revelation 4:11 NLT)

All Glory to God, Able, At Work, To Accomplish, Ask

> Now All Glory to God, who is Able, through His mighty power At Work within us, To Accomplish infinitely more than we might Ask or think. (Ephesians 3:20 NLT)

Provide All You Need, Always

> And God will generously Provide All You Need. Then you will Always have everything you need and plenty left over to share with others. (2 Corinthians 9:8 NLT)

God Is Able

> He was fully convinced that God Is Able to do whatever He promises. (Romans 4:21 NLT)

Abound in Love for One Another, for All

> And may the Lord make you increase and Abound in Love For One Another and For All, as we do for you. (1 Thessalonians 3:12 ESV)

All Joy and Peace, Abound in Hope

> May the God of hope fill you with All Joy and Peace in believing, so that by the power of the Holy Spirit you may Abound in Hope. (Romans 15:13 ESV)

<u>PRAYERS</u> (Using A Words)

You are *amazing*. You give us blessed *assurance* because You have *all authority* and are *able* to guide us and guard us from the evil one. You are my *Advisor*, and I *adore* You. You are my *All in All*. You are *all-knowing, all-sufficient,* and *all powerful.* You are the *Author* of my faith. We praise and thank You for healing us, setting us free from *anxiety*, and *activating* our faith. We are in *awe* because You are always present! We will *abide* in You forever! *Abba*, Father, we lift our *arms* high *above* to the sky and praise Your *almighty* name. We *appreciate* You, God, for *all* You have done! We are extremely grateful that You *adopted* us as Your children. Father God, thank You for protecting us with the full *Armor of God!*

In Your *almighty* name, Jesus, we pray.

Amen.

B

Bread of Life, Believes in Me

> Then Jesus declared, "I am the Bread of Life. Whoever comes to me will never go hungry, and whoever Believes in Me will never be thirsty." (John 6:35 NIV)

Behold, Beloved Son

> And Behold, a voice from heaven said, "This is my Beloved Son, with whom I am well pleased." (Matthew 3:17 ESV)

Burden Bearer

> Cast thy Burden upon the Lord, and He shall sustain thee: He shall never suffer the righteous to be moved. (Psalm 55:22 KJ21)

Beginning and the End

> I am the A and the Z, the Beginning and the End, the First and Last. (Revelation 22:13 TLB)

Made Everything Beautiful, Beginning to the End

> He has made everything Beautiful in its time. Moreover, He has set eternity in their heart—yet without the possibility that humankind can ever discover the work that God has done from the Beginning to The End. (Ecclesiastes 3:11 TLV)

Believe

> If you Believe, you will receive whatever you ask for in prayer. (Matthew 21:22 GNT)

Blessings Will Come

> All these Blessings Will Come on you and accompany you if you obey the Lord Your God. (Deuteronomy 28:2 NIV)

Beatitudes

> Blessed are the poor in spirit, those who mourn, the meek, those who hunger and thirst for righteousness, the merciful, pure in heart, the peacemakers and those who are persecuted because of righteousness for theirs is the kingdom of heaven. (Matthew 5:3–10 RSV)

Blood of Jesus Christ

> But if we walk in the light, as He is in the light, we have fellowship one with another, and the Blood of Jesus Christ His Son cleanseth us from all sin. (1 John 1:7 KJ21)

Sacrificed His Blood

> Christ Sacrificed His life's Blood to set us free, which means that our sins are now forgiven. Christ did this because God was so kind to us. God has great wisdom and understanding. (Ephesians 1:7–8 CEV)

Before All Else Began

> He was Before All Else Began and it is His power that holds everything together. (Colossians 1:17 TLB)

Bright Morning Star

> I, Jesus, have sent my angel to give you this testimony for the churches. I am the Root and the Offspring of David, and the Bright Morning Star. (Revelation 22:16 EHV)

Brilliant Dawning Light

> For God, who said, "Let Brilliant Light shine out of darkness," is the one who has cascaded His Light into us—the Brilliant Dawning Light of the glorious knowledge of God as we gaze into the face of Jesus Christ. (2 Corinthians 4:6 TPT)

Biblical Hope

> "For I know the plans I have for you," declares the Lord, "plans to prosper you and not to harm you, plans to give you Hope and a future." (Jeremiah 29:11 NIV)

Blessed and Only Almighty God

> For in due season Christ will be revealed from heaven by the Blessed and Only Almighty God, the King of Kings and Lord of Lords. (1 Timothy 6:15 TLB)

Blessed for Evermore

> The God and Father of our Lord Jesus Christ, who is Blessed for Evermore, knoweth that I lie not. (2 Corinthians 11:31 KJ21)

Fresh Olive Branch in Its Beak (Symbol of Peace and Forgiveness)

> After waiting another seven days, Noah released the dove again. This time the dove returned to him in the evening with a Fresh Olive Branch in Its Beak. Then Noah knew that the floodwaters were almost gone. (Genesis 8:10–11 NLT)

Brokenhearted

> The Lord is close to the Brokenhearted and saves those who are crushed in spirit. (Psalm 34:18 NIVUK)

Bear the Sins

> So, Christ also, having been offered once to Bear the Sins of many, will appear a second time for salvation without reference to sin, to those who eagerly await Him. (Hebrews 9:28 NASB)

Blessed Hope

> While we wait for the Blessed Hope—the appearing of the glory of our great God and Savior, Jesus Christ. (Titus 2:13 NIV)

Balance

> My life constantly hangs in the Balance, but I will not stop obeying Your instructions. (Psalm 119:109 NLT)

Jesus at Birth

> And when eight days were accomplished for the circumcising of the Child, His name was called Jesus, who was so named by the angel before He was conceived in the womb. (Luke 2:21 KJ21)

Baby Jesus

> When Mary and Joseph brought Jesus to the temple to do what the Law of Moses says should be done for a new Baby, the Spirit told Simeon to go into the temple. Simeon took the Baby Jesus in his arms and praised God. (Luke 2:27–28 CEV)

Backslidings, Be My People, I Will Be Their God

> They shall not defile themselves anymore with their idols and their detestable things, or with any of their transgressions. But I will save them from all the Backslidings in which they have sinned, and will cleanse them; and they shall Be My People, and I Will Be Their God. (Ezekiel 37:23 ESV)

Not Be Overcome By Evil, Bad News

> Such people will Not Be Overcome By Evil. Those who are righteous will be long remembered. They do not fear Bad News; they confidently trust the Lord to care for them. (Psalm 112:6–7 NLT)

Baptized

> You were Baptized into union with Christ, and now you are clothed, so, to speak, with the life of Christ Himself. (Galatians 3:27 GNT)

True Beauty, Lasting Beauty

> Let your True Beauty come from your inner personality, not a focus on the external. For Lasting Beauty comes from a gentle and peaceful spirit, which is precious in God's sight and is much more important than the outward adornment of elaborate hair, jewelry, and fine clothes. (1 Peter 3:3–4 TPT)

Beholding the Marvelous Beauty

> Here's the one thing I crave from Yahweh, the one thing I seek above all else: I want to live with Him every moment in His house, Beholding the Marvelous Beauty of Yahweh, filled with awe, delighting in His glory and grace. I want to contemplate in His temple. (Psalm 27:4 TPT)

Be in Awe Before, Bowing in Worship, Beauty of Holiness

> Be in Awe Before His majesty. Be In Awe Before such power and might! Come worship wonderful Yahweh, arrayed in all His splendor, Bowing in Worship as He appears in the Beauty of holiness. Give Him the honor due His name. Worship Him wearing the glory-garments of your holy, priestly calling! (Psalm 29:2 TPT)

Sunrise Brilliance, Sunset Beauty Both

O God, to the farthest corners of the planet people will stand in awe, startled and stunned by your signs and wonders. Sunrise Brilliance and Sunset Beauty Both take turns singing their songs of joy to You. (Psalm 65:8 TPT)

Sunrise Brilliance, Sunset Beauty

From Sunrise-Brilliance to Sunset-Beauty, lift up His praise from dawn to dusk! (Psalm 113:3 TPT)

Beauty Fills Each Day

Do you want to live a long, good life, enjoying the Beauty that fills each day? Then never speak a lie or allow wicked words to come from your mouth. (Psalm 34:12–13 TPT)

Beauty in Your People

God of Heaven's Armies, you find so much Beauty in Your People! They're like lovely sanctuaries of your presence. (Psalm 84:1 TPT)

Beauty Fills Your House

Nothing could ever change Your royal decrees; they will last forever! Holiness is the Beauty that Fills Your House; You are the one who abides forevermore! (Psalm 93:5 TPT)

His Beauty

For He enjoys His faithful lovers. He adorns the humble with His Beauty, and He loves to give them victory. (Psalm 149:4 TPT)

By Your Hands, Beauty

The four corners of the earth were formed By Your Hands, and every changing season owes its Beauty to You. (Psalm 74:17 TPT)

Sweet Beauty

> O Lord our God, let your Sweet Beauty rest upon us. Come work with us, and then our works will endure; You will give us success in all we do. (Psalm 90:17 TPT)

Breathtaking Brilliance, Stunning Beauty, Come before Him

> Breathtaking Brilliance and awe-inspiring majesty radiate from His shining presence. His Stunning Beauty overwhelms all who Come Before Him. (Psalm 96:6 TPT)

Bless the Lord, Breath, Beauty

> Everything I am will praise and Bless the Lord! O Lord, my God, Your greatness takes my Breath away, overwhelming me by Your majesty, Beauty, and splendor! (Psalm 104:1 TPT)

Bubble, Beauty, Bringing Bliss, Breakthrough

> Our hearts Bubble over as we celebrate the fame of Your marvelous Beauty, Bringing Bliss to our hearts. We shout with ecstatic joy over Your Breakthrough for us. (Psalm 145:7 TPT)

Beauty

> Everything He does is full of splendor and Beauty! Each miracle demonstrates His eternal perfection. (Psalm 111:3 TPT)

> We admire the young for their strength and Beauty, but the dignity of the old is their wisdom. (Proverbs 20:29 TPT)

Beautiful Crown

> If you prize wisdom, she will make you great. Embrace her, and she will honor you. She will place a lovely wreath on your head; she will present you with a Beautiful Crown. (Proverbs 4:8–9 NLT)

Beauty, Better Person

> When you humbly receive wise correction, it adorns your life with Beauty and makes you a Better Person. (Proverbs 25:12 TPT)

Be with Beauty of Our Lord, Bring, Because of Christ

> Let every activity of your lives and every word that comes from your lips Be drenched With the Beauty of Our Lord Jesus, the Anointed One. And bring your constant praise to God the Father Because of what Christ has done for you! (Colossians 3:17 TPT)

Beyond Description, Be in Awe of Him

> For the Lord's greatness is Beyond Description, and He deserves all the praise that comes to Him. He is our King-God, and it's right to Be In holy Awe of Him. (Psalm 96:4 TPT)

Future Is Bright

> Your Future Is Bright and filled with a living hope that will never fade away. (Proverbs 23:18 TPT)

Future Will Be Bright

> For then you will perceive what is true wisdom, your Future Will Be Bright, and this hope living within you will never disappoint you. (Proverbs 24:14 TPT)

PRAYERS (USING B WORDS)

We praise You Jesus for shedding Your **blood**. You have set us free from **brokenness, bondage,** and **bitterness.** We are truly grateful for this, Jesus. Thank You, God, for the many **blessings** You have given us in our lives. We love You for the **blessed** hope we have in You. The **Bible** is a glorious **book** filled with Your **beautiful** words that are of utmost importance in our lives. We **believe** in You totally, our **beloved** Father, Son, and Holy Spirit! We are in awe of Your **brilliant** light because You are our **Bright Morning Star.** God, You are **beyond** description, and You are **blessing** us with **bright** futures. Thank You for the **belt** of truth and the **breastplate** of righteousness, which Your armor protects us with. We praise You for the **beautiful** flowers that **bloom** around us.

We thank You, Jesus, for giving Your **body** & **blood,** and we pray in Your **blessed** name.

Amen.

C

Companion

> And the Lord God said, "It isn't good for man to be alone; I will make a Companion for him, a helper suited to his needs." (Genesis 2:18 TLB)

Stay Close, Companionship

> Run from anything that gives you the evil thoughts that young men often have, but Stay Close to anything that makes you want to do right. Have faith and love, and enjoy the Companionship of those who love the Lord and have pure hearts. (2 Timothy 2:22 TLB)

Courageous

> Be strong and Courageous. Do not be afraid or terrified because of them, for the Lord Your God goes with you; He will never leave you nor forsake you. (Deuteronomy 31:6 NIV)

Commanded, Courageous

> Have I not Commanded you? Be strong and Courageous. Do not be afraid; do not be discouraged, for the Lord your God will be with you wherever you go. (Joshua 1:9 NIV)

Content

> I know what it is to be in need, and I know what it is to have plenty. I have learned the secret of being Content in any and every situation, whether well fed or hungry, whether living in plenty or in want. (Philippians 4:12 NIV)

Godliness with Contentment Is Great, Clothing, Content

> But Godliness with Contentment Is Great gain. For we brought nothing into the world, and we can take nothing out of it. But if we have food and Clothing, we will be Content with that. (1 Timothy 6:6–8 NIV)

Christ Gives Us Courage and Confidence, Come to God

> Christ now Gives Us Courage and Confidence, so that we can Come To God by faith. (Ephesians 3:12 CEV)

Confidence

> Let us then with Confidence draw near to the throne of grace, that we may receive mercy and find grace to help in time of need. (Hebrews 4:16 ESV)

God of Compassion

> But you, O Lord, are a God of Compassion and mercy slow to get angry and filled with unfailing love and faithfulness. (Psalm 86:15 NLT)

Compassion

> Once again you will have Compassion on us. You will trample our sins under your feet and throw them into the depths of the ocean! (Micah 7:19 NLT)

Comforted His People, Compassion

> Sing for joy, O heavens! Rejoice, O earth! Burst into song, O mountains! For the Lord has Comforted His People and will have Compassion on them in their suffering. (Isaiah 49:13 NLT)

Childlike Faith

> The Lord takes care of the Childlike. I was brought down, and He saved me. (Psalm 116:6 NLV)

Commit Everything to the Lord

> Commit Everything you do to the Lord. Trust Him, and He will help you. (Psalm 37:5 NLT)

Commit, Listen Carefully

> Commit yourself to instruction; Listen Carefully to words of knowledge. (Proverbs 23:12 NLT)

Cleanse Us, Committed

> He gave His life to free us from every kind of sin, to Cleanse Us, and to make us His very own people, totally Committed to doing good deeds. (Titus 2:14 NLT)

Confess to God

> For it is written: "'As I live,' saith the Lord, 'every knee shall bow to Me, and every tongue shall Confess to God.'" So, then every one of us shall give account of himself to God. (Romans 14:11–12 KJ21)

Complete Conviction of Truth

> For we brought the Good News to you, not with words only, but also with power and the Holy Spirit, and with Complete Conviction of its Truth. You know how we lived when we were with you; it was for your own good. (1 Thessalonians 1:5 GNT)

Counselor

> I will instruct thee and teach thee in the way which thou shalt go: I will guide thee with mine eye. I will instruct you (says the Lord) and guide you along the best pathway for your life; I will advise you and watch your progress. (Psalm 32:8 KJ21; Psalm 32:8 TLB)

Cast, He Cares for You

> Cast all your anxiety on Him because He Cares for You. (1 Peter 5:7 EHV)

Calmly for God, Salvation Comes from Him

> My soul waits Calmly for God alone. My Salvation Comes from Him. (Psalm 62:1 GW)

Cares of My Heart, Consolations Cheer My Soul

> When the Cares of My Heart are many, Your Consolations Cheer My Soul. (Psalm 94:19 ESV)

God Says Calm Down

> Our God says, "Calm Down, and learn that I am God! All nations on earth will honor Me." (Psalm 46:10 CEV)

Calm

> You rule the roaring sea and Calm its waves. (Psalm 89:9 CEV)

Staying Calm

> Losing your temper Causes a lot of trouble, but Staying Calm settles arguments. (Proverbs 15:18 CEV)

No Condemnation

> So now there is No Condemnation for those who belong to Christ Jesus. (Romans 8:1 NLT)

Cool, Calm, Collected

> Can you bridle your tongue when your heart is under pressure? That's how you show that you are wise. An understanding heart keeps you Cool, Calm, and Collected, no matter what you're facing. (Proverbs 17:27 TPT)

Chosen

> You belong exclusively to the Lord Your God, and He has Chosen you to be His own possession, more so than any other nation on the face of the earth. (Deuteronomy 14:2 TLB)

People He Has Chosen

> Blessed is the nation whose God is the Lord, whose People He Has Chosen as His own. (Psalm 33:12 TLB)

Chosen Ones

> Let me share in the prosperity of Your Chosen Ones. Let me rejoice in the joy of Your people; let me praise You with those who are Your heritage. (Psalm 106:5 NLT)

More than Conquerors

> No, in all these things we are More than Conquerors through Him who loved us. (Romans 8:37 NRSVA)

Commander in Chief of the Lord's Army, Give Me Your Commands

> "I am the Commander-In-Chief of The Lord's Army," He replied. Joshua fell to the ground before Him and worshiped Him and said, "Give Me Your Commands." "Take off your shoes," the Commander told him, "For this is holy ground." And Joshua did. (Joshua 5:14–15 TLB)

Created by His Power, God's Children

> Everything belongs to God, and all things were Created by His Power. So, God did the right thing when He made Jesus perfect by suffering, as Jesus led many of God's Children to be saved and to share in His glory. (Hebrews 2:10 CEV)

Crowd, Come Closer, Take Up Your Cross

> Jesus then told the Crowd and the disciples to Come Closer, and He said: If any of you want to be my followers, you must forget about yourself. You must Take Up Your Cross and follow Me. (Mark 8:34 CEV)

Jesus Never Changes

> Jesus Christ Never Changes! He is the same yesterday, today, and forever. (Hebrews 13:8 CEV)

> Descendants of Jacob, I am the Lord All-Powerful, and I Never Change. That's why you haven't been wiped out. (Malachi 3:6 CEV)

Coming to Christ, Living Cornerstone, Chosen by God

> You are Coming to Christ, who is the Living Cornerstone of God's temple. He was rejected by people, but He was Chosen by God for great honor. (1 Peter 2:4 NLT)

Christ, Child of God, Children

> Everyone who believes that Jesus is the Christ has become a Child of God. And everyone who loves the Father loves His Children, too. (1 John 5:1 NLT)

Counselor, Comforter

> I will pray to the Father, and He will give you another Counselor (Comforter), that He may be with you forever. (John 14:16 WEB)

Created, Creator

> They exchanged the truth about God for a lie; they worship and serve what God has Created instead of the Creator Himself, who is to be praised forever! Amen. (Romans 1:25 GNT)

Creator

> Don't you yet understand? Don't you know by now that the everlasting God, the Creator of the farthest parts of the earth, never grows faint or weary? No one can fathom the depths of His understanding. (Isaiah 40:28 TLB)

Crowning Glory

> Then at last the Lord Almighty Himself will be their Crowning Glory, the diadem of beauty to His people who are left. (Isaiah 28:5 TLB)

Cleanse Us, Conscience

> Let us draw near to God with a sincere heart and with the full assurance that faith brings, having our hearts sprinkled to Cleanse Us from a guilty Conscience and having our bodies washed with pure water. (Hebrews 10:22 NIV)

Complete Victory through God

> But in all these troubles we have Complete Victory through God, who has shown His love for us. (Romans 8:37 ERV)

Compulsion, Cheerful Giver

> Each one must give as he has decided in his heart, not reluctantly or under Compulsion, for God loves a Cheerful Giver. (2 Corinthians 9:7 ESV)

Convinced

> We do this because we are Convinced that He who raised Jesus will raise us up with Him, and together we will all be brought into His presence. (2 Corinthians 4:14 TPT)

> We're fully Convinced that You are the Anointed One, the Son of the Living God, and we believe in You! (John 6:69 TPT)

> I am Convinced that My God will fully satisfy every need you have, for I have seen the abundant riches of glory revealed to me through Jesus Christ! (Philippians 4:19 TPT)

Convinced, Compared

> I am Convinced that any suffering we endure is less than nothing Compared to the magnitude of glory that is about to be unveiled within us. (Romans 8:18 TPT)

Confidence, Convinced, Circumstances

> So now I live with the Confidence that there is nothing in the universe with the power to separate us from God's love. I'm Convinced that His love will triumph over death, life's troubles, fallen angels, or dark rulers in the heavens. There is nothing in our present or future Circumstances that can weaken His love. (Romans 8:38 TPT)

PRAYERS (Using C Words)

We are in awe! **Christ** Jesus was **crucified** on the **cross**. He took the **crown** of thorns upon Himself and gave us the **crown** of eternal life. He **conquered** death, hell, and the grave in order to **calm** our storms in life. Thank You, Lord! Jesus, You are the solid rock upon which we stand, and You are the **center** of our lives. We are in awe, God, that You have **chosen** us! We exalt You that we have been **called** according to Your will, plan, and purpose. We praise You, God, for **creating** us and for providing our wonderful careers and for teaching us Your **Christlike character**. Jesus, you are our **Counselor** and **Comforter**, and we are grateful for that. I am Your **child**, dear God, and I love that You never **change**.

Thank You, **Christ** Jesus, for **caring** so much. In Your **cherished** name we pray.

Amen.

D

Dead, Delivers Us

> And to wait for His Son from heaven, whom He raised from the Dead, Jesus who Delivers Us from the wrath to come. (1 Thessalonians 1:10 RSV)

Do Not Be Lazy

> Do Not Be Lazy but always work hard. Work for the Lord with a heart full of love for Him. (Romans 12:11 NLV)

Do It for the Lord

> Whatever work you Do, Do it with all your heart. Do It for The Lord and not for men. (Colossians 3:23 NLV)

Discretion

> Discretion will protect you, and understanding will guard you. (Proverbs 2:11 NET)

Do Not Let Wisdom Out of Your Sight, Discretion

> My son, Do Not Let Wisdom and understanding Out of Your Sight, preserve sound judgment and Discretion. (Proverbs 3:21 NIV)

Things You Do Will Be Pleasing and Perfect

Do not act like the sinful people of the world. Let God change your life. First of all, let Him give you a new mind. Then you will know what God wants you to Do. And the things you Do Will Be good and Pleasing and Perfect. (Romans 12:2 NLV)

Word Is Trustworthy and Dependable

And God-Enthroned spoke to me and said, "Consider this! I am making everything to be new and fresh. Write down at once all that I have told you, because each Word Is Trustworthy and Dependable." (Revelation 21:5 TPT)

Holy Determination, Do His Will

The Lord Yahweh empowers me, so I am not humiliated. For that reason, with Holy Determination, I will Do His Will and not be ashamed. (Isaiah 50:7 TPT)

Day of Judgment

I have fought well. I have finished the race, and I have been faithful. So, a crown will be given to me for pleasing the Lord. He judges fairly, and on the Day of Judgment He will give a crown to me and to everyone else who wants Him to appear with power. (2 Timothy 4:7–8 CEV)

Deeply, Devotion to Him

Your spiritual roots go Deeply into His life as you are continually infused with strength, encouraged in every way. For you are established in the faith you have absorbed and enriched by your Devotion to Him. (Colossians 2:7 TPT)

Discernment

> And it is my prayer that your love may abound more and more, with knowledge and all Discernment. (Philippians 1:9 ESV)

> Teach me good judgment (Discernment) and knowledge, For I have believed and trusted and relied on Your commandments. (Psalm 119:66 AMP)

Discern Good and Evil

> But solid food is for the mature, who through practice have their senses trained to Discern both Good and Evil. (Hebrews 5:14 TLV)

Deliverer

> The Lord is my rock, my fortress and my Deliverer; my God is my rock, in whom I take refuge, my shield and the horn of my salvation, my stronghold. (Psalm 18:2 NIV)

> He is always kind and loving to me; He is my fortress, my tower of strength and safety, my Deliverer. He stands before me as a shield. He subdues my people under me. (Psalm 144:2 TLB)

God Disciplines You

> Think about it: Just as a parent Disciplines a child, the Lord Your God Disciplines you for your own good. (Deuteronomy 8:5 NLT)

Do Not Despise the Discipline

> But consider the joy of those corrected by God! Do Not Despise the Discipline of the Almighty when you sin. (Job 5:17 NLT)

Do Not Be Conformed, Discern God's Will

> Do Not Be Conformed to this age, but be transformed by the renewing of your mind, so that you may Discern what is the good, pleasing, and perfect Will of God. (Romans 12:2 HCSB)

Defender

> O God, our Defender and our Shield, have mercy on the one you have anointed as your king. (Psalm 84:9 TLB)

> The Lord is your protector (Defender), there at your right side to shade you from the sun. (Psalm 121:5 CEV)

Champion Defender

> He alone is my safe place; His wraparound presence always protects me. For He is my Champion Defender; there's no risk of failure with God. So why would I let worry paralyze me, even when troubles multiply around me? (Psalm 62:2 TPT)

Directing Our Steps

> Since the Lord is Directing Our Steps, why try to understand everything that happens along the way? (Proverbs 20:24 TLB)

Steps Are Directed by the Lord, He Delights in His Way

> The Steps of a [good and righteous] man Are Directed and established By The Lord, And He Delights in His way [and blesses His path]. (Psalm 37:23 AMP)

The Lord Directs Your Life, Your Destiny

> It is the Lord who Directs Your Life, for each step you take is ordained by God to bring you closer to Your Destiny. So much of your life, then, remains a mystery! (Proverbs 20:24 TPT)

Destiny

> Lord, I know that none of us are in charge of our own Destiny; none of us have control over our own life. (Jeremiah 10:23 GNT)

Desire

> Seek Your happiness in the Lord, and He will give you your heart's Desire. (Psalm 37:4 GNT)

Do Good Things, Decide to Worship Him

> And He will bless you with many children, large herds and flocks, and abundant crops. The Lord will be happy to Do Good Things for you, just as He did for your ancestors. But you must Decide once and for all To Worship Him with all your heart and soul and to obey everything in The Book of God's Law. (Deuteronomy 30:9–10 CEV)

Delight in Your Word

> I have recited Your laws and rejoiced in them more than in riches. I will meditate upon them and give them my full respect. I will Delight In them and not forget them. Bless me with life so that I can continue to obey You. Open my eyes to see wonderful things in Your Word. (Psalm 119:13–18 TLB)

The Lord Takes Delight in His People

> For the Lord takes Delight in His People; He crowns the humble with victory. (Psalm 149:4 NLT)

Delight in You

> The Lord your God is with you, the Mighty Warrior who saves. He will take great Delight in You; in His love He will no longer rebuke you, but will rejoice over you with singing. (Zephaniah 3:17 NIV)

Dazzling Light

> Dazzling Light, Came Down, Six Days the Dazzling Light of the Lord's presence Came Down on the mountain. To the Israelites the light looked like a fire burning on top of the mountain. The cloud covered the mountain for Six Days, and on the seventh Day the Lord called to Moses from the cloud. (Exodus 24:16–17 GNT)

Divine Power

> By His Divine Power, God has given us everything we need for living a godly life. We have received all of this by coming to know Him, the one who called us to Himself by means of His marvelous glory and excellence. (2 Peter 1:3 NLT)

Divine Guidance

> When people do not accept Divine Guidance, they run wild. But whoever obeys the law is joyful. (Proverbs 29:18 NLT)

Divine Discipline, Disciplined

> As you endure this Divine Discipline, remember that God is treating you as His own children. Who ever heard of a child who is never Disciplined by its father? (Hebrews 12:7 NLT)

Dwelling Place, Dwell

> And I heard a loud voice from the throne saying, "Look! God's Dwelling Place is now among the people, and He will Dwell with them. They will be His people, and God Himself will be with them and be their God." (Revelation 21:3 NIV)

> Lord, You have been our Dwelling Place in all generations. (Psalm 90:1 ESV)

Turns My Darkness into Light

> You, Lord, are my lamp; the Lord Turns My Darkness into Light. (2 Samuel 22:29 NIV)

Separated Light from Darkness

> God saw that the light was good, and He Separated the Light from the Darkness. (Genesis 1:4 NIV)

Light Shines in the Darkness

> The Light Shines in The Darkness, and the Darkness has not overcome it. (John 1:5 ESV)

Light Is Better than Darkness

> Oh, I know, "Wisdom is better than foolishness, just as Light Is Better than Darkness." (Ecclesiastes 2:13 GNT)

> Woe unto them that call evil good, and good evil; that count Darkness as light, and light as Darkness; that put bitter for sweet, and sweet for bitter! (Isaiah 5:20 KJ21)

Lead the Blind, Turn Darkness into Light

> I will Lead the Blind by ways they have not known, along unfamiliar paths I will guide them; I will Turn the Darkness into Light before them and make the rough places smooth. These are the things I Will Do; I will not forsake them. (Isaiah 42:16 NIV)

Disappear, Darkness

> He protects the lives of His faithful people, but the wicked Disappear in Darkness; a man does not triumph by His own strength. (1 Samuel 2:9 GNT)

Darkness

> I have come into the world as a light, so that no one who believes in me should stay in Darkness. (John 12:46 NIV)

Deeply, Deeds Are Done, Dark Place

> Woe (judgment is coming) to those who [try to] Deeply hide their plans from the Lord, Whose Deeds Are Done in a Dark Place, and who say, "Who sees us?" or "Who knows us?" (Isaiah 29:15 AMP)

Do Well, Dark Place, Day Dawns

> And we have the prophetic word more fully confirmed, to which you will Do Well to pay attention as to a lamp shining in a Dark Place, until the Day Dawns and the morning star rises in your hearts. (2 Peter 1:19 ESV)

Defends Me

> But the Lord Defends me; my God protects me. (Psalm 94:22 GNT)

Do Not Be Afraid

> My Spirit remains among you, just as I promised when you came out of Egypt. So Do Not Be Afraid. (Haggai 2:5 NLT)

Day, Daily Bread

> Give us this Day our Daily Bread. (Matthew 6:11 KJ21)

Day, Diadem of Beauty

> In that Day the Lord of Hosts shall become a crown of glory and a Diadem of Beauty (a symbol of sovereignty) to the remnant of His people. (Isaiah 28:5 MEV)

Door of the Sheep

> Then Jesus said to them again, "Truly, truly I say to you, I am the Door of The Sheep. I am the Door. If anyone enters through Me, he will be saved and will go in and out and find pasture." (John 10:7, 9 MEV)

Despised and Rejected, Deepest Grief, Did Not Care

> He was Despised and Rejected—a man of sorrows, acquainted with Deepest Grief. We turned our backs on Him and looked the other way. He was Despised, and we Did Not Care. (Isaiah 53:3 NLT)

Delivered, Not Disappointed

> In You our fathers put their trust. They trusted, and You Delivered them. They cried to You and were Delivered. In You they trusted, and were Not Disappointed. (Psalm 22:5–6 TLV)

Desires Life, Good Days, Deceit

> The one who Desires Life, to love and see Good Days, must keep his tongue from evil and his lips from speaking Deceit. (1 Peter 3:10 NASB)

Destroyed Death

> But it has now been revealed through the appearing of our Savior, Christ Jesus, who has Destroyed Death and has brought life and immortality to light through the gospel. (2 Timothy 1:10 NIV)

Diseases

> He forgives all my sins. He heals all my Diseases. (Psalm 103:3 NLV)

Day, Declared

> And God blessed the seventh Day and Declared it holy, because it was the Day when He rested from all His work of creation. (Genesis 2:3 NLT)

Declare

> I can assure you of this: If you freely Declare in public that I am the Son of Man, the Messiah, then I will freely Declare to all the angels of God that you are Mine. (Luke 12:8 TPT)

Deeds Are Perfect, Does No Wrong

> He is the Rock; his Deeds Are Perfect. Everything He Does is just and fair. He is a faithful God who Does No Wrong; how just and upright He is! (Deuteronomy 32:4 NLT)

Day by Day, Good Deeds

> Day By Day the Lord watches the Good Deeds of the godly, and He prepares for them His forever-reward. (Psalm 37:18 TPT)

Dignity

> Old age with wisdom will crown you with Dignity and honor, for it takes a lifetime of righteousness to acquire it. (Proverbs 16:31 TPT)

Deepen

> I pray for you that the faith we share may effectively Deepen your understanding of every good thing that belongs to you in Christ. (Philemon 1:6 TPT)

Right Direction, Deeper into Godliness

> God has transmitted His very substance into every Scripture, for it is God-breathed. It will empower you by its instruction and correction, giving you the strength to take the Right Direction and lead you Deeper into the path of Godliness. (2 Timothy 3:16 TPT)

Divine Authority, Decisions

The king speaks with Divine Authority; His Decisions are always right. (Proverbs 16:10 GNT)

Divine Holiness, Raised from Death

As to His Divine Holiness, He was shown with great power to be the Son of God by being Raised from Death. (Romans 1:4 GNT)

Divine Majesty

The whole point of what we are saying is that we have such a High Priest, who sits at the right of the throne of the Divine Majesty in heaven. (Hebrews 8:1 GNT)

Not Driven to Despair

We are pressured in every way [hedged in], but not crushed; perplexed [unsure of finding a way out], but Not Driven to Despair. (2 Corinthians 4:8 AMP)

Do Not Sin

Tremble in awe before the Lord, and Do Not Sin against Him. Be still upon your bed and search your heart before Him. (Psalm 4:4 TPT)

Do Not Judge

I Do Not Judge as people judge. They look at the outward appearance, but I look at the heart. (1 Samuel 16:7b GNT)

Don't Be Pulled in Different Directions, Each Day, Detail

Don't Be Pulled in Different Directions or worried about a thing. Be saturated in prayer throughout Each Day, offering your faith-filled requests before God with overflowing gratitude. Tell him every Detail of your life. (Philippians 4:6 TPT)

Do Not Waver, Divided

> But when you ask Him, be sure that your faith is in God alone. Do Not Waver, for a person with Divided loyalty is as unsettled as a wave of the sea that is blown and tossed by the wind. (James 1:6 NLT)

PRAYERS (USING D WORDS)

We *delight* in Your Word so much because it gives us Your *divine* truth. We are in awe that we have seen Your light and are not walking in *darkness*. We experience Your *divine* power. Your *divine* guidance and *direction* guide our steps, and we praise You for that. We are *delivered* from *death*. Amen! You are my heart's *desire* because it's all about Your *divine* grace. I am so grateful, Father God, that You healed our *disease*, cancer. We are *devoted* and *depend* on You, God. You *display* Your supernatural power through Your *divine* glory. We are grateful for Your *divine discipline*. We are the *daughters* of the King and are *deeply* loved. We *delight* in You, Father God, and we *dedicate* our lives to You, Jesus.

We praise You, our *dear* Lord and Savior, and we pray in Your *divine* name.

Amen.

E

Encouragement of the Holy Spirit

> The church then had peace throughout Judea, Galilee, and Samaria, and it became stronger as the believers lived in the fear of the Lord. And with the Encouragement of The Holy Spirit, it also grew in numbers. (Acts 9:31 NLT)

Encouragement to Each Other

> Then, by the will of God, I will be able to come to you with a joyful heart, and we will be an Encouragement To Each Other. (Romans 15:32 NLT)

Encouragement Belonging to Christ

> Is there any Encouragement from Belonging to Christ? Any comfort from His love? Any fellowship together in the Spirit? Are your hearts tender and compassionate? (Philippians 2:1 NLT)

Encourage

> I weep with grief; my heart is heavy with sorrow; Encourage and cheer me with Your words. (Psalm 119:28 TLB)

Encourage Each Other

> So, Encourage Each Other to build Each Other up, just as you are already doing. (1 Thessalonians 5:11 TLB)

Encouragement, Each Other

> Such things were written in the Scriptures long ago to teach us. And the Scriptures give us hope and Encouragement as we wait patiently for God's promises to be fulfilled. May God, who gives this patience and Encouragement, help you live in complete harmony with Each Other, as is fitting for followers of Christ Jesus. (Romans 15:4–5 NLT)

Everything, Encouragement

> Don't use foul or abusive language. Let Everything you say be good and helpful, so that your words will be an Encouragement to those who hear them. (Ephesians 4:29 NLT)

God-Enthroned, Everlasting Ages

> God Himself will hear me! God-Enthroned through Everlasting Ages, the God of unchanging faithfulness— He will put them in their place, all those who refuse to love and revere Him! (Psalm 55:19 TPT)

Everlasting Mountain

> God, You are so resplendent and radiant! Your majesty shines from Your Everlasting Mountain. Nothing could be compared to You in glory! (Psalm 76:4 TPT)

Earth, Everlasting to Everlasting

> Long before You gave birth to the Earth and before the mountains were born, You have been from Everlasting to Everlasting, the one and only true God. (Psalm 90:2 TPT)

Everlasting Life

> For God so loved the world that He gave His only begotten Son that whosoever believeth in Him should not perish but have Everlasting Life. (John 3:16 KJ21)

Everlasting God

> Don't you know? Haven't you been listening? Yahweh is the one and only Everlasting God, the Creator of all you can see and imagine! He never gets weary or worn out. His intelligence is unlimited; He is never puzzled over what to do! (Isaiah 40:28 TPT)

Enthusiasm

> Enthusiasm without knowledge is not good; impatience will get you into trouble. (Proverbs 19:2 GNT)

> He had been instructed in the Way of the Lord, and with great Enthusiasm He proclaimed and taught correctly the facts about Jesus. However, He knew only the baptism of John. (Acts 18:25 GNT)

> "Don't be frightened," Samuel reassured them. "You have certainly done wrong, but make sure now that you worship the Lord with true Enthusiasm, and that you don't turn your back on Him in any way." (1 Samuel 12:20 TLB)

> He died under God's judgment against our sins so that He could rescue us from constant falling into sin and make us His very own people, with cleansed hearts and real Enthusiasm for doing kind things for others. (Titus 2:14 TLB)

Efficient

> Do you see a person who is Efficient in his work? He will serve kings. He will not serve unknown people. (Proverbs 22:29 GW)

Eternal God, Everlasting Arms, Thrust Enemy

> The Eternal God is thy refuge, and underneath are the Everlasting Arms: and He shall Thrust out the Enemy from before thee; and shall say, Destroy them. (Deuteronomy 33:27 KJ21)

Eternal Life, Never Experience

> And anyone who believes in God's Son has Eternal Life. Anyone who doesn't obey the Son will Never Experience Eternal Life but remains under God's angry judgment. (John 3:36 NLT)

Eternal Life

> For it is my Father's will that all who see His Son and believe in Him should have Eternal Life. I will raise them up at the last day. (John 6:40 NLT)

> But those who drink the water I give will never be thirsty again. It becomes a fresh, bubbling spring within them, giving them Eternal Life. (John 4:14 NLT)

> I tell you the truth, anyone who believes has Eternal Life. (John 6:47 NLT)

> When this life became visible, we saw it; so, we speak of it and tell you about the Eternal Life which was with the Father and was made known to us. (1 John 1:2 GNT)

Christ Is Eternal Life

> This one who is life from God has been shown to us, and we guarantee that we have seen Him; I am speaking of Christ, who Is Eternal Life. He was with the Father and then was shown to us. (1 John 1:2 TLB)

Experience Eternal Life, Evil Will Experience Judgment

> And they will rise again. Those who have done good will rise to Experience Eternal Life, and those who have continued in Evil Will rise to Experience Judgment. (John 5:29 NLT)

Patient Endurance

> I know all the things You do. I have seen Your love, Your faith, Your service, and Your Patient Endurance. And I can see Your constant improvement in all these things. (Revelation 2:19 NLT)

> Patient Endurance is what you need now, so that you will continue to do God's will. Then you will receive all that He has promised. (Hebrews 10:36 NLT)

Endurance

> We can rejoice, too, when we run into problems and trials, for we know that they help us develop Endurance. And Endurance develops strength of character, and character strengthens our confident hope of salvation. (Romans 5:3–4 NLT)

> We also pray that you will be strengthened with all His glorious power so you will have all the Endurance and patience you need. May you be filled with joy. (Colossians 1:11 NLT)

Enthusiasm, Example, Patient Endurance

> So don't allow your hearts to grow dull or lose your Enthusiasm, but follow the Example of those who fully received what God has promised because of their strong faith and Patient Endurance. (Hebrews 6:12 TPT)

Every Weight, Especially, Easily, Endurance

> Therefore, since we are surrounded by such a huge crowd of witnesses to the life of faith, let us strip off Every

Weight that slows us down, Especially the sin that so Easily trips us up. And let us run with Endurance the race God has set before us. (Hebrews 12:1 NLT)

Endurance

Dear brothers and sisters, when troubles of any kind come your way, consider it an opportunity for great joy. For you know that when your faith is tested, your Endurance has a chance to grow. So let it grow, for when your Endurance is fully developed, you will be perfect and complete, needing nothing. (James 1:2–4 NLT)

Expectantly

In the morning, Lord, you hear my voice; in the morning I lay my requests before you and wait Expectantly. (Psalm 5:3 NIV)

Equipped, Every Good Work

All Scripture is God-breathed and is useful for teaching, rebuking, correcting and training in righteousness, so that the servant of God may be thoroughly Equipped for Every Good Work. (2 Timothy 3:16–17 NIV)

God Exalted Him, Every Name, Every Knee, Earth

Therefore, God Exalted Him to the highest place and gave Him the name that is above Every Name, that at the name of Jesus Every Knee should bow, in heaven and on Earth and under the Earth. (Philippians 2:9–10 NIV)

Everything in Heaven, Earth, Exalted

Yours, Lord, is the greatness and the power and the glory and the majesty and the splendor, for Everything in Heaven and Earth is Yours. Yours, Lord, is the kingdom; You are Exalted as head over all. (1 Chronicles 29:11 NIV)

Exalted, Earth

> He says, "Be still, and know that I am God; I will be Exalted among the nations, I will be Exalted in the Earth." (Psalm 46:10 NIV)

> Be Exalted, O God, above the heavens; let your glory be over all the Earth. (Psalm 57:11 NIV)

> Let them praise the name of the Lord, for His name alone is Exalted; His splendor is above the Earth and the heavens. (Psalm 148:13 EHV)

Exalted

> The Lord lives! Praise be to my Rock! Exalted be God my Savior! (Psalm 18:46 NIV)

> But you, Lord, are forever Exalted. (Psalm 92:8 NIV)

> In that day you will say: "Give praise to the Lord, proclaim His name; make known among the nations what He has done, and proclaim that His name is Exalted." (Isaiah 12:4 NIV)

Exceedingly

> Now to Him who is able to do Exceedingly abundantly above all that we ask or think, according to the power that works in us. (Ephesians 3:20 NKJV)

Excellent

> Finally, brothers and sisters, whatever is true, whatever is noble, whatever is right, whatever is pure, whatever is lovely, whatever is admirable—if anything is Excellent or praiseworthy—think about such things. (Philippians 4:8 NIV)

Eyes, Egyptians

> He said, "If you listen carefully to the Lord your God and do what is right in His Eyes, if you pay attention to His commands and keep all His decrees, I will not bring on you any of the diseases I brought on the Egyptians, for I am the Lord, who heals you." (Exodus 15:26 NIV)

Everything, Eyes

> Nothing in all creation is hidden from God's sight. Everything is uncovered and laid bare before the Eyes of Him to whom we must give account. (Hebrews 4:13 NIV)

Eyes

> I will lift up mine Eyes unto the hills, from whence cometh my help! (Psalm 121:1 KJ21)

Eye

> See, the Eye of the Lord is on those who fear Him, and on those who hope for His loving-kindness. (Psalm 33:18 NLV)

Eyes, Each

> Lift up your Eyes and look to the heavens: Who created all these? He who brings out the starry host one by one and calls forth Each of them by name. Because of His great power and mighty strength, not one of them is missing. (Isaiah 40:26 NIV)

Eyes, Eternal

> So, we fix our Eyes not on what is seen, but on what is unseen, since what is seen is temporary, but what is unseen is Eternal. (2 Corinthians 4:18 NIV)

Wipe Every Tear, Eyes

> He will Wipe Every tear from their Eyes, and there will be no more death or sorrow or crying or pain. All these things are gone forever. (Revelation 21:4 NLT)

Eyes, Enlightened

> I pray that the Eyes of your heart may be Enlightened in order that you may know the hope to which He has called you, the riches of His glorious inheritance in His holy people. (Ephesians 1:18 NIV)

Eyes, Endured the Cross

> Fixing our Eyes on Jesus, the pioneer and perfecter of faith. For the joy set before Him He Endured the Cross, scorning its shame, and sat down at the right hand of the throne of God. (Hebrews 12:2 NIV)

End to the Law, Everyone

> For Christ has put an End to the Law, so Everyone who has put His trust in Christ is made right with God. (Romans 10:4 NLV)

Equality with God

> Though He was God, He did not think of Equality with God as something to cling to. (Philippians 2:6 NLT)

Everyone, Pray Earnestly, Turn from Evil

> People and animals alike must wear garments of mourning, and Everyone must Pray Earnestly to God. They must Turn from their Evil ways and stop all their violence. (Jonah 3:8 NLT)

Equipped, Mercy Endures

> And he consulted with the people and then appointed singers for the Lord and those praising Him in holy attire

as they went before those Equipped for battle saying, "Praise the Lord, for His Mercy Endures forever." (2 Chronicles 20:21 MEV)

Exercise Self-Control

So, prepare your minds for action and Exercise Self-Control. Put all your hope in the gracious salvation that will come to you when Jesus Christ is revealed to the world. (1 Peter 1:13 NLT)

Express

Then you will show discernment, and your lips will Express what you've learned. (Proverbs 5:2 NLT)

Enriched in Everything

By Him you are Enriched in Everything, in all speech and in all knowledge. (1 Corinthians 1:5 MEV)

Enriched, Every Way, Eloquent Words

Through Him, God has Enriched your church in Every Way— with all of your Eloquent Words and all of your knowledge. (1 Corinthians 1:5 NLT)

Eloquent Wisdom, Emptied

For Christ did not send me to baptize but to preach the gospel, and not with words of Eloquent Wisdom, lest the cross of Christ be Emptied of its power. (1 Corinthians 1:17 ESV)

Entrusted

Through the power of the Holy Spirit who lives within us, carefully guard the precious truth that has been Entrusted to you. (2 Timothy 1:14 NLT)

That teaching is found in the gospel that was Entrusted to me to announce, the Good News from the glorious and blessed God. (1 Timothy 1:11 GNT)

Entrusted, Examines Our Hearts

Instead, just as we have been approved by God to be Entrusted with the gospel, so we speak, not to please people, but rather God, who Examines Our Hearts. (1 Thessalonians 2:4 CSB)

Ever-Present Help

God is our refuge and strength, an Ever-Present Help in times of trouble. (Psalm 46:1 GW)

Enter the Temple Gates

Enter the Temple Gates with thanksgiving; go into its courts with praise. Give thanks to Him and praise Him. (Psalm 100:4 GNT)

Embrace

Cherish wisdom. It will raise you up. It will bring you honor when you Embrace it. (Proverbs 4:8 GW)

Enable

Think about what I am saying, because the Lord will Enable you to understand it all. (2 Timothy 2:7 GNT)

<u>PRAYERS</u> (Using E Words)

We are grateful, God, for Your Son, Jesus, who provides a way for *eternal life* throughout all *eternity.* Thank You, Jesus, for *enduring* the cross. We *exalt* You *exceedingly.* We praise you, God, that we can make our requests known and wait *expectantly* upon You. You have *equipped* us to love and serve You in a more *excellent* way. We praise you, heavenly Father, that You have given us *spiritual eyes* to see Your love, Your Word, and Your truth. Thank You for helping us pray *earnestly* and to trample out *evil.* Thank You for Your *empathy* toward us. We are *empowered* to seek You *earnestly.* We praise You, God, for Your *encouragement.*

We pray in Your *excellent* name, Jesus.

Amen.

F

Future

> For I know the plans I have for you," says the Lord. "They are plans for good and not for disaster, to give you a Future and a hope." (Jeremiah 29:11 NLT)

Full of Joy, Future

> Her clothes are strength and honor. She is Full of Joy about the Future. (Proverbs 31:25 NLV)

Follow Me, Fishers of Men

> And he saith unto them, Follow Me, and I will make you Fishers of Men. (Matthew 4:19 KJV)

Glorious Freedom from Sin

> For on that day thorns and thistles, sin, death, and decay— the things that overcame the world against its will at God's command—will all disappear, and the world around us will share in the Glorious Freedom from Sin which God's children enjoy. (Romans 8:20–21 TLB)

Freedom, Forgave

> Who bought our Freedom with His blood and Forgave us all our sins. (Colossians 1:14 TLB)

Free

> So, if the Son sets you Free, you will be Free indeed. (John 8:36 ESV)

Fragrant Aroma

> And walk in love, just as Messiah also loved us and gave Himself up for us as an offering and sacrifice to God for a Fragrant Aroma. (Ephesians 5:2 TLV)

> But I have received everything and have more than enough. I am amply supplied, having received from Epaphroditus what you sent—a Fragrant Aroma, an acceptable sacrifice, pleasing to God. (Philippians 4:18 TLV)

Fire

> For our God is a consuming Fire. (Hebrews 12:29 KJ21)

Flame, Forest Fire

> And so, the tongue is a small part of the body yet it carries great power! Just think of how a small Flame can set a huge Forest Fire ablaze. (James 3:5 TPT)

Father to the Fatherless

> A Father to The Fatherless, a defender of widows, is God in His holy dwelling. (Psalm 68:5 NIV)

Fear the Lord, Faithfulness

> Now Fear the Lord and serve him with all Faithfulness. Throw away the gods your ancestors worshiped beyond the Euphrates River and in Egypt, and serve the Lord. (Joshua 24:14 NIV)

It is Finished, Scripture Fulfilled

> Later, knowing that everything had now been Finished, and so that Scripture would be Fulfilled, Jesus said, "I am

thirsty." A jar of wine vinegar was there, so they soaked a sponge in it, put the sponge on a stalk of the hyssop plant, and lifted it to Jesus' lips. When He had received the drink, Jesus said, "It is Finished." With that, He bowed His head and gave up His spirit. (John 19:28–30 NIV)

Faithfulness

For great is Your love, reaching to the heavens; Your Faithfulness reaches to the skies. (Psalm 57:10 NIV)

I will praise You with the harp for Your Faithfulness, my God; I will sing praise to You with the lyre, Holy One of Israel. (Psalm 71:22 NIV)

But You, Lord, are a compassionate and gracious God, slow to anger, abounding in love and Faithfulness. (Psalm 86:15 NIV)

Who is like You, Lord God Almighty? You, Lord, are mighty and Your Faithfulness surrounds you. (Psalm 89:8 NIV)

Forever, Faithfulness, Love Stands Firm Forever

I will sing of the Lord's great love Forever; with my mouth I will make Your Faithfulness known through all generations. I will declare that Your Love Stands Firm Forever, that You have established Your Faithfulness in heaven itself. (Psalm 89:1–2 NIV)

Feathers, Find Refuge, Faithfulness

He will cover you with His Feathers, and under His wings you will Find Refuge; His Faithfulness will be your shield and rampart. (Psalm 91:4 NIV)

Love Endures Forever, Faithfulness

> For the Lord is good and His Love Endures Forever; His Faithfulness continues through all generations. (Psalm 100:5 NIV)

Faithfulness, Fear

> Through love and Faithfulness sin is atoned for; through the Fear of the Lord evil is avoided. (Proverbs 16:6 NIV)

Compassions Fail Not, Faithfulness

> It is of the Lord's mercies that we are not consumed, because His Compassions Fail Not. They are new every morning: great is thy Faithfulness. (Lamentations 3:22–23 KJV)

Perfect Faithfulness

> Lord, You are my God; I will exalt You and praise Your name, for in Perfect Faithfulness You have done wonderful things, things planned long ago. (Isaiah 25:1 NIV)

God of Forgiveness, Full of Love and Mercy

> They refused to obey and didn't pay any attention to the miracles You did for them; instead, they rebelled and appointed a leader to take them back into slavery in Egypt! But you are a God of Forgiveness, always ready to pardon, gracious and merciful, slow to become angry, and Full of Love and Mercy; You didn't abandon them. (Nehemiah 9:17 TLB)

Forgiveness of Sins

> And that this message of salvation should be taken from Jerusalem to all the nations: There is Forgiveness of Sins for all who turn to Me. (Luke 24:47 TLB)

Full of Loving Forgiveness, Heavenly Father

> And Christ became a human being and lived here on earth among us and was Full of Loving Forgiveness and truth. And some of us have seen His glory—the glory of the only Son of the Heavenly Father! (John 1:14 TLB)

For Forgiveness of Your Sins

> And Peter replied, "Each one of you must turn from sin, return to God, and be baptized in the name of Jesus Christ For the Forgiveness of Your Sins; then you also shall receive this gift, the Holy Spirit." (Acts 2:38 TLB)

Fellowship with God, Forgiveness For Our Sins

> He is the one who took God's wrath against our sins upon Himself and brought us into Fellowship with God; and He is the Forgiveness For Our Sins, and not only ours but all the world's. (1 John 2:2 TLB)

Fellowship of Holy Spirit

> May the grace of the Lord Jesus Christ, the love of God, and the Fellowship of the Holy Spirit be with you all. (2 Corinthians 13:14 NLT)

Faithful, Fellowship with Son and Father

> So, you must remain Faithful to what you have been taught from the beginning. If you do, you will remain in Fellowship with the Son and with the Father. (1 John 2:24 NLT)

Faithful Followers

> They will wage war against the Lamb, but the Lamb will triumph over them because He is Lord of Lords and King of Kings—and with Him will be His called, chosen and Faithful Followers. (Revelation 17:14 NIV)

Fruit of the Spirit, Forbearance, Faithfulness

> But the Fruit of the Spirit is love, joy, peace, Forbearance, kindness, goodness, Faithfulness, gentleness and Self-Control. (Galatians 5:22–23a NIV)

Faithful Creator

> So then, those who suffer according to God's will should commit themselves to their Faithful Creator and continue to do good. (1 Peter 4:19 NIV)

No Spirit of Fear

> For God has not given us a Spirit of Fear and timidity, but of power, love, and self-discipline. (2 Timothy 1:7 NLT)

Firm Foundation

> In this way they will lay up treasure for themselves as a Firm Foundation for the coming age, so that they may take hold of the life that is truly life. (1 Timothy 6:19 NIV)

Foundation

> For no one can lay any Foundation other than the one we already have—Jesus Christ. (1 Corinthians 3:11 NLT)

Forever and Ever

> Before the mountains were born, before You gave birth to the earth and the world, Forever and Ever, You are God. (Psalm 90:2 NLV)

Everlasting Father

> For unto us a child is born; unto us a son is given; and the government shall be upon His shoulder. These will be

His royal titles: "Wonderful," "Counselor," "The Mighty God," "The Everlasting Father," "The Prince of Peace." (Isaiah 9:6 TLB)

Faithful People

Sing the praises of the Lord, You His Faithful People; praise His Holy Name. (Psalm 30:4 NIV)

Faithful

For the Word of the Lord is right and true; He is Faithful in all He does. (Psalm 33:4 NIV)

Let those who love the Lord hate evil, for He guards the lives of His Faithful ones and delivers them from the hand of the wicked. (Psalm 97:10 NIV)

Wisdom From Above, First, Full of Mercy, Fruit, No Favoritism

But the Wisdom From Above is First of all pure. It is also peace loving, gentle at all times, and willing to yield to others. It is Full of Mercy and the Fruit of good deeds. It shows No Favoritism and is always sincere. (James 3:17 NLT)

Fountain of Life

For You are the Fountain of Life, the light by which we see. (Psalm 36:9 NLT)

Live Forever, Flesh

I am the living bread that came down from heaven. Anyone who eats this bread will Live Forever; and this bread, which I will offer so the world may live, is my Flesh. (John 6:51 NLT)

Eats My Flesh

> But anyone who Eats My Flesh and drinks my blood has eternal life, and I will raise that person at the last day. (John 6:54 NLT)

Fighting, Flesh

> For we are not fighting against Flesh-and-blood enemies, but against evil rulers and authorities of the unseen world, against mighty powers in this dark world, and against evil spirits in the heavenly places. (Ephesians 6:12 NLT)

Fortress

> God is my strong Fortress, and He makes my way perfect. (2 Samuel 22:33 NLT)

> The Lord is my rock, my Fortress, and my Savior; my God is my rock, in whom I find protection. He is my shield, the power that saves me, and my place of safety. (Psalm 18:2 NLT)

> The Lord is my light and my salvation—so why should I be afraid? The Lord is my Fortress, protecting me from danger, so why should I tremble? (Psalm 27:1 NLT)

> The Lord rescues the godly; He is their Fortress in times of trouble. (Psalm 37:39 NLT)

> He alone is my rock and my salvation, my Fortress where I will never be shaken. (Psalm 62:2 NLT)

Friends

> You are my Friends if you do what I command. (John 15:14 NLT)

> Look! I stand at the door and knock. If you hear My voice and open the door, I will come in, and we will share a meal together as Friends. (Revelation 3:20 NLT)

Friends of God

> So now we can rejoice in our wonderful new relationship with God because our Lord Jesus Christ has made us Friends of God. (Romans 5:11 NLT)

Friends, Friendly, Friend

> A man who has Friends must show himself Friendly, and there is a Friend who sticks closer than a brother. (Proverbs 18:24 MEV)

Fine Young Men, Faint and Weary

> Beautiful girls and Fine Young Men alike will grow Faint and Weary, thirsting for the Word of God. (Amos 8:13 TLB)

Faint

> But they that wait upon the Lord shall renew their strength. They shall mount up with wings like eagles; they shall run and not be weary; they shall walk and not Faint. (Isaiah 40:31 KJ21)

Fellow Worker, Faith, Fainthearted

> And send Timothy, our brother and Fellow Worker, God's minister, to visit you to strengthen your Faith and encourage you and to keep you from becoming Fainthearted in all the troubles you were going through. (But of course, you know that such troubles are a part of God's plan for us Christians?) (1 Thessalonians 3:2–3 TLB)

Fault, Find, Far from Me

> This is what the Lord says: "What Fault did your ancestors Find in Me that led them to stray so Far from Me? They worshiped worthless idols, only to become worthless themselves." (Jeremiah 2:5 NLT)

Fault

> If your brother sins against you, go to him and show him his Fault. But do it privately, just between yourselves. If he listens to you, you have won your brother back. (Matthew 18:15 GNT)

Faults, Forgive, Fault

> None of us know our Faults. Forgive me when I sin without knowing it. Don't let me do wrong on purpose, Lord, or let sin have control over my life. Then I will be innocent, and not guilty of some terrible Fault. (Psalm 19:12–13 CEV)

Free from Love of Money, Forsake

> Keep your lives Free from the Love of Money, and be content with what you have; for He has said, "I will never leave you or Forsake you." (Hebrews 13:5 NRSVA)

Fear of the Lord, Forsake Evil

> And this is what He says to all humanity: "The Fear of the Lord is true wisdom; to Forsake Evil is real understanding." (Job 28:28 NLT)

Finisher of Our Faith

> Let us look to Jesus, the author and Finisher of Our Faith, who for the joy that was set before Him endured the cross, despising the shame, and is seated at the right hand of the throne of God. (Hebrews 12:2 MEV)

Firstborn

> And again, when He brings the Firstborn into the world, He says: "Let all the angels of God worship Him." (Hebrews 1:6 MEV)

Foreknew, Firstborn

> For those whom He Foreknew, He predestined to be conformed to the image of His Son, so that He might be the Firstborn among many brothers. (Romans 8:29 MEV)

Fact, From, First Fruits, Fallen Asleep

> But in Fact, Christ has been raised From the dead, the First Fruits of those who have Fallen asleep. (1 Corinthians 15:20 EHV)

> But the truth is that Christ has been raised From death, as the guarantee that those who sleep in death will also be raised. (1 Corinthians 15:20 GNT)

Forsake, Forsaken, Fountain of Living Waters

> O Lord, the Hope of Israel, all who Forsake You will be ashamed. "Those who depart from Me in the earth will be written down, because they have Forsaken the Lord, the Fountain of Living Waters." (Jeremiah 17:13 MEV)

Fountain of Life Flows From You

> The Fountain of Life Flows From You. Your light lets us see light. (Psalm 36:9 ERV)

Feasts, Friend of Tax Collectors and Sinners, Follow Wisdom

> The Son of Man, on the other hand, Feasts and drinks, and you say, "He's a glutton and a drunkard, and a Friend of Tax Collectors and other Sinners!" But wisdom is shown to be right by the lives of those who Follow it. (Luke 7:34–35 NLT)

Finds, Favor of the Lord

> Whoever Finds a wife Finds a good thing, and obtains Favor of the Lord. (Proverbs 18:22 MEV)

Fullness of Joy, Forevermore

> Because of You, I know the path of life, as I taste the Fullness of Joy in Your presence. At Your right side I experience divine pleasures Forevermore! (Psalm 16:11 TPT)

Full Life, I Do For You, Enjoy Fullness

> I will satisfy you with a Full Life and with all that I Do For You. For you will Enjoy the Fullness of my salvation! (Psalm 91:16 TPT)

Feel, Joy and Fullness

> Everything seems to go wrong when you Feel weak and depressed. But when you choose to be cheerful, every day will bring you more and more Joy and Fullness. (Proverbs 15:15 TPT)

Pray For, Fullness of Faith

> Everything you Pray For with the Fullness of Faith you will receive! (Matthew 21:22 TPT)

Fulfillment, Fullness, Hope-Filled Gospel

> His message was this: "At last the Fulfillment of the age has come! It is time For God's kingdom to be experienced in its Fullness! Turn your lives back to God and put your trust in the Hope-Filled Gospel!" (Mark 1:15 TPT)

Function, Faith, Fullness, Finally, Full, Fully Developed

> These grace ministries will Function until we all attain oneness into the Faith, until we all experience the Fullness of what it means to know the Son of God, and Finally we become one into a perfect man with the Full dimensions of spiritual maturity and Fully Developed into the abundance of Christ. (Ephesians 4:13 TPT)

PRAYERS (USING F WORDS)

Thank You, God, for setting us *free* as we *follow* You. May we keep our minds *focused* on You so the enemy cannot touch us! We are grateful that You are our *Firm Foundation* and *Fountain* of life. We praise Your *friendship, fellowship,* and *faithfulness*. *Father* God, thank You for *filling* us with the *fruit* of the Spirit and increasing our *faith*. We are grateful that You are a *forgiving Father*. We love You, Lord, and are in awe that You will never leave us or *forsake* us! It is *fantastic* that You have helped us become *fully* mature, *fully* developed, and *fully* alive in Christ. We thank You, *Father* God, for the shield of *faith*, which helps us extinguish the *flaming* arrows of the *fiery* evil one! It is a *fact*, God, that You are such a *forgiving Father*, and the more we become *familiar* with You, the more *fruitful* we become. We are very *fortunate* to have You in our lives.

We praise You, *Father* God, and we pray in Your *faithful* name. Amen.

G

In the beginning GOD created the heavens and the earth. Now the earth was formless and empty, darkness was over the surface of the deep, and the Spirit of God was hovering over the waters. And God said, "Let there be light" and there was Light. (Genesis 1:1–3 NIV)

The Beginning: God started creation.

The First Day: God created light.

The Second Day: God created the sky.

The Third Day: God created dry land, seas, plants, and trees.

The Fourth Day: God created the sun, moon, and stars.

The Fifth Day: God created creatures that live in the sea and creatures that fly.

The Sixth Day: God created animals that live on land and male and female made in the image of God.

By Day Seven: God finished His work of creation and rested, making the seventh day a special holy day.

God separated the light from the darkness. God called the light Day, and the darkness He called Night. And there was evening and there was morning, one day. (Genesis 1:4b–5 CSB)

God called the dry land Earth, and the accumulated waters He called Seas. And God saw that this was good (fitting, admirable) and He approved it. God said, Let the Earth put forth [tender] vegetation, plants yielding seed and fruit trees yielding fruit whose seed is in itself, each according to its kind, upon the earth. And it was so. (Genesis 1:10–11 AMPC)

God made the two great lights—the greater light (the sun) to rule the day and the lesser light (the moon) to rule the night. He also made the stars. (Genesis 1:16 AMPC)

And God said, "Let the waters bring forth abundantly and swarm with living creatures and let birds fly over the earth in the open expanse of the heavens." (Genesis 1:20 AMPC)

And God said, "Let the earth bring forth living creatures according to their kinds—livestock and creeping things and beasts of the earth according to their kinds." (Genesis 1:24 ESV)

So, God created man in His own image, in the image and likeness of God He created him; male and female He created them. (Genesis 1:27 AMPC)

And God blessed them, and God said to them, "Be fruitful and multiply, and fill the earth and subdue it; and have dominion over the fish of the sea, and over the birds of the air and over every living thing that moves upon the earth." (Genesis 1:28 RSV)

God

But God has shown us how much He loves us—it was while we were still sinners that Christ died for us! (Romans 5:8 GNT)

Good Shepherd

> I am the Good Shepherd. The Good Shepherd lays down His life for the sheep. (John 10:11 CEB)

> I am the Good Shepherd; I know My own sheep, and they know Me. (John 10:14 CEB)

Great High Priest, Son of God

> Therefore, since we have a Great High Priest who has passed through the heavens, Jesus the Son of God, let us hold fast to our confession. (Hebrews 4:14 CSB)

Great High Priest, God's House

> We have a Great High Priest who is in charge of God's House. (Hebrews 10:21 CEV)

Life Pleases God, Given to Us, God's Power, Share in Goodness

> We have everything we need to live a Life that Pleases God. It was all Given to Us by God's own Power, when we learned He had invited us to Share in His Wonderful Goodness. (2 Peter 1:3 CEV)

Goodness and Mercy

> Surely Goodness and Mercy shall follow me all the days of my life: and I will dwell in the house of the Lord forever. (Psalm 23:6 KJ21)

Holy Spirit Produces Goodness, Gentleness

> But the Holy Spirit Produces this kind of fruit in our lives: love, joy, peace, patience, kindness, Goodness, faithfulness, Gentleness, and self-control. (Galatians 5:22–23a NLT)

Love and Goodness

> Forgive the sins and errors of my youth. In your constant Love and Goodness, remember me, Lord! (Psalm 25:7 GNT)

Add Goodness, Add Knowledge, Add Self-Control, Add Endurance, Add Godliness

> For this very reason do your best to add Goodness to your faith; to your Goodness add knowledge; to your knowledge add self-control; to your self-control add endurance; to your endurance add Godliness; to your Godliness add Christian affection; and to your Christian affection add love. These are the qualities you need, and if you have them in abundance, they will make you active and effective in your knowledge of our Lord Jesus Christ. (2 Peter 1:5–8 GNT)

Goodness, Gracious

> And He said, "I will make all My Goodness pass before you and will proclaim before you My name 'The Lord.' And I will be Gracious to whom I will be Gracious, and will show mercy on whom I will show mercy." (Exodus 33:19 ESV)

Lord God, Merciful and Gracious, Goodness

> And the Lord passed by before Him, and proclaimed, The Lord, The Lord God, Merciful and Gracious, longsuffering, and abundant in Goodness and truth. (Exodus 34:6 KJ21)

All Good Things Come from You

> I said to the Lord, "You are my Lord. All the Good Things I have come from You." (Psalm 16:2 NLV)

> Lord Is Good O taste and see that the Lord Is Good: blessed is the man that trusteth in Him. (Psalm 34:8 KJ21)

Good Things

> How wonderful are the Good Things you keep for those who honor You! Everyone knows how Good You are, how securely You protect those who trust You. (Psalm 31:19 GNT)

Glory and Honor, People will See the Good

> Then this city will bring me joy, Glory, and Honor before all the nations of the earth! The People of the world will See all the Good I do for My people, and they will tremble with awe at the peace and prosperity I provide for them. (Jeremiah 33:9 NLT)

Great Works, Good Things

> Let them give thanks to the Lord for His loving-kindness and His Great Works to the children of men! For He fills the thirsty soul. And He fills the hungry soul with Good Things. (Psalm 107:8–9 NLV)

Wisdom Leads Us to be Gentle, Genuine

> But the Wisdom that comes from above Leads us to be pure, friendly, Gentle, sensible, kind, helpful, Genuine, and sincere. (James 3:17 CEV)

Pursue Godliness, Gentleness

> But you, man of God, flee from all this, and Pursue righteousness, Godliness, faith, love, endurance, & Gentleness. (1 Timothy 6:11 NIV)

Gentleness Be Evident

> Let your Gentleness Be Evident to all. The Lord is near. (Philippians 4:5 NIV)

Humility and Gentleness

> With complete Humility and Gentleness, with patience, putting up with one another in love. (Ephesians 4:2 TLV)

Give an answer, Gentleness and Respect

> But in your hearts revere Christ as Lord. Always be prepared to Give an answer to everyone who asks you to Give the reason for the hope that you have. But do this with Gentleness and Respect. (1 Peter 3:15 NIV)

God's Chosen People, Gentleness

> Therefore, as God's Chosen People, holy and dearly loved, clothe yourselves with compassion, kindness, humility, Gentleness and patience. (Colossians 3:12 NIV)

Recognized by Gentleness

> He cannot be a drunkard, or someone who lashes out at others, or argumentative, or someone who simply craves more money, but instead, Recognized by His Gentleness. (1 Timothy 3:3 TPT)

Gentle Answer

> A Gentle Answer turns away wrath, but a harsh word stirs up anger. (Proverbs 15:1 NIV)

Gentle Words

> Gentle Words are a tree of life; a deceitful tongue crushes the spirit. (Proverbs 15:4 NLT)

Gentle and Humble

> Take My yoke upon you and learn from Me, for I am Gentle and Humble in heart, and you will find rest for your souls. (Matthew 11:29 NIV)

Gentle among You

> Even though we could have imposed upon you our demands as apostles of Christ, instead we showed you

kindness and were Gentle Among You. We cared for you in the same way a nursing mother cares for her own children. (1 Thessalonians 2:7 TPT)

Gentle toward Everyone

To slander no one, to be peaceable and considerate and always to be Gentle toward Everyone. (Titus 3:2 NIV)

Gratitude, The Lord Himself Is God

Know and fully recognize with Gratitude that The Lord Himself Is God; It is He who has made us, not we ourselves [and we are His]. We are His people and the sheep of His pasture. (Psalm 100:3 AMP)

Meets Needs of God's People, Gratitude to God

For this service You perform not only Meets the Needs of God's People, but also produces an outpouring of Gratitude to God. (2 Corinthians 9:12 GNT)

Sing to God with Gratitude

Christ's message in all its richness must live in your hearts. Teach and instruct one another with all wisdom. Sing psalms, hymns, and sacred songs; Sing to God with thanksgiving (Gratitude) in your hearts. (Colossians 3:16 GNT)

Should have Gratitude, Pleasing to God

Therefore, we who are receiving the unshakable kingdom Should have Gratitude, with which we should offer worship Pleasing to God in reverence and awe. (Hebrews 12:28 NABRE)

Glorious Gospel, Gratitude for God's Mercy

According to the Glorious Gospel of the blessed God, with which I have been entrusted. Gratitude for God's Mercy. (1 Timothy 1:11 NABRE)

Give Glory to God, Generosity, Good News of Christ

> As a result of your ministry, they will Give Glory to God. For your Generosity to them and to all believers will prove that you are obedient to the Good News of Christ. (2 Corinthians 9:13 NLT)

Given us a Special Gift, Generosity of Christ

> However, He has Given each one of us a Special Gift through the Generosity of Christ. (Ephesians 4:7 NLT)

Great Joy and Generosity

> They worshiped together at the Temple each day, met in homes for the Lord's Supper, and shared their meals with Great Joy and Generosity. (Acts 2:46 NLT)

God, Great Harvest of Generosity

> For God is the one who provides seed for the farmer and then bread to eat. In the same way, He will provide and increase your resources and then produce a Great Harvest of Generosity in you. (2 Corinthians 9:10 NLT)

Generosity

> They are being tested by many troubles, and they are very poor. But they are also filled with abundant joy, which has overflowed in rich Generosity. (2 Corinthians 8:2 NLT)

Generosity, Good Things

> And I am praying that you will put into action the Generosity that comes from your faith as you understand and experience all the Good Things we have in Christ. (Philemon 1:6 NLT)

Give

> Give as you are able, according as the Lord has blessed you. (Deuteronomy 16:17 TLB)

He Will Give You

> And I will ask the Father, and He Will Give You another Advocate, who will never leave you. (John 14:16 NLT)

Holy Spirit Gives Birth

> Humans can reproduce only human life, but the Holy Spirit Gives Birth to spiritual life. (John 3:6 NLT)

God will Give

> But even now I know that God will Give you whatever you ask. (John 11:22 NLT)

Given Him Authority, Return to God

> Jesus knew that the Father had Given Him Authority over everything and that He had come from God and would Return to God. (John 13:3 NLT)

Given, Glory You have Given me

> Father, I want those you have Given me to be with me where I am, and to see my Glory, the Glory You have Given me because you loved me before the creation of the world. (John 17:24 NIV)

Gift, Peace I Give

> I am leaving you with a Gift—peace of mind and heart. And the Peace I Give is a Gift the world cannot Give. So don't be troubled or afraid. (John 14:27 NLT)

God Is Glorified, Glorify the Son

> If God Is Glorified in Him, God will Glorify the Son in Himself, and will Glorify Him at once. (John 13:32 NIV)

Loved by God, Give Grace and Peace

> I am writing to all of you in Rome who are Loved by God and are called to be His own holy people. May God our Father and the Lord Jesus Christ Give you Grace and Peace. (Romans 1:7 NLT)

Give Eternal Life, Will of God, Unseen Glory and Honor

> He will Give Eternal Life to those who patiently do the Will of God, seeking for the Unseen Glory and Honor and Eternal Life that He offers. (Romans 2:7 TLB)

Grace, God Has Given us Different Gifts

> In His Grace, God Has Given us different Gifts for doing certain things well. So, if God has Given you the ability to prophesy, speak out with as much faith as God has Given you. (Romans 12:6 NLT)

Gift, Giving, Give Generously, God Has Given You, Do It Gladly

> If your Gift is to encourage others, be encouraging. If it is Giving, Give Generously. If God has Given you leadership ability, take the responsibility seriously. And if you have a Gift for showing kindness to others, do it Gladly. (Romans 12:8 NLT)

Gospel, Power of God

> For I am not ashamed of the Gospel; it is the Power of God for salvation to everyone who has faith, to the Jew first and also to the Greek. (Romans 1:16 NRSVA)

Proclaim the Gospel

> In the same way, the Lord commanded that those who Proclaim the Gospel should get their living by the Gospel. (1 Corinthians 9:14 NRSVA)

Gospel of Your Salvation

> In Him you also, when you had heard the word of truth, the Gospel of Your Salvation, and had believed in Him, were marked with the seal of the promised Holy Spirit. (Ephesians 1:13 NRSVA)

Light of the Gospel, Glory of Christ, Image of God

> In their case the god (Enemy Satan) of this world has blinded the minds of the unbelievers, to keep them from seeing the Light of the Gospel of the Glory of Christ, who is the Image of God. (2 Corinthians 4:4 NRSVA)

Gospel of Christ

> Only, live your life in a manner worthy of the Gospel of Christ, so that, whether I come and see you or am absent and hear about you, I will know that you are standing firm in one spirit, striving side by side with one mind for the faith of the Gospel. (Philippians 1:27 NRSVA)

Grace of God, Truth of the Gospel

> It's no wonder I pray with such confidence, since you have a permanent place in my heart! You have remained partners with me in the wonderful Grace of God even though I'm here in chains for standing up for the Truth of the Gospel. (Philippians 1:7 TPT)

Glorify God, Gospel of Christ, Generosity

> Through the testing of this ministry, you Glorify God by your obedience to the confession of the Gospel of Christ and by the Generosity of your sharing with them and with all others. (2 Corinthians 9:13 NRSVA)

Godly Lives

> It teaches us to say "No" to ungodliness and worldly passions, and to live self-controlled, upright and Godly Lives in this present age. (Titus 2:12 NIV)

> And so, since everything around us is going to melt away, what holy, Godly Lives we should be living! (2 Peter 3:11 TLB)

Godly Life, Glory and Goodness

> His divine power has Given us everything we need for a Godly Life through our knowledge of Him who called us by his own Glory and Goodness. (2 Peter 1:3 NIV)

Godliness

> For physical training is of some value, but Godliness has value for all things, holding promise for both the present life and the life to come. (1 Timothy 4:8 NIV)

Great Gain

> But Godliness with contentment is Great Gain. (1 Timothy 6:6 NIV)

His Glory, Full of Grace and Truth

> The Word became flesh and made His dwelling among us. We have seen His Glory, the Glory of the one and only Son, who came from the Father, Full of Grace and Truth. (John 1:14 NIV)

God's Grace

> With great power the apostles continued to testify to the resurrection of the Lord Jesus. And God's Grace was so powerfully at work in them all. (Acts 4:33 NIV)

Good News of God's Grace

> However, I consider my life worth nothing to me; my only aim is to finish the race and complete the task the Lord Jesus has given me—the task of testifying to the Good News of God's Grace. (Acts 20:24 NIV)

Grace, Glory of God

> All this is for your benefit, so that the Grace that is reaching more and more people may cause thanksgiving to overflow to the Glory of God. (2 Corinthians 4:15 NIV)

Grace of Our Lord Jesus Christ

> You know the Grace of Our Lord Jesus Christ; rich as He was, He made Himself poor for your sake, in order to make you rich by means of His poverty. (2 Corinthians 8:9 GNT)

My Grace Is Sufficient, Gladly

> But He said to me, "My Grace Is sufficient for you, for my power is made perfect in weakness." Therefore, I will boast all the more Gladly of my weaknesses, so that the power of Christ may rest upon me. (2 Corinthians 12:9 ESV)

By Grace, Gift of God

> For it is By Grace you have been saved, through Faith and this is not from yourselves, it is the Gift of God. (Ephesians 2:8 NIV)

Guidance

> Let the wise listen to these proverbs and become even wiser. Let those with understanding receive Guidance. (Proverbs 1:5 NLT)

And I will destroy those who used to worship me but now no longer do. They no longer ask for the Lord's Guidance or seek my blessings. (Zephaniah 1:6 NLT)

Give You Spiritual Guidance

Dear brothers and sisters, honor those who are your leaders in the Lord's work. They work hard among you and Give You Spiritual Guidance. (1 Thessalonians 5:12 NLT)

He will Guide you

When the Spirit of truth comes, He will Guide you into all truth. He will not speak on His own but will tell you what He has heard. He will tell you about the future. (John 16:13 NLT)

Guide Them

Give them someone who will Guide them wherever they go and will lead them into battle, so the community of the Lord will not be like sheep without a shepherd. (Numbers 27:17 NLT)

He Gives me Wisdom, Guides me

I will bless the Lord who counsels me; He Gives me Wisdom in the night. He tells me what to do. (Psalm 16:7 TLB)

Greatness, Glory and the Majesty

Yours, Lord, is the Greatness and the power and the Glory and The Majesty and the splendor, for everything in heaven and earth is yours. Yours, Lord, is the kingdom; You are exalted as head over all. (1 Chronicles 29:11 NIV)

Lord's Greatness, King-God

> For the Lord's Greatness is beyond description, and He deserves all the praise that comes to Him. He is our King-God, and it's right to be in holy awe of Him. (Psalm 96:4 TPT)

Ye Are of God, Greater is He

> Ye Are of God, little children, and have overcome them, because Greater is He that is in you than He that is in the world. (1 John 4:4 KJ21)

Generations

> Your faithfulness continues through all Generations; You established the earth, and it endures. (Psalm 119:90 NIV)

God's Handiwork, Do Good Works

> For we are God's Handiwork, created in Christ Jesus to Do Good Works, which God prepared in advance for us to do. (Ephesians 2:10 NIV)

Grow

> Do you not know? Have you not heard? The Lord is the everlasting God, the Creator of the ends of the earth. He will not Grow tired or weary, and His understanding no one can fathom. (Isaiah 40:28 NIV)

Growing

> Instead, we will speak the truth in love, Growing in every way more and more like Christ, who is the head of His body, the church. (Ephesians 4:15 NLT)

Good Work, Growing in the Knowledge of God

> To walk in a manner worthy of the Lord, to please Him in all respects, bearing fruit in every Good Work and Growing in the Knowledge of God. (Colossians 1:10 TLV)

Grow in the Grace, To Him Be Glory

> But Grow in the Grace and knowledge of our Lord and Savior Jesus Christ. To Him Be Glory both now and forever! Amen. (2 Peter 3:18 ASV)

Gift of God, Given Living Water

> Jesus answered her, "If you knew the Gift of God, and who it is who is saying to you, 'Give Me a drink,' you would have asked Him, and He would have Given you Living Water." (John 4:10 EHV)

My Glory

> But you, Lord, are a shield that protects me, you are My Glory and the one who restores me. (Psalm 3:3 NET)

Great Men of God, Praise God Forever

> Great Men of God were your fathers, and Christ Himself was one of you, a Jew so far as His human nature is concerned, He who now rules over all things. Praise God Forever! (Romans 9:5 TLB)

God

> Lord our God, you answered their prayers. You showed them that you are a forgiving God and that you punish people for the evil they do. (Psalm 99:8 ERV)

O God, Given Me Relief

> Hear me when I call, O God of my righteousness! You have Given Me Relief when I was in distress; have mercy on me, and hear my prayer. (Psalm 4:1 MEV)

God of My Salvation

> The Lord lives! And blessed be my Rock! May the God of My Salvation be exalted. (Psalm 18:46 MEV)

Goodness, God of My Life

> The Lord will send His Goodness in the daytime; And His song will be with me in the night, A prayer to the God of My Life. (Psalm 42:8 NASB)

Glad the City of God

> There is a river whose streams make Glad the City of God, the holy dwelling place of the Most High. God is in the midst of her; she will not be moved; God will help her in the early dawn. (Psalm 46:4–5 MEV)

Grace

> The Grace of our Lord Jesus Christ be with you all. Amen. (Romans 16:24 KJ21)

Glory of Our Great God

> As we await the blessed hope and the appearing of the Glory of Our Great God and Savior Jesus Christ. (Titus 2:13 MEV)

God of Peace, Great Shepherd of the Sheep

> Now may the God of Peace, who through the blood of the eternal covenant brought again from the dead our Lord Jesus, the Great Shepherd of the Sheep. (Hebrews 13:20 MEV)

God Forever and Ever, our Guide

> For this God is our God Forever and Ever; He will be our Guide even unto death. (Psalm 48:14 KJ21)

Never Grieve the Spirit of God, Granted

> The Holy Spirit of God has sealed you in Jesus Christ until you experience your full salvation. So Never Grieve the Spirit of God or take for Granted His holy influence in your life. (Ephesians 4:30 TPT)

Gladness

> Serve the Lord with Gladness; come before His presence with singing! (Psalm 100:2 KJ21)

O God, Give us a fresh start, Joy and Gladness

> Revive us again, O God! I know you will! Give us a fresh start! Then all Your people will taste Your Joy and Gladness. (Psalm 85:6 TPT)

Gladden Hearts, Give Us Daily Bread, Glowing Health

> You provide sweet wine to Gladden Hearts. You Give Us Daily Bread to sustain life, Giving Us Glowing Health for our bodies. (Psalm 104:15 TPT)

<u>PRAYERS</u> (Using G Words)

Father **God**, thank You for Your **goodness**, Your **glorious good news** and Your **grace**. We are **grateful** for Your **godly gifts** such as **gentleness**, **guidance**, and the **Gospel of Christ**. We are in awe of the spiritual **growth** that You have shown and **given** us. **God**, You are so **good** to us, and we **glorify** You in a **glorious** way! We praise You, **God**, for creating the heavens and the earth. May You be **glorified**, **God**, for teaching us to be **godly**. Thank You, **God**. When we are sad, You **give** us a **garland** and a crown of beauty. You **give** us Your anointing oil of **gladness**, and we can clothe ourselves in a **garment** of praise. You **gladden** our hearts and **give** us **glowing**, spiritual, emotional, and physical health. Thank You, **God**, for the **Gospel** of peace, which is part of Your armor. Jesus, You are the **greatest**, You help us to be **gentle** and **grow** in Your love, and we **glow** inside our hearts.

We praise You, Father **God**, and we pray in Your **gracious** name.

Amen.

H

Hope of Salvation, Holy Spirit

> And endurance develops strength of character, and character strengthens our confident Hope of Salvation. And this Hope will not lead to disappointment. For we know how dearly God loves us, because He has given us the Holy Spirit to fill our hearts with His love. (Romans 5:4–5 NLT)

Hope in the Lord, Our Help

> We put our Hope in the Lord. He is Our Help and our shield. (Psalm 33:20 NLT)

Hope in God, Heart

> Why am I discouraged? Why is my Heart so sad? I will put my Hope in God! I will praise Him again—my Savior and my God! (Psalm 43:5 NLT)

Hope in the Lord

> So be strong and courageous, all you who put your Hope in the Lord! (Psalm 31:24 NLT)

> Let your unfailing love surround us, Lord, for our Hope is in you alone. (Psalm 33:22 NLT)

> So, each generation should set its Hope anew on God, not forgetting His glorious miracles and obeying His commands. (Psalm 78:7 NLT)

You are my refuge and my shield; your word is my source of Hope. (Psalm 119:114 NLT)

Discipline your children while there is Hope. Otherwise, you will ruin their lives. (Proverbs 19:18 NLT)

Hope and Confidence

But blessed are those who trust in the Lord and have made the Lord their Hope and Confidence. (Jeremiah 17:7 NLT)

Head of the Church

And He put all things under His feet and gave Him as Head over all things to the church. (Ephesians 1:22 ESV)

Holy Servant, Hand, Heal

And now, Lord, observe their threats [take them into account] and grant that Your bond-servants may declare Your message [of salvation] with great confidence, while You extend Your Hand to Heal, & signs and wonders (attesting miracles) take place through the name [and the authority and power] of Your Holy Servant and Son Jesus. (Acts 4:29–30 AMP)

Humble

He was Humble and walked the path of obedience all the way to death—His death on the cross. (Philippians 2:8 GNT)

Humble, Honor

Showing respect to the Lord will make you wise, and being Humble will bring Honor to you. (Proverbs 15:33 CEV)

Humble, Humility

> You younger men, likewise, be subject to your elders; and all of you, clothe yourselves with Humility toward one another, because God is opposed to the proud, but He gives grace to the Humble. (1 Peter 5:5 NASB)

Holy People He Loves, Humility

> Since God chose you to be the Holy People He Loves, you must clothe yourselves with tenderhearted mercy, kindness, Humility, gentleness, and patience. (Colossians 3:12 NLT)

Honest

> We want to do the right thing. We want God and men to know we are Honest. (2 Corinthians 8:21 NLV)

> A good man is guided by his Honesty; the evil man is destroyed by his dishonesty. (Proverbs 11:3 TLB)

High Priest, Holy, Heavens

> Jesus, then, is the High Priest that meets our needs. He is Holy; He has no fault or sin in Him; He has been set apart from sinners and raised above the Heavens. (Hebrews 7:26 GNT)

Practice Hospitality

> Share with the Lord's people who are in need. Practice Hospitality. (Romans 12:13 NIV)

Holy Hill

> Exalt the Lord our God, and worship at His Holy Hill; for the Lord our God is Holy. (Psalm 99:9 KJ21)

Help, Heaven

> Our Help is in the name of the Lord, who made Heaven and earth. (Psalm 124:8 KJ21)

Heaven, Hallelujah

> After this I heard what sounded like the roar of a great multitude in Heaven shouting: "Hallelujah! Salvation and glory and power belong to our God." (Revelation 19:1 NIV)

High Priest, He Is Holy, Higher than the Heavens

> For such a High Priest was fitting for us, for He Is Holy, innocent, undefiled, separate from sinners, and is Higher than the Heavens. (Hebrews 7:26 MEV)

Complete in Him, Head

> And you are Complete in Him, who is the Head of all authority and power. (Colossians 2:10 MEV)

His Son, Appointed Heir, He Made the World

> Has in these last days spoken to us by His Son, whom He has Appointed Heir of all things, and through whom He made the world. (Hebrews 1:2 MEV)

Helper

> So, we may boldly say: "The Lord is my Helper; I will not fear. What can man do to me?" (Hebrews 13:6 MEV)

Hiding Place

> You are my Hiding Place; You will preserve me from trouble; You will surround me with shouts of deliverance. (Psalm 32:7 MEV)

High Priest, Honor

> Where Christ has gone ahead to plead for us from His position as our High Priest, with the Honor and rank of Melchizedek. (Hebrews 6:20 TLB)

High Tower of Refuge

> But as for me, I will sing each morning about your power and mercy. For you have been my High Tower of Refuge, a place of safety in the day of my distress. (Psalm 59:16 TLB)

Himself, He, The Holy One

> Yes, our protection is from the Lord Himself and He, The Holy One of Israel, has given us our king. (Psalm 89:18 TLB)

Horn of Salvation, House

> And has raised up a Horn of Salvation for us in the House of His servant David. (Luke 1:69 ESV)

Heaven, Holy City, Heavenly, Husband

> Then in a vision I saw a new Heaven and a new earth. The first Heaven and earth had passed away, and the sea no longer existed. I saw the Holy City, the New Jerusalem, descending out of the Heavenly realm from the presence of God, like a pleasing bride that had been prepared for her Husband. (Revelation 21:1–2 TPT)

Head of the Church, His Body, He

> Christ is also the Head of the Church, which is His Body. He is the beginning, supreme over all who rise from the dead. So, He is first in everything. (Colossians 1:18 NLT)

Heaven, Hallowed

> He said to them, "When you pray, say, 'Our Father in Heaven, Hallowed be Your name. Your kingdom come. Your will be done on earth as it is in Heaven." (Luke 11:2 EHV)

HOLY SPIRIT
(DOES ALL THESE THINGS)

The Spirit Convicts the World of Sin, Righteousness, and Judgment

> When the Helper comes, He will show the world the truth about sin. He will show the world about being right with God. And He will show the world what it is to be guilty. (John 16:8 NLV)

The Spirit Guides Us into All Truth

> The Holy Spirit is coming. He will lead you into all truth. He will not speak His Own words. He will speak what He hears. He will tell you of things to come. (John 16:13 NLV)

The Spirit Regenerates Us

> Jesus replied, "I assure you; no one can enter the Kingdom of God without being born of water and the Spirit. Humans can reproduce only human life, but the Holy Spirit gives birth to spiritual life. So don't be surprised when I say, 'You must be born again.' The wind blows wherever it wants. Just as you can hear the wind but can't tell where it comes from or where it is going, so you can't explain how people are born of the Spirit." (John 3:5–8 NLT)

He saved us, not because of the righteous things we had done, but because of His mercy. He washed away our sins, giving us a new birth and new life through the Holy Spirit. (Titus 3:5 NLT)

The Spirit Glorifies and Testifies of Christ

But I will send you the Advocate—the Spirit of truth. He will come to you from the Father and will testify all about me. (John 15:26 NLT)

He shall praise me and bring me great Honor by showing you, my glory. (John 16:14 TLB)

The Spirit Reveals Christ to us and in us

The Spirit will bring glory to me by taking my message and telling it to you. Everything the Father has is mine. That is why I have said that the Spirit takes my message and tells it to you. (John 16:14–15 CEV)

The Spirit Leads Us

For all who are led by the Spirit of God are sons of God. (Romans 8:14 AMPC)

But if you are led by the Spirit, you are not under the law. (Galatians 5:18 CSB)

Then Jesus was led by the Spirit into the wilderness to be tempted by the devil. (Matthew 4:1 EHV)

Jesus, full of the Holy Spirit, returned from the Jordan and was led by the Spirit in the wilderness. (Luke 4:1 EHV)

The Spirit Sanctifies Us

Christian brothers, the Lord loves you. We always thank God for you. It is because God has chosen you from the beginning to save you from the punishment of sin. He chose to make you holy by the Holy Spirit and to give you faith to believe the truth. (2 Thessalonians 2:13 NLV)

God the Father knew you and chose you long ago, and His Spirit has made you holy. As a result, you have obeyed Him and have been cleansed by the blood of Jesus Christ. May God give you more and more grace and peace. (1 Peter 1:2 NLT)

The Spirit Empowers Us

Then Jesus returned to Galilee, and the power of the Holy Spirit was with Him. The news about Him spread throughout all that territory. (Luke 4:14 GNT)

They were convinced by the power of miraculous signs and wonders and by the power of God's Spirit. In this way, I have fully presented the Good News of Christ from Jerusalem all the way to Illyricum. (Romans 15:19 NLT)

But you will receive power when the Holy Spirit comes upon you. And you will be my witnesses, telling people about Me everywhere—in Jerusalem, throughout Judea, in Samaria, and to the ends of the earth. (Acts 1:8 NLT)

The Spirit Fills Us

Don't be drunk with wine, because that will ruin your life. Instead, be filled with the Holy Spirit. (Ephesians 5:18 NLT)

And everyone present was filled with the Holy Spirit and began speaking in other languages, as the Holy Spirit gave them this ability. (Acts 2:4 NLT)

Then Peter, filled with the Holy Spirit, said to them, "Rulers and elders of our people." (Acts 4:8 NLT)

> After this prayer, the meeting place shook, and they were all filled with the Holy Spirit. Then they preached the word of God with boldness. (Acts 4:31 NLT)

> So, Ananias went and found Saul. He laid his hands on him and said, "Brother Saul, the Lord Jesus, who appeared to you on the road, has sent me so that you might regain your sight and be filled with the Holy Spirit." (Acts 9:17 NLT)

The Spirit Teaches Us to Pray

> And the Holy Spirit helps us in our weakness. For example, we don't know what God wants us to pray for. But the Holy Spirit prays for us with groanings that cannot be expressed in words. And the Father who knows all hearts knows what the Spirit is saying, for the Spirit pleads for us believers in harmony with God's own will. (Romans 8:26–27 NLT)

> But you, dear friends, must build each other up in your most holy faith, pray in the power of the Holy Spirit. (Jude 1:20 NLT)

The Spirit Bears Witness in us that we are Children of God

> For His Spirit joins with our spirit to affirm that we are God's children. (Romans 8:16 NLT)

The Spirit produces in us the fruit or evidence of His work and presence

> But the Holy Spirit produces this kind of fruit in our lives: love, joy, peace, patience, kindness, goodness, faithfulness, gentleness, and self-control. There is no law against these things! (Galatians 5:22–23 NLT)

The Spirit Distributes Spiritual Gifts and Manifestations (the Outshining) of His Presence to and through the Body

> There are different kinds of spiritual gifts, but the same Spirit is the source of them all. (1 Corinthians 12:4 NLT)

To one person the Spirit gives the ability to give wise advice; to another the same Spirit gives a message of special knowledge. The same Spirit gives great faith to another, and to someone else the one Spirit gives the gift of healing. He gives one person the power to perform miracles, and another the ability to prophesy. He gives someone else the ability to discern whether a message is from the Spirit of God or from another spirit. Still another person is given the ability to speak in unknown language while another is given the ability to interpret what is being said. (1 Corinthians 12:8–10 NLT)

And God confirmed the message by giving signs and wonders and various miracles and gifts of the Holy Spirit whenever He chose. (Hebrews 2:4 NLT)

The Spirit Anoints us for Ministry

The Spirit of the Lord is upon me; He has appointed me to preach Good News to the poor; He has sent me to heal the brokenhearted and to announce that captives shall be released and the blind shall see, that the downtrodden shall be freed from their oppressors, and that God is ready to give blessings to all who come to Him. (Luke 4:18–19 TLB)

And you no doubt know that Jesus of Nazareth was anointed by God with the Holy Spirit and with power, and He went around doing good and healing all who were possessed by demons, for God was with Him. (Acts 10:38 TLB)

The Spirit Washes and Renews us

Then He saved us—not because we were good enough to be saved but because of His kindness and pity—by washing away our sins and giving us the new joy of the indwelling Holy Spirit. (Titus 3:5 TLB)

The Spirit Seals us unto the Day of Redemption

> And because of what Christ did, all you others too, who heard the Good News about how to be saved, and trusted Christ, were marked as belonging to Christ by the Holy Spirit, who long ago had been promised to all of us Christians. (Ephesians 1:13 TLB)

> Don't cause the Holy Spirit sorrow by the way you live. Remember, He is the one who marks you to be present on that day when salvation from sin will be complete. (Ephesians 4:30 TLB)

The Spirit Sets Us Free from the Law of Sin and Death

> For the power of the life-giving Spirit—and this power is mine through Christ Jesus—has freed me from the vicious circle of sin and death. (Romans 8:2 TLB)

The Spirit Quickens Our Mortal Bodies

> And if the Spirit of God, who raised up Jesus from the dead, lives in you, He will make your dying bodies live again after you die, by means of this same Holy Spirit living within you. (Romans 8:11 TLB)

The Spirit Brings Unity and Oneness to the Body

> Try always to be led along together by the Holy Spirit and so be at peace with one another. (Ephesians 4:3 TLB)

> We have peace because of Christ. He has made the Jews and those who are not Jews one people. He broke down the wall that divided them. He stopped the fighting between them by His death on the cross. He put an end to the Law. Then He made of the two people one new kind of people like Himself. In this way, He made peace. He brought both groups together to God. Christ finished the fighting between them by His death on the cross. Then Christ came and preached the Good News of peace to you who were far away from God. And He preached

it to us who were near God. Now all of us can go to the Father through Christ by way of the one Holy Spirit. (Ephesians 2:14–18 NLV)

The Spirit Is Our Guarantee and Deposit of the Future Resurrection

He has put His mark on us to show we belong to Him. His Spirit is in our hearts to prove this. (2 Corinthians 1:22 NLV)

It is God Who has made us ready for this change. He has given us His Spirit to show us what He has for us. (2 Corinthians 5:5 NLV)

The Spirit Reveals the Deep Things of God to us

God has shown these things to us through His Holy Spirit. It is the Holy Spirit Who looks into all things, even the secrets of God, and shows them to us. (1 Corinthians 2:10 NLV)

The Spirit Reveals What Has Been Given to us by God

We have not received the spirit of the world. God has given us His Holy Spirit that we may know about the things given to us by Him. (1 Corinthians 2:12 NLV)

The Spirit Dwells in Us

But you are not doing what your sinful old selves want you to do. You are doing what the Holy Spirit tells you to do, if you have God's Spirit living in you. No one belongs to Christ if he does not have Christ's Spirit in him. (Romans 8:9 NLV)

Do you not know that you are a house of God and that the Holy Spirit lives in you? (1 Corinthians 3:16 NLV)

Keep safe that which He has trusted you with by the Holy Spirit Who lives in us. (2 Timothy 1:14 NLV)

He is the Spirit of Truth. The world cannot receive Him. It does not see Him or know Him. You know Him because He lives with you and will be in you. (John 14:17 NLV)

The Spirit Speaks to, in, and through Us

So, I tell you that no one speaking by the help of the Holy Spirit can say that he hates Jesus. No one can say, "Jesus is Lord," except by the help of the Holy Spirit. (1 Corinthians 12:3 NLV)

The Holy Spirit tells us in plain words that in the last days some people will turn away from the faith. They will listen to what is said about spirits and follow the teaching about demons. (1 Timothy 4:1 NLV)

If you have ears, listen to what the Spirit says to the churches. Whoever wins the victory will not be hurt by the second death. (Revelation 2:11 CEV)

The first death is physical death, and the "second death" is eternal death.

So, as the Holy Spirit says: "Today, if you hear His voice, do not harden your hearts as you did in the rebellion, during the time of testing in the wilderness." (Hebrews 3:7–8 NIV)

It will not be you who will speak the words. The Spirit of your Father will speak through you. (Matthew 10:20 NLV)

They were all filled with the Holy Spirit. Then they began to speak in other languages which the Holy Spirit made them able to speak. (Acts 2:4 NLV)

Peter was still thinking about the dream when the Holy Spirit said to him, "See, three men are looking for you." (Acts 10:19 NLV)

The Holy Spirit told me to go with them and not doubt about going. These six men also went with me to this man's house. (Acts 11:12 NLV)

While they were worshiping the Lord and eating no food so they could pray better, the Holy Spirit said, "Let Barnabas and Saul be given to Me for the work I have called them to." (Acts 13:2 NLV)

We looked for the Christians and stayed with them seven days. The Christians had been told by the Holy Spirit to tell Paul not to go to Jerusalem. (Acts 21:4 NLV)

He came to see us. Then he took Paul's belt and used it to tie his own feet and hands. He said, "This is what the Holy Spirit says, 'The Jews at Jerusalem will tie the man who owns this belt. Then they will hand him over to the people who are not Jews.'" (Acts 21:11 NLV)

The Spirit Is the Agent by which we are Baptized into the Body of Christ

It is the same way with us. Jews or those who are not Jews, men who are owned by someone or men who are free to do what they want to do, have all been baptized into the one body by the same Holy Spirit. We have all received the one Spirit. (1 Corinthians 12:13 NLV)

The Spirit Brings Liberty

The heart is free where the Spirit of the Lord is. The Lord is the Spirit. (2 Corinthians 3:17 NLV)

The Spirit Transforms us into the Image of Christ

All of us, with no covering on our faces, show the shining-greatness of the Lord as in a mirror. All the time we are being changed to look like Him, with more and more of His shining- greatness. This change is from the Lord Who is the Spirit. (2 Corinthians 3:18 NLV)

The Spirit cries in our hearts, "Abba, Father."

> Because you are the sons of God, He has sent the Spirit of His Son into our hearts. The Spirit cries, "Father!" (Galatians 4:6 NLV)

The Spirit Enables us to Wait

> We are waiting for the Hope of being made right with God. This will come through the Holy Spirit and by faith. (Galatians 5:5 NLV)

The Spirit Supplies us with Christ

> Because of your prayers and the help the Holy Spirit gives me, all of this will turn out for good. (Philippians 1:19 NLV)

The Spirit Grants Everlasting Life

> If a man does things to please his sinful old self, his soul will be lost. If a man does things to please the Holy Spirit, He will have life that lasts forever. (Galatians 6:8 NLV)

The Spirit Gives us Access to God the Father

> Now all of us can go to the Father through Christ by way of the one Holy Spirit. (Ephesians 2:18 NLV)

The Spirit Makes us (Corporately) God's Habitation

> You are also being put together as a part of this building because God lives in you by His Spirit. (Ephesians 2:22 NLV)

The Spirit Reveals the Mystery of God to us

> Long ago men did not know these things. But now they have been shown to His missionaries and to the early preachers by the Holy Spirit. (Ephesians 3:5 NLV)

The Spirit Strengthens Our Spirits

> I pray that because of the riches of His shining-greatness, He will make you strong with power in your hearts through the Holy Spirit. (Ephesians 3:16 NLV)

The Spirit Enables us to Obey the Truth

> You have made your souls pure by obeying the truth through the Holy Spirit. This has given you a true love for the Christians. Let it be a true love from the heart. (1 Peter 1:22 NLV)

The Spirit Enables us to Know that Jesus Abides in us

> The person who obeys Christ lives by the help of God and God lives in him. We know He lives in us by the Holy Spirit, He has given us. (1 John 3:24 NLV)

> He has given us His Spirit. This is how we live by His help and He lives in us. (1 John 4:13 NLV)

The Spirit Confesses that Jesus Came in the Flesh

> You can tell if the spirit is from God in this way: Every spirit that says Jesus Christ has come in a human body is from God. (1 John 4:2 NLV)

The Spirit says, "Come, Lord Jesus," along with the Bride

> The Holy Spirit and the Bride say, "Come!" Let the one who hears, say, "Come!" Let the one who is thirsty, come. Let the one who wants to drink of the water of life, drink it. It is a free gift. (Revelation 22:17 NLV)

The Spirit Dispenses God's Love into Our Hearts

> Hope never makes us ashamed because the love of God has come into our hearts through the Holy Spirit Who was given to us. (Romans 5:5 NLV)

The Spirit Bears Witness to the Truth in Our Conscience

> I am telling the truth because I belong to Christ. The Holy Spirit tells my heart that I am not lying. (Romans 9:1 NLV)

The Spirit Teaches us

> We speak about these things also. We do not use words of man's wisdom. We use words given to us by the Holy Spirit. We use these words to tell what the Holy Spirit wants to say to those who put their trust in Him. (1 Corinthians 2:13 NLV)

> But when the Father sends the Advocate as my representative— that is, the Holy Spirit—He will teach you everything and will remind you of everything I have told you. (John 14:26 NLT)

The Spirit Gives us Joy

> You followed our way of life and the life of the Lord. You suffered from others because of listening to us. But you had the joy that came from the Holy Spirit. (1 Thessalonians 1:6 NLV)

The Spirit Enables Some to Preach the Gospel

> They knew these things would not happen during the time they lived but while you are living many years later. These are the very things that were told to you by those who preached the Good News. The Holy Spirit Who was sent from heaven gave them power and they told of things that even the angels would like to know about. (1 Peter 1:12 NLV)

The Spirit Moves us

> No part of the Holy Writings came long ago because of what man wanted to write. But holy men who belonged to God spoke what the Holy Spirit told them. (2 Peter 1:21 NLV)

The Spirit Knows the Things of God

> Who can know the things about a man, except a man's own spirit that is in him? It is the same with God. Who can understand Him except the Holy Spirit? (1 Corinthians 2:11 NLV)

The Spirit Casts Out Demons

> But if I am casting out demons by the Spirit of God, then the Kingdom of God has arrived among you. (Matthew 12:28 NLT)

The Spirit Brings Things to Our Remembrance

> The Helper, the Holy Spirit, whom the Father will send in my name, will teach you everything and make you remember all that I have told you. (John 14:26 GNT)

The Spirit Comforts us

> Then the church throughout Judea, Galilee and Samaria enjoyed a time of peace and was strengthened. Living in the fear of the Lord and encouraged by the Holy Spirit, it increased in numbers. (Acts 9:31 NIV)

The Spirit makes some overseers in the church and sends some out to the work of church planting [through the body].

> Keep watch over yourselves and all the flock of which the Holy Spirit has made you overseers. Be shepherds of the church of God, which He bought with His own blood. (Acts 20:28 NIV)

While they were worshiping the Lord and fasting, the Holy Spirit said, "Set apart for me Barnabas and Saul for the work to which I have called them." (Acts 13:2 NIV)

SUMMARY

The Holy Spirit unites us to Jesus Christ and to His body. The Spirit reveals Christ to us, gives us His life, and makes Christ alive in us. The Spirit takes the experiences of Jesus—His Incarnation, Ministry, Crucifixion, Resurrection, and Ascension—and brings them into our own experience. Because of the Holy Spirit, the history of Jesus Christ becomes our story and experience.

PRAYERS (USING H WORDS)

We are in awe of Your **helmet** of salvation to wear daily. We are grateful that we can put our **hope** in You, Lord because You are our **Helper**, and our **help** is in You alone. We are thankful that He extends **His hand** to **heal** us. We praise You for making us wise and **humble**, Lord, because our **humbleness honors** You. Thank You, God, for choosing us to be Your **holy** people and for clothing us in **humility**. We are blessed with the power of the **Holy Spirit** who lives in us. **Holy** Father, thank You for revealing these attributes that are from Your Spirit God. We are in awe, **Holy Spirit**, that You unite us to Jesus and make **Him** alive in us. Our **hearts** are filled with Your light and glory. Yes, **Holy Spirit**, You **help** us and give us **hope**, and we become so much **happier** than we could ever be with You in our lives. **Hallowed** is Your name! We love You!

We praise You, **Holy Spirit**, and we pray in Your **heavenly** name!

Amen.

I

I Am

> Jesus said to them, "Truly, truly, I say to you, before Abraham was, I Am." (John 8:58 ESV)

I Am the Way

> Jesus saith unto Him, I Am the Way, the truth, and the life: no man cometh unto the Father, but by me. (John 14:6 BRG)

I Am Who I Am

> And God said to Moses, "I AM WHO I AM." And He said, "Say to the Israelites, 'I AM has sent me to you.'" (Exodus 3:14 NLV)

I Am He

> When Jesus said, "I Am He," they drew back and fell to the ground. (John 18:6 AMP)

I Am the Living One, I Am Alive Forever

> I Am the Living One. I was dead, but look, I Am Alive Forever. I have power over death and hell. (Revelation 1:18 NLV)

PERSONAL REFLECTIONS IN PRAISING GOD

Immanuel

Therefore, the Lord Himself will give you a sign. Behold, a young woman shall conceive and bear a son, and shall call His name Immanuel. (Isaiah 7:14 RSV)

His Indescribable Gift

Thanks be to God for His Indescribable Gift! (2 Corinthians 9:15 NIV)

I Can Do All Things

I Can Do All Things through Christ who strengtheneth me. (Philippians 4:13 KJ21)

Integrity of Heart

And David shepherded them with Integrity of Heart; with skillful hands He led them. (Psalm 78:72 NIV)

Infirmities, Intercession

Likewise, the Spirit also helpeth our Infirmities (signs of old age: being frail, weak, fragile, sickness): for we know not what we should pray for as we ought: but the Spirit itself maketh Intercession for us with groanings which cannot be uttered. (Romans 8:26 KJ21)

In the Light of God, God's Inheritance

To open their eyes to their true condition so that they may repent and live In the Light of God instead of in Satan's darkness, so that they may receive forgiveness for their sins and God's Inheritance along with all people everywhere whose sins are cleansed away, who are set apart by faith in Me. (Acts 26:18 TLB)

Image of the Invisible God

He is the Image of The Invisible God, the firstborn of every creature. (Colossians 1:15 KJ21)

Innocent

> "I have sinned by betraying an Innocent man to death!" he said. (Matthew 27:4a GNT)

Inhabits the Praises of Israel

> But You are holy, O You who Inhabits the Praises of Israel. (Psalm 22:3 MEV)

Interceded

> I will give Him the honors of a victorious soldier, because He exposed Himself to death. He was counted among the rebels. He bore the sins of many and Interceded for rebels. (Isaiah 53:12 NLT)

Intercedes for Us

> Who is He who condemns? It is Christ who died, yes, who is risen, who is also at the right hand of God, who also Intercedes for Us. (Romans 8:34 MEV)

Immortal, Invisible

> To the King of the ages, Immortal (living forever and never dying), Invisible (unseen), the only God, be honor and glory forever and ever. Amen. (1 Timothy 1:17 ESV)

Infinite

> Great is our Lord and mighty in power—His understanding is Infinite (Impossible to measure, limitless, never ends)! (Psalm 147:5 ASV)

> Yes, everything else is worthless when compared with the Infinite value of knowing Christ Jesus my Lord. For His sake I have discarded everything else, counting it all as garbage, so that I could gain Christ. (Philippians 3:8 NLT)

Immutable, Impossible

> God did this so that, by two unchangeable (Immutable) things in which it is Impossible for God to lie, we who have fled to take hold of the hope set before us may be greatly encouraged. (Hebrews 6:18 NIV)

Immense Patience

> But for that very reason I was shown mercy so that in me, the worst of sinners, Christ Jesus might display His Immense Patience as an example, for those who would believe in Him and receive eternal life. (1 Timothy 1:16 NIV)

Infallible

> To whom also He shewed Himself alive after His passion by many Infallible (Incapable of ever being wrong) proofs, being seen of them forty days, and speaking of the things pertaining to the kingdom of God: (Acts 1:3 BRG)

Inner

> You made all the delicate, Inner parts of my body and knit me together in my mother's womb. (Psalm 139:13 NLT)

Idolatry

> Nothing evil will be allowed to enter, nor anyone who practices shameful Idolatry and dishonesty—but only those whose names are written in the Lamb's Book of Life. (Revelation 21:27 NLT)

Idols

> And what union can there be between God's temple and Idols? For we are the temple of the living God. As God said: "I will live in them and walk among them. I will be their God, and they will be my people." (2 Corinthians 6:16 NLT)

Ignorant

> For, being Ignorant of the righteousness of God, and seeking to establish their own, they did not submit to God's righteousness. (Romans 10:3 ESV)

> Whomever you forgive anything, I also forgive. For if I forgave someone anything, for your sakes I forgave it in Christ, lest Satan should take advantage of us. For we are not Ignorant of his devices. (2 Corinthians 2:10–11 MEV)

> But I would not have you Ignorant, brothers, concerning those who are asleep, that you may not grieve as others who have no hope. For if we believe that Jesus died and arose again, so God will bring with Him those who sleep in Jesus. (1 Thessalonians 4:13–14 MEV)

Impart

> A rod and a reprimand Impart wisdom, but a child left undisciplined disgraces its mother. (Proverbs 29:15 NIV)

Impartial

> But the wisdom that comes from heaven is first of all pure; then peace-loving, considerate, submissive, full of mercy and good fruit, Impartial and sincere. (James 3:17 NIV)

Imperfect

> But when that which is perfect comes, then that which is Imperfect shall pass away. (1 Corinthians 13:10 MEV)

Impossible

> Jesus said to them, "Because of your unbelief. For truly I say to you, if you have faith as a grain of mustard seed, you will say to this mountain, 'Move from here to there,' and it will move. And nothing will be Impossible for you." (Matthew 17:20 MEV)

MY NEW IDENTITY IN CHRIST

- Amazing gifts come from God.

- This is who we are in Christ.

- I Am … in Christ

I am the salt of the earth:

> You are the salt of the earth, but if salt has lost its taste, how shall its saltiness be restored? It is no longer good for anything except to be thrown out and trampled under people's feet. (Matthew 5:13 ESV)

I am the light of the world:

> You are the light of the world. A town built on a hill cannot be hidden. (Matthew 5:14 NIV)

I am valuable to God:

> Consider the birds—do you think they worry about their existence? They don't plant or reap or store up food, yet your heavenly Father provides them each with food. Aren't you much more valuable to Your Father than they? So, which one of you by worrying could add anything to your life? (Matthew 6:26–27 TPT)

I am indwelled by Christ. His Spirit lives in me:

> On that day you will realize that I am in my Father, and you are in me, and I am in you. (John 14:20 NIV)

I am a branch of the True Vine:

> I am the true Vine. My Father is the One Who cares for the Vine. I am the Vine and you are the branches. Get your life from Me. Then I will live in you and you will give much fruit. You can do nothing without Me. (John 15:1, 5 NLV)

I am Christ's friend:

> I do not call you servants that I own anymore. A servant does not know what his owner is doing. I call you friends, because I have told you everything I have heard from My Father. (John 15:15 NLV)

I am chosen and appointed by Christ to go and bear fruit:

> You have not chosen Me; I have chosen you. I have set you apart for the work of bringing in fruit. Your fruit should last. And whatever you ask the Father in My name, He will give it to you. (John 15:16 NLV)

I am justified by Christ's blood:

> Now that we have been saved from the punishment of sin by the blood of Christ, He will save us from God's anger also. (Romans 5:9 NLV)

I am set free from sin and a slave of righteousness:

> You were made free from the power of sin. Being right with God has power over you now. (Romans 6:18 NLV)

I am saved from the punishment of sin by the death of Christ:

> We hated God. But we were saved from the punishment of sin by the death of Christ. He has brought us back to God and we will be saved by His life. (Romans 5:10 NLV)

I am justified by Christ's blood:

> Since we have now been justified by His blood, how much more shall we be saved from God's wrath through Him! (Romans 5:9 NIV)

I am reconciled to God through Christ's death, and I am saved through Christ's life:

> For if, while we were God's enemies, we were reconciled to Him through the death of His Son, how much more, having been reconciled, shall we be saved through His life! (Romans 5:10 NIV)

I am free from condemnation:

> There is therefore now no condemnation for those who are in Christ Jesus, who walk not according to the flesh, but according to the Spirit. (Romans 8:1 KJ21)

I am free in Christ:

> The power of the Holy Spirit has made me free from the power of sin and death. This power is mine because I belong to Christ Jesus. (Romans 8:2 NLV)

I am a child of God and a coheir with Christ:

> If we are children of God, we will receive everything He has promised us. We will share with Christ all the things God has given to Him. But we must share His suffering if we are to share His shining-greatness. (Romans 8:17 NLV)

I am more than a conqueror through Christ:

> No, in all these things we are more than conquerors through Him who loved us. (Romans 8:37 ESV)

I am accepted by Christ:

> Honor God by accepting each other, as Christ has accepted you. Receive each other as Christ received you. (Romans 15:7 CEV)

I have the mind of Christ:

> For who has the thoughts of the Lord? Who can tell Him what to do? But we have the thoughts of Christ. (1 Corinthians 2:16 NLV)

I am a house of God:

> His Spirit lives in me. Do you not know that you are a house of God and that the Holy Spirit lives in you? (1 Corinthians 3:16 NLV)

I am washed, justified, and sanctified through Christ:

> Some of you were like that. But now your sins are washed away. You were set apart for God-like living to do His work. You were made right with God through our Lord Jesus Christ by the Spirit of our God. (1 Corinthians 6:11 NLV)

I am a temple of God:

> Don't you realize that your body is the temple of the Holy Spirit, who lives in you and was given to you by God? You do not belong to yourself. (1 Corinthians 6:19 NLT)

I am part of Christ's body:

> All of you together are Christ's body, and each of you is a part of it. (1 Corinthians 12:27 NLT)

I am the fragrance of Christ:

> We are a sweet smell of Christ that reaches up to God. It reaches out to those who are being saved from the punishment of sin and to those who are still lost in sin. (2 Corinthians 2:15 NLV)

I am a new creation:

> This means that anyone who belongs to Christ Has become a new person. The old life is gone; a new life has begun! (2 Corinthians 5:17 NLT)

I am righteous in Christ:

> For God made Christ, who never sinned, to be the offering for our sin, so that we could be made right with God through Christ. (2 Corinthians 5:21 NLT)

I am an ambassador for Christ and a minister of reconciliation:

> Here we are, then, speaking for Christ, as though God Himself were making His appeal through us. We plead on Christ's behalf: let God change you from enemies into His friends! (2 Corinthians 5:20 GNT)

I am redeemed from the curse of the law:

> But Christ rescued us from the Law's curse, when He became a curse in our place. This is because the Scriptures say that anyone who is nailed to a tree is under a curse. (Galatians 3:13 CEV)

I am a child of God and an heir of God:

> You are no longer slaves. You are God's children, and you will be given what He has promised. (Galatians 4:7 CEV)

I am a saint:

> Paul, an apostle of Jesus Christ by the will of God, To the saints who are at Ephesus, and to the faithful in Christ Jesus: Grace be to you and peace from God our Father and from the Lord Jesus Christ. (Ephesians 1:1–2 KJ21)

I am adopted into God's family:

> He predestined and lovingly planned for us to be adopted to Himself as [His own] children through Jesus Christ, in accordance with the kind intention and good pleasure of His will. (Ephesians 1:5 AMP)

I am blessed with every spiritual blessing in Christ:

> Blessed and worthy of praise be the God and Father of our Lord Jesus Christ, who has blessed us with every spiritual blessing in the heavenly realms in Christ, just as [in His love] He chose us in Christ [actually selected us for Himself as His own] before the foundation of the world, so that we would be holy [that is, consecrated, set apart for Him, purpose-driven] and blameless in His sight. In love. (Ephesians 1:3–4 AMP)

I am redeemed and forgiven through Christ's blood:

> In Him we have redemption [that is, our deliverance and salvation] through His blood, [which paid the penalty for our sin and resulted in] the forgiveness and complete pardon of our sin, in accordance with the riches of His grace. (Ephesians 1:7 AMP)

I am chosen by God:

> All things are done according to God's plan and decision; and God chose us to be His own people in union with Christ because of His own purpose, based on what He had decided from the very beginning. (Ephesians 1:11 GNT)

I am sealed by God with the Holy Spirit:

> And because of what Christ did, all you others too, who heard the Good News about how to be saved, and trusted Christ, were marked as belonging to Christ by the Holy Spirit, who long ago had been promised to all of us Christians. (Ephesians 1:13 TLB)

I am now alive with Christ:

> Even when we were dead because of our sins, He made us alive by what Christ did for us. You have been saved from the punishment of sin by His loving-favor. (Ephesians 2:5 NLV)

I am God's workmanship, created in Christ Jesus to do good works, which God prepared in advance for me to do:

> For we are God's masterpiece. He has created us anew in Christ Jesus, so we can do the good things He planned for us long ago. (Ephesians 2:10 NLT)

I am a fellow citizen with God's people and a member of God's household:

> So, then ye are no more strangers and sojourners, but ye are fellow citizens with the saints, and of the household of God. (Ephesians 2:19 ASV)

I am able to do all things through Christ, who gives me strength:

> I can do all things through Christ, who strengthens me. (Philippians 4:13 EHV)

I am a citizen of heaven:

> For our citizenship is in heaven, from which we also eagerly wait for the Savior, the Lord Jesus Christ. (Philippians 3:20 NKJV)

I am complete in Christ:

> And our own completeness is now found in Him. We are completely filled with God as Christ's fullness overflows within us. He is the Head of every kingdom and authority in the universe! (Colossians 2:10 TPT)

I am rescued from the dominion of darkness and brought into the kingdom of light:

> For He has rescued us from the kingdom of darkness and transferred us into the Kingdom of His dear Son. (Colossians 1:13 NLT)

I am holy in God's sight—without blemish and free of accusation:

> But Christ has brought you back to God by His death on the cross. In this way, Christ can bring you to God, holy and pure and without blame. (Colossians 1:22 NLV)

I am chosen by God, holy, and dearly loved:

> So, as those who have been chosen of God, holy and beloved, put on a heart of compassion, kindness, humility, gentleness, and patience. (Colossians 3:12 NASB)

I am hidden with Christ in God:

> For you have died, and your life is hidden with Christ in God. (Colossians 3:3 ESV)

I am forgiven of my sins:

> If we confess our sins, He is faithful and just to forgive us our sins and to cleanse us from all unrighteousness. (1 John 1:9 KJ21)

I am of a chosen people, a royal priesthood, a holy nation, a people belonging to God to declare the praises of He who called me out of darkness and into His wonderful light:

But you are a chosen race, a royal priesthood, a holy nation, a people for God's own possession, so that you may declare the goodness of Him who has called you out of darkness into His marvelous light. In times past, you were not a people, but now you are the people of God. You had not received mercy, but now you have received mercy. (1 Peter 2:9–10 MEV)

I am an alien and stranger in this world:

Dear friends, your real home is not here on earth. You are strangers here. I ask you to keep away from all the sinful desires of the flesh. These things fight to get hold of your soul. (1 Peter 2:11 NLV)

I am an enemy of the devil:

Stay alert! Watch out for your great enemy, the devil. He prowls around like a roaring lion, looking for someone to devour. (1 Peter 5:8 NLT)

I am now a child of God:

See what great love the Father has for us that He would call us His children. And that is what we are. For this reason, the people of the world do not know who we are because they did not know Him. (1 John 3:1 NLV)

I am born of God and the evil one (the devil) cannot harm me:

We know that no child of God keeps on sinning. The Son of God watches over him and the devil cannot get near him. (1 John 5:18 NLV)

I am the bride of Christ:

One of the seven angels who had the seven bowls full of the seven last plagues came to me and said, "Come, and I will show you the bride, the wife of the Lamb." (Revelation 21:9 GNT)

Our identities in Christ give us:

> Love, hope, strength, joy, value, worth, peace, victory, patience, kindness, optimism, better attitude, confidence, assurance, faith, life, light, comfort, courage, calmness, and contentment. People seek all these things.

PRAYERS (USING I WORDS)

Thank You for being the great *I Am*. Father God, You are ***Immanuel***. You are ***infinite***, ***infallible***, and ***immortal***. Thank You for ***interceding*** for us, which is such an ***indescribable*** gift. Thank You for the ***immense*** patience that You ***impart*** on our behalf. We know nothing is ***impossible*** without You, God, and our ***identities*** are in You. *I* can do all things through You, Christ, and *I* love You for that. We thank You, God, for giving us Your ***integrity***. Heavenly Father, we are thrilled that we can live in the light of Your ***inheritance*** so we may receive forgiveness for our sins. We thank You, God, for creating us in Your ***image***. We praise You, heavenly Father, for this beautiful ***identification*** in Christ! Your Spirit ***impresses*** us with Your ***inspiration*** for how to ***improve*** our lives so we can become ***impactful*** to others in our community. We want to show others how ***important*** You are to us.

We praise You, Father God, and pray in Your ***infinite*** name.

Amen.

J

Birth to Jesus

> Jacob was the father of Joseph, the husband of Mary. Mary gave Birth to Jesus, who is called the Messiah. (Matthew 1:16 NLT)

Jesus the Messiah

> This is how Jesus the Messiah was born. His mother, Mary, was engaged to be married to Joseph. But before the marriage took place, while she was still a virgin, she became pregnant through the power of the Holy Spirit. (Matthew 1:18 NLT)

Name Him Jesus

> And she will have a Son, and you are to name Him Jesus, for He will save His people from their sins. (Matthew 1:21 NLT)

Jesus to Be Baptized

> Then Jesus went from Galilee to the Jordan River to Be Baptized by John. (Matthew 3:13 NLT)

Jesus Saw the Spirit of God

> After His baptism, as Jesus came up out of the water, the heavens were opened and He Saw the Spirit of God descending like a dove and settling on Him. (Matthew 3:16 NLT)

Jesus Was Tempted by the Devil

> Then Jesus was led by the Spirit into the wilderness to be Tempted there by the Devil. (Matthew 4:1 NLT)

Jesus Told Satan to Worship Your God Only

> "Get out of here, Satan," Jesus Told him. "For the Scriptures say, 'You must Worship the Lord Your God and serve Only Him.'" (Matthew 4:10 NLT)

Jesus Began to Preach

> From then on Jesus Began to Preach, "Repent of your sins and turn to God, for the Kingdom of Heaven is near." (Matthew 4:17 NLT)

Jesus Knew Their Thoughts

> And Jesus Knew Their Thoughts, and said unto them, "Every kingdom divided against itself is brought to desolation; and every city or house divided against itself shall not stand." (Matthew 12:25 KJ21)

Jesus Spoke, "Do Not Be Afraid."

> But immediately Jesus Spoke to them, saying, "Be of good cheer. It is I. Do Not Be Afraid." (Matthew 14:27 MEV)

Jesus Said He Would Be Killed

> From then on Jesus began to tell His disciples plainly that it was necessary for Him to go to Jerusalem, and that He would suffer many terrible things at the hands of the elders, the leading priests, and the teachers of religious law. He Would Be Killed, but on the third day He would be raised from the dead. (Matthew 16:21 NLT)

Follower of Jesus

> Then Jesus said to His disciples, "If any of you wants to be my Follower, you must give up your own way, take up your cross, and follow Me." (Matthew 16:24 NLT)

Jesus Said Nothing Shall Be Impossible

> And Jesus said unto them, "Because of your unbelief; for verily I say unto you, if ye have faith as a grain of mustard seed, ye shall say unto this mountain, 'Remove hence to yonder place,' and it shall remove. And Nothing Shall Be Impossible unto you." (Matthew 17:20 KJ21)

Jesus Said Greatest Commandment

> Jesus Said to him, "You shall love the Lord your God with all your heart, with all your soul, and with all your mind." This is the first and the Greatest Commandment. "The second is like it: 'Love your neighbor as yourself.'" (Matthew 22:37–39 NET)

Jesus Spoke All Authority Given to Him

> Then Jesus came and spoke to them, saying, "All Authority has been Given to Me in heaven and on earth." (Matthew 28:18 MEV)

Jesus Is Called Christ

> Pilate said to them, "Then what am I to do with Jesus Who Is Called Christ?" They all said to him, "Nail Him to a cross!" (Matthew 27:22 NLV)

Jesus Wearing the Crown of Thorns

> So, when Jesus emerged, bleeding, Wearing the purple robe and The Crown of Thorns on His head, Pilate said to them, "Look at Him! Here is your man!" (John 19:5 TPT)

Jesus Beaten and Nailed to a Cross

> Pilate wanted to please the people. He gave Barabbas to them and had Jesus Beaten. Then he handed Him over to be Nailed to a Cross. (Mark 15:15 NLV)

Jesus Cried, "Why Have You Forsaken Me?"

> And about three o'clock Jesus Cried with a loud voice, "Eli, Eli, lema sabachthani?" that is, "My God, my God, Why Have You Forsaken Me?" (Matthew 27:46 NRSVA)

Jesus Died

> Then Jesus gave a loud cry. He gave up His spirit and died. (Mark 15:37 NLV)

Jesus's Body Laid in a Tomb

> Joseph bought a long sheet of linen cloth. Then he took Jesus' Body down from the cross, wrapped it in the cloth, and Laid it in a Tomb that had been carved out of the rock. Then he rolled a stone in front of the entrance. (Mark 15:46 NLT)

Jesus Is Risen

> He said, "Do not be afraid. You are looking for Jesus of Nazareth Who was nailed to a cross. He is risen! He is not here! See, here is the place where they laid Him." (Mark 16:6 NLV)

Jesus Appeared First

> Now when Jesus was risen early the first day of the week, He Appeared First to Mary Magdalene, out of whom He had cast seven devils. (Mark 16:9 KJ21)

God Appointed Jesus as Judge

And He ordered us to preach everywhere and to testify that Jesus is the one Appointed by God to be the Judge of all—the living and the dead. (Acts 10:42 NLT)

Judge

They will give an account to the One who is ready to Judge the living and the dead. (1 Peter 4:5 GW)

Judged by the Lord

Yet when we are Judged by the Lord, we are being disciplined so that we will not be condemned along with the world. (1 Corinthians 11:32 NLT)

Day of Judgment

I will not Judge those who hear me but don't obey me, for I have come to save the world and not to Judge it. But all who reject me and my message will be Judged on the Day of Judgment by the truth I have spoken. (John 12:47–48 NLT)

Do Not Judge Others

Do Not Judge Others, and you will not be Judged. Do not condemn others, or it will all come back against you. Forgive others, and you will be forgiven. (Luke 6:37 NLT)

The Lord Will Judge His People

For we know Him who said, "Vengeance is Mine," says the Lord, "I will repay." And again, He says, "The Lord Will Judge His People." (Hebrews 10:30 MEV)

Justice

> When the Lord comes to rule the earth. He will rule the peoples of the world with Justice and fairness. (Psalm 96:13 GNT)

Heart Full of Joy

> A Heart Full of Joy and goodness makes a cheerful face, but when a heart is full of sadness the spirit is crushed. (Proverbs 15:13 AMP)

Joy and Delight

> I have told you these things so that My Joy and Delight may be in you, and that your Joy may be made full and complete and over-flowing. (John 15:11 AMP)

Joy

> I am on my way to you. But I say these things while I am still in the world, so, my followers will have the same complete Joy that I do. (John 17:13 CEV)

> The commandments of the Lord are right, bringing Joy to the heart. The commands of the Lord are clear, giving insight for living. (Psalm 19:8 NLT)

> Yet I will rejoice in the Lord, I will Joy in the God of my salvation. (Habakkuk 3:18 KJ21)

> Then they all returned, every man from Judah and Jerusalem, with Jehoshaphat as their head, to Jerusalem with Joy because the Lord made them rejoice because of the death of their enemies. (2 Chronicles 20:27 MEV)

Joyous Treasure

> Your laws are my Joyous Treasure forever. I am determined to obey You until I die. (Psalm 119:111–112 TLB)

Joy of the Lord

> And Nehemiah continued, "Go and celebrate with a feast of rich foods and sweet drinks, and share gifts of food with people who have nothing prepared. This is a sacred day before our Lord. Don't be dejected and sad, for the Joy of the Lord is Your strength!" (Nehemiah 8:10 NLT)

Serve the Lord with Joy

> If you do not Serve the Lord Your God with Joy and enthusiasm for the abundant benefits you have received, you will serve your enemies whom the Lord will send against you. (Deuteronomy 28:47–48a NLT)

Joy to the Lord

> Let the godly sing for Joy to the Lord; it is fitting for the pure to praise Him. (Psalm 33:1 NLT)

Joyful Songs

> Deep in my heart I long for your temple, and with all that I am, I sing Joyful Songs to You. (Psalm 84:2 CEV)

Sing Joyfully to the Lord, Shout Joyfully

> O come, let us Sing Joyfully to The Lord; let us Shout Joyfully to the Rock of our salvation! (Psalm 95:1 AMP)

Be Joyful in Him

> Hear this message from the Lord, all you who tremble at His words: "Your own people hate you and throw you out for being loyal to my name. 'Let the Lord be honored!' they scoff. 'Be Joyful in Him!' But they will be put to shame." (Isaiah 66:5 NLT)

Bring Joy to My Sorrowing Heart

> Your words are what sustain me; they are food to my hungry soul. They Bring Joy to My Sorrowing Heart and delight me. How proud I am to bear your name, O Lord. (Jeremiah 15:16 TLB)

Do What Is Right and Just

> I have chosen Him in order that He may command His sons and His descendants to obey me and to Do What Is Right and Just. If they do, I will do everything for Him that I have promised. (Genesis 18:19 GNT)

Love Justice

> For I, the Lord, Love Justice; I hate robbery and wrongdoing. In my Faithfulness I will reward my people and make an everlasting covenant with them. (Isaiah 61:8 NIV)

Joy, Just, Judgment

> It is a Joy to the Just to do Judgment, but destruction shall come to the workers of iniquity. (Proverbs 21:15 KJ21)

Judges, Judge, Judgment

> You must appoint Judges and officers in all your gates, which the Lord your God gives you, throughout your tribes, and they shall Judge the people with righteous Judgment. (Deuteronomy 16:18 MEV)

Judgments

> He is the Lord our God; His Judgments are in all the earth. (1 Chronicles 16:14 KJ21)

Judges, Judgment of God, Judge

> Therefore, you have no excuse, O man, every one of you who Judges. For in passing Judgment on another you condemn yourself, because you, the Judge, practice the very same things. We know that the Judgment of God rightly falls on those who practice such things. Do you suppose, O man—you who Judge those who practice such things and yet do them yourself—that you will escape the Judgment of God? (Romans 2:1–3 ESV)

Jehovah Jireh

> And Abraham called the name of that place Jehovah Jireh [that is, The Lord Will Provide]; as it is said to this day, "In the mount of the Lord it shall be seen." (Genesis 22:14 KJ21)

Jehovah Nissi

> And Moses built an altar, and called the name of it Jehovah Nissi [that is, The Lord my banner]. (Exodus 17:15 KJ21)

Jehovah Shalom

> Then Gideon built an altar there unto the Lord and called it Jehovah Shalom [that is, The Lord send peace]. (Judges 6:24a KJ21)

Jehovah

> Sing unto God, sing praises to His name! Extol Him that rideth upon the heavens by His name Jehovah; and rejoice before Him. (Psalm 68:4 KJ21)

> That men may know that Thou, whose name alone is Jehovah, art the Most High over all the earth. (Psalm 83:18 KJ21)

Behold, God is my salvation; I will trust and not be afraid; for the Lord Jehovah is my strength and my song; He also has become my salvation. (Isaiah 12:2 KJ21)

Trust ye in the Lord forever, for in the Lord Jehovah is everlasting strength. (Isaiah 26:4 KJ21)

Jealous God

You shall not bow down to them or worship them; for I, the Lord Your God, am a Jealous God, punishing the children for the sin of the parents to the third and fourth generation of those who hate me. (Exodus 20:5 NIV)

Journey

Those who live in one city will Journey to another, saying, "Let us surely go to seek the Lord of Hosts. I myself am going." (Zechariah 8:21 MEV)

Patience of Job

Indeed, we count them happy who endure. You have heard of the Patience of Job and have seen the purpose of the Lord, that the Lord is very gracious and merciful. (James 5:11 MEV)

Justified, Our Lord Jesus Christ

Therefore, since we have been Justified by faith, we have peace with God through Our Lord Jesus Christ. (Romans 5:1 MEV)

Jesus Christ, Joined Together, Judgment

Now I ask you, brothers, by the name of our Lord Jesus Christ, that you all speak in agreement and that there be no divisions among you. But be perfectly Joined Together in the same mind and in the same Judgment. (1 Corinthians 1:10 MEV)

Justified by His Grace

> That being Justified by His grace, we should be made heirs according to the hope of eternal life. (Titus 3:7 KJ21)

Joint Heirs with Christ

> And if children, then heirs, heirs of God and Joint Heirs with Christ, if indeed, we suffer with Him, that we may also be glorified with Him. (Romans 8:17 MEV)

Jesus Christ

> Anyone can be made right with God by the free gift of His loving-favor. It is Jesus Christ Who bought them with His blood and made them free from their sins. (Romans 3:24 NLV)

Joined

> Melodies of praise will fill the air as every musical instrument, joined with every heart, overflows with worship. (Psalm 92:3 TPT)

Joy, Joined

> We laughed and laughed and overflowed with gladness. We were left shouting for Joy and singing Your praise. All the nations saw it and Joined in, saying, "The Lord has done great miracles for them!" (Psalm 126:2 TPT)

Joined to Jesus

> For it is not from man that we draw our life but from God as we are being Joined to Jesus, the Anointed One. And now He is our God-given wisdom, our virtue, our holiness, and our redemption. (1 Corinthians 1:30 TPT)

Joined (Joined Together in Perfect Unity)

> Look at how much encouragement you've found in your relationship with the Anointed One! You are filled to overflowing with His comforting love. You have experienced a deepening friendship with the Holy Spirit and have felt His tender affection and mercy. (Philippians 2:2 TPT)

PRAYERS (USING J WORDS)

Jehovah Rophe, You are our Healer, the Great Physician, and we praise You for that. We are in total and complete awe of You, King *Jesus*, for shedding Your blood on the cross so we can be saved and have eternal life with You. We know You are a *jealous* God because You want everyone to believe in You. We are so thankful that You are our *joyous* Treasure. We love making a *joyful* noise and singing *joyful* songs to You. We love You, Savior *Jesus*, and we know we are *justified* by Your grace. We are *joined* to You, *Jesus*. We are on a *journey* of praising and worshipping You. *Jesus*, You are a *Jewel*, and You become *jubilant*. We praise You that we can be *jolly* and *joyful*.

We pray in the precious name of *Jesus*.

Amen.

NAMES OF JESUS

You can pray these names of Jesus to become closer to Him:

- Immanuel (God with Us)

- Light of the World

- Child

- Bread of Life

- Physician

- Lamb, Lamb of God

- King of Kings

- Prince of Peace

- Christ, Messiah

- Rabbi, Rabboni

- Teacher

- Word

- Cornerstone, Capstone

- Bright Morning Star

- Lion of the Tribe of Judah

- Lord

- Friend

- Alpha and Omega

- Jesus the Savior

- Bridegroom, Husband

- Son of David

- Priest, Prophet

- Son of God

- Son of Man

- Good Shepherd

- Servant, Servant of God

- Man of Sorrows

- The Redeemer

- I Am

K

King of All Kings

> Together they will go to war against the Lamb, but the Lamb will defeat them because He is Lord of all Lords and King of All Kings. And His called and chosen and faithful ones will be with Him. (Revelation 17:14 NLT)

> For, at just the right time Christ will be revealed from heaven by the blessed and only almighty God, the King of All Kings and Lord of all Lords. (1 Timothy 6:15 NLT)

Kings, Knowledge

> That night the secret was revealed to Daniel in a vision. Then Daniel praised the God of heaven. He said, "Praise the name of God forever and ever, for He has all wisdom and power. He controls the course of world events; He removes Kings and sets up other Kings. He gives wisdom to the wise and Knowledge to the scholars." (Daniel 2:19–21 NLT)

King Who Lives Forever, One Who Knows All Things

> We give honor and thanks to the King Who Lives Forever. He is the One Who never dies and Who is never seen. He is the One Who Knows all Things. He is the only God. Let it be so. (1 Timothy 1:17 NLV)

Keeper

> The Lord is your Keeper; the Lord is your shade on your right hand. (Psalm 121:5 AMP)

King of Heaven

> And now, I, Nebuchadnezzar, praise, honor, and glorify the King of Heaven. Everything He does is right and just, and He can humble anyone who acts proudly. (Daniel 4:37 GNT)

King of Glory

> Lift up your heads, O you gates; lift up, you everlasting doors, that the King of Glory may enter. Who is He— this King Of glory? The Lord of Hosts, He is the King Of glory. Selah (Psalm 24:9–10 MEV)

King of Kings

> On His robe and thigh was written this title: "King of Kings and Lord of Lords." (Revelation 19:16 TLB)

King of Righteousness, King of Salem, King of Peace

> In the first place, His name is translated "King of Righteousness," and then also He is King of Salem, which means "King of Peace." (Hebrews 7:2b MEV)

King of Saints

> They sang the song of Moses, the servant of God, and the song of the Lamb, saying: "Great and marvelous are Your works, Lord God Almighty! Just and true are Your ways, O King of Saints!" (Revelation 15:3 MEV)

His Kingdom

> He has gathered us into His Kingdom and made us priests of God His Father. Give to Him everlasting glory! He rules forever! Amen! (Revelation 1:6 TLB)

Kings of the Earth

> And from Jesus Christ, who is the faithful witness, and the first-begotten of the dead, and the prince over the Kings of the Earth. Unto Him that loved us, and washed us from our sins in His own blood. (Revelation 1:5 KJ21)

King

> Saying, "Blessed is the King who comes in the name of the Lord! Peace in heaven, and glory in the highest heaven!" (Luke 19:38 MEV)

> It is you, O King! You have grown great and strong. Your greatness has increased and reaches to heaven, and Your sovereignty to the ends of the earth. (Daniel 4:22 NRSVA)

Eternal King

> All honor and glory to God forever and ever! He is the Eternal King, the unseen one who never dies; He alone is God. Amen. (1 Timothy 1:17 NLT)

Kingdom

> They shall speak of the glory of Your Kingdom and talk of Your power. (Psalm 145:11 MEV)

Kind

> The Lord is right and good in all His ways, and Kind in all His works. (Psalm 145:17 NLV)

Kind, Kindness

> Don't you see how wonderfully Kind, tolerant, and patient God is with you? Does this mean nothing to you? Can't you see that His Kindness is intended to turn you from your sin? (Romans 2:4 NLT)

Notice how God is both Kind and severe. He is severe toward those who disobeyed, but Kind to you if you continue to trust in His Kindness. But if you stop trusting, you also will be cut off. (Romans 11:22 NLT)

Kindness

Long ago I gave these commands to My people: "You must see that justice is done, and must show Kindness and mercy to one another." (Zechariah 7:9 GNT)

Kindness, Keep My Promises

I will treat you with such Kindness that your nation will grow strong, and I will also Keep My Promises to you. (Leviticus 26:9 CEV)

Kindness

But when God our Savior's Kindness and love appeared, He saved us because of His mercy, not because of righteous things we had done. He did it through the washing of new birth and the renewing by the Holy Spirit. (Titus 3:4–5 CEB)

But the Lord watches over all who honor Him and trust His Kindness. (Psalm 33:18 CEV)

He is so rich in Kindness and grace that He purchased our freedom with the blood of His Son and forgave our sins. (Ephesians 1:7 NLT)

We praise you, Lord God! You treat us with Kindness Day after day, and you rescue us. (Psalm 68:19 CEV)

Our Lord and our God, You are like the sun and also like a shield. You treat us with Kindness and with honor, never denying any good thing to those who live right. (Psalm 84:11 CEV)

You, the source of my life, showered me with Kindness and watched over me. (Job 10:12 CEV)

Our Lord, you bless those who live right, and you shield them with your Kindness. (Psalm 5:12 CEV)

Kindness of God

Now Christ Jesus has come to show us the Kindness of God. Christ our Savior defeated death and brought us the good news. It shines like a light and offers life that never ends. (2 Timothy 1:10 CEV)

Deeds of Kindness Are Known

Your Deeds of Kindness Are Known in the heavens. No one is like you! (Psalm 71:19 CEV)

Kept Your Promise, Kindness

I am your servant, Lord, and You have Kept Your Promise to treat me with Kindness. (Psalm 119:65 CEV)

King, Speak with Kindness

The King is the friend of all who are sincere and Speak with Kindness. (Proverbs 22:11 CEV)

God's Love and Kindness

God's Love and Kindness will shine upon us like the sun that rises in the sky. (Luke 1:78 CEV)

Undeserved Kindness

Christ has also introduced us to God's Undeserved Kindness (gift of undeserved grace) on which we take our stand. So, we are happy, as we look forward to sharing in the glory of God. (Romans 5:2 CEV)

God's Kindness Now Rules

The Law came, so that the full power of sin could be seen. Yet where sin was powerful, God's Kindness (gift of undeserved grace) was even more powerful. Sin ruled by means of death. But God's Kindness (gift of grace)

Now Rules, and God has accepted us because of Jesus Christ our Lord. This means that we will have eternal life. (Romans 5:20–21 CEV)

Kindness, Kind

In fact, God treats us with even greater Kindness, just as the Scriptures say, "God opposes everyone who is proud, but He is Kind and blesses all who are humble with undeserved grace." (James 4:6 CEV)

Kindness, Keep on Growing

Let the wonderful Kindness and the gift of undeserved grace and the understanding that come from our Lord and Savior Jesus Christ, help you Keep on Growing. Praise Jesus now and forever! Amen. (2 Peter 3:18 CEV)

Know

I have written these things to you who believe in the name of the Son of God so that you may Know that you have eternal life. (1 John 5:13 CSB)

Knowing

Nothing is as wonderful as Knowing Christ Jesus my Lord. I have given up everything else and count it all as garbage. All I want is Christ. (Philippians 3:8 CEV)

Keeps His Promises

God is no mere human! He doesn't tell lies or change His mind. God always Keeps His Promises. (Numbers 23:19 CEV)

Kind, Keeps His Promises

The Lord is always Kind to those who worship Him, and He Keeps His Promises to their descendants. (Psalm 103:17 CEV)

Knowledge

God always does right—and this Knowledge comes straight from God. (Job 36:3 CEV)

God instructs the nations and gives Knowledge to us all. Won't He also correct us? (Psalm 94:10 CEV)

Your Knowledge of me is too deep; it is beyond my understanding. (Psalm 139:6 GNT)

If you really want to gain Knowledge, you must begin by having respect for the Lord. But foolish people hate wisdom and instruction. (Proverbs 1:7 NIRV)

By His wisdom and Knowledge the Lord created heaven and earth. (Proverbs 3:19 CEV)

This wonderful Knowledge comes from the Lord All-Powerful, who has such great wisdom. (Isaiah 28:29 CEV)

Now thanks be to God who always leads us in Christ's triumphal procession and through us spreads the aroma of the Knowledge of Him in every place. (2 Corinthians 2:14 CSB)

For the earth shall be filled with the Knowledge of the glory of the Lord, as the waters cover the sea. (Habakkuk 2:14 KJ21)

My people are destroyed for lack of Knowledge; because you have rejected Knowledge, I will reject you from serving as my priest. (Hosea 4:6a CSB)

The fear of the Lord is the beginning of wisdom, and the Knowledge of the Holy One is understanding. (Proverbs 9:10 CSB)

He who has Knowledge restrains and is careful with his words, and a Man of understanding and wisdom has a cool spirit (self- control, an even temper.) (Proverbs 17:27 AMP)

Know, Knowledge

I, Wisdom, live together with good judgment. I Know where to discover Knowledge and discernment. (Proverbs 8:12 NLT)

Kingdoms of the Earth, Know

So now, O Lord our God, save us from His hand, that all the Kingdoms of the Earth may Know that You, O Lord, are God alone. 2 Kings 19:19 MEV)

Kingdoms of the Earth

Sing to the Lord, O Kingdoms of The Earth—sing praises to the Lord. (Psalm 68:32 TLB)

Kingdom of God

But seek first the Kingdom of God and His righteousness, and all these things shall be given to you. (Matthew 6:33 MEV)

The time is fulfilled, and the Kingdom of God is at hand. Repent and believe the gospel. (Mark 1:15 MEV)

Truly I say to you, whoever does not receive the Kingdom of God as a little child shall not enter it. (Mark 10:15 MEV)

Nor will people say, Look! Here [it is]! or, See, [it is] there! For behold, the Kingdom of God is within you [in your hearts] and among you [surrounding you]. (Luke 17:21 AMPC)

Jesus answered him, "Truly, truly, I say to you, unless one is born again, he cannot see the Kingdom of God." (John 3:3 ESV)

Jesus answered, "Truly, truly, I say to you, unless one is born of water and the Spirit, he cannot enter the Kingdom of God. (John 3:5 RSV)

For the Kingdom of God is not in word, but in power. (1 Corinthians 4:20 KJ21)

Kept, Kind, Kingdom

We encouraged you; we comforted you, and we Kept urging you to live the Kind of life that pleases God, who calls you to share in His own Kingdom and glory. (1 Thessalonians 2:12 GNT)

Kingdoms of the Earth

O Lord of hosts, God of Israel, who is enthroned above the cherubim, You are the God, You alone, of all the Kingdoms of the Earth; You have made heaven and earth. (Isaiah 37:16 AMP)

King, King of Kings, Kingdom

You, O King, are the King of Kings. For the God of heaven has given you a Kingdom, power, and strength, and glory. (Daniel 2:37 MEV)

Keys, Kingdom of Heaven

I will give you the Keys of the Kingdom of Heaven, and whatever you bind on earth shall be bound in heaven, and whatever you loose on earth shall be loosed in heaven. (Activating God's Will) (Matthew 16:19 ESV)

Knees

> Come, let us bow down in worship. Let us get down on our Knees before the Lord who made us. (Psalm 95:6 NLV)

King Forever and Ever

> The Lord is King Forever and Ever: the heathen have perished out of his land. (Psalm 10:16 KJ21)

Know

> We Know that God has chosen you, dear brothers, much beloved of God. (1 Thessalonians 1:4 TLB)

Knit Them Together

> You made all the delicate, inner parts of my body and Knit Them Together in my mother's womb. (Psalm 139:13 TLB)

Knit Together by Love, Knowing Christ, Made Known

> This is what I have asked of God for you: that you will be encouraged and Knit Together by strong ties of Love, and that you will have the rich experience of Knowing Christ with real certainty and clear understanding. For God's secret plan, now at last Made Known, is Christ Himself. (Colossians 2:2 TLB)

Keep on Asking, Keep on Getting, Keep on Looking, Keep on Finding, Knock

> And so, it is with prayer—Keep on Asking and you will Keep on Getting; Keep on Looking and you will Keep on Finding; Knock and the door will be opened. Everyone who asks, receives; all who seek, find; and the door is opened to everyone who Knocks. (Luke 11:9–10 TLB)

Ask, Seek, Knock

> Ask, and you will be given what you ask for. Seek, and you will find. Knock, and the door will be opened. (Matthew 7:7 TLB)

Knocking

> Look! I have been standing at the door, and I am constantly Knocking. If anyone hears Me calling him and opens the door, I will come in and fellowship with Him and He with Me. (Revelation 3:20 TLB)

Knocked Down, Get Up, and Keep Going

> We are hunted down, but God never abandons us. We get Knocked Down, but we Get Up again and Keep Going. (2 Corinthians 4:9 TLB)

PRAYERS (USING K WORDS)

Thank You for being our *King* who is *all-knowing* and *knowledgeable*. We praise You for Your *kindness* and for *keeping* Your promises. We are grateful to be in the *kingdom* of God. We worship You and *kneel* before our *King of kings*. We seek first the *kingdom* of God. I am in awe of *knowing* how much You *know* and love me. Thank You, my *King* of glory! We are thankful that You *knit* us together in our mothers' wombs. What a miraculous creation! We have *knocked*, and You have opened the door so we can *know* You better. As believers in You, we have *kindred* spirits, and the *key* is You, dear Lord. We have come to *know* You in a deeper way, and we become more *knowledgeable*. Thank You, God, for being *keen* with us.

We praise You, our *King of kings!*

Amen.

L

Look, Lamb of God

> The next day John saw Jesus coming toward Him and said, "Look, the Lamb of God, who takes away the sin of the world!" (John 1:29 NLT)

Lamb's Book of Life, Lamb

> All who live on earth will worship the beast. These are all the people since the beginning of the world whose names are not written in the Lamb's Book of Life. The Lamb is the One who was killed. (Revelation 13:8 ICB)

Lamb That Was Slain

> Saying with a Loud voice: "Worthy is the Lamb That Was Slain, to receive power and riches and wisdom and strength, and honor and glory and blessing!" (Revelation 5:12 KJ21)

Lamb, Lead them to Springs of Living Water

> For the Lamb who is in the midst of the throne will shepherd them and He will Lead them to Springs of Living Water, and God will wipe away every tear from their eyes. (Revelation 7:17 MEV)

Light of Life

> For He came as a witness, to point the way to the Light of Life, and to help everyone believe. (John 1:7 TPT)

Light of the World, Light of Life

> Again, Jesus spoke to them, saying, "I am the Light of The World. Whoever follows Me shall not walk in darkness, but shall have the Light of Life." (John 8:12 MEV)

Light, Lord, Everlasting Light

> No longer will you need the sun or moon to give you Light, for the Lord Your God will be your Everlasting Light, and He will be your glory. Your sun shall never set; the moon shall not go down—for the Lord will be your Everlasting Light; your days of mourning all will end. (Isaiah 60:19–20 TLB)

Light So Shine

> Let your Light So Shine before men, that they may see your good works and glorify your Father in heaven. (Matthew 5:16 KJ21)

Living in the Light, God is in the Light

> But if we are Living in the Light, as God is in the Light, then we have Fellowship with each other, and the blood of Jesus, His Son, cleanses us from all sin. (1 John 1:7 NLT)

Lion of the Tribe of Judah

> And I began to weep bitterly, because no one was found worthy to open the scroll or look inside it. Then one of the elders said to me, "Do not weep! Behold, the Lion of the Tribe of Judah, the Root of David, has triumphed to open the scroll and its seven seals." (Revelation 5:5 Berean Study Bible)

Loved

> Now before the Passover Feast, Jesus knew that His hour had come to depart from this world to the Father. Having Loved His own who were in the world, He Loved them to the end. (John 13:1 MEV)

Jesus Christ Is Lord

> For this reason, also, God highly exalted Him, and bestowed on Him the name which is above every name, so that at the name of Jesus every knee will bow, of those who are in heaven and on earth and under the earth, and that every tongue will confess that Jesus Christ is Lord, to the glory of God, the Father. (Philippians 2:9–11 NASB)

Love

> For God has not given us a spirit of fear, but of power, and of Love, and of a sound mind. (2 Timothy 1:7 NKJV)

> But now abideth faith, hope, and Love, these three; and the greatest of these is Love. (1 Corinthians 13:13 ASV)

> Consider how much Love the Father has given to us, that we should be called children of God. Therefore, the world does not know us, because it did not know Him. (1 John 3:1 MEV)

Greater Love, Lay Down His Life

> Greater Love hath no man than this: that a man Lay Down His Life for His friends. (John 15:13 KJ21)

Lord, Love

> The grace of our Lord overflowed with the faith and Love which is in Christ Jesus. (1 Timothy 1:14 MEV)

Loved the World, Have Everlasting Life

> For God so Loved the World that He gave His only begotten Son, that whosoever believeth in Him should not perish, but Have Everlasting Life. (John 3:16 KJ21)

Lord Your God, Full of Faithful Love

> Return to the Lord Your God, for He is merciful and compassionate, very patient, Full of Faithful Love, and ready to forgive. (Joel 2:13b CEB)

Lord, Loved You, Love that Lasts Forever, Loving-Kindness

> The Lord came to us from far away, saying, "I have Loved you with a Love that Lasts Forever. So, I have helped you come to Me with Loving-Kindness." (Jeremiah 31:3 NLV)

Live, Christ Liveth in me, Life, Live in the Flesh, Live by Faith, Loved me

> I am crucified with Christ, nevertheless I Live, yet not I, but Christ Liveth in me. And the Life which I now Live in the Flesh, I Live by Faith of the Son of God, who Loved me and gave Himself for me. (Galatians 2:20 KJ21)

Love, Lord Jesus Christ, Eternal Life

> Keep yourselves in God's Love as you wait for the mercy of our Lord Jesus Christ to bring you to Eternal Life. (Jude 1:21 NIV)

Love Me, Obey My Laws

> But I show my Love to thousands of generations of those who Love Me and Obey My Laws. (Exodus 20:6 GNT)

Loves, Loving-Kindness of the Lord

> He Loves righteousness and justice; The earth is full of the Loving-Kindness of the Lord. (Psalm 33:5 AMP)

Loves you

> A friend Loves you all the time, but a brother was born to help in times of trouble. (Proverbs 17:17 ERV)

I Am the Way, the Truth, the Life

> Jesus answered, "I Am the Way and the Truth and the Life. No one comes to the Father except through Me." (John 14:6 NIV)

Listen to Me, First and Last

> Listen To Me, my people, my chosen ones! I alone am God. I am the First; I am the Last. (Isaiah 48:12 TLB)

Living Being, Last Adam, Life-Giving Spirit

> So, it is written, The first man, Adam became a Living Being; the Last Adam became a Life-Giving Spirit. (1 Corinthians 15:45 CSB)

Living Bread, Live Forever, Life of the World

> I am the Living Bread which came down from heaven. If any man eat of this Bread, he shall Live Forever; and the Bread that I will give is My flesh, which I will give for the Life of the World. (John 6:51 KJ21)

Lawgiver

> There is only one Lawgiver and Judge, the one who is able to save and destroy. But you—who are you to judge your neighbor? (James 4:12 NIV)

Lord, One Who Lifts My Head

> But You, O Lord, are a covering around me, my shining-greatness, and the One Who Lifts My Head. (Psalm 3:3 NLV)

My Lord and My God

> And Thomas answered and said unto Him, "My Lord and My God!" (John 20:28 KJ21)

Lord, Kingdom that will Last Forever

> Then our Lord and Savior Jesus Christ will give you a glorious welcome into His Kingdom that will Last Forever. (2 Peter 1:11 CEV)

Life, Lord of the Dead and of the Living

> This is because Christ died and rose to Life, so that He would be the Lord of the Dead and of the Living. (Romans 14:9 CEV)

Lord God Almighty

> Then I heard a voice from the altar saying, "Lord God Almighty! True and just indeed are your judgments!" (Revelation 16:7 GNT)

Lord God Omnipotent

> Then I heard something like the sound like a great multitude, as the sound of many waters and as the sound of mighty thundering's, saying: "Alleluia! For the Lord God Omnipotent (all powerful) reigns!" (Revelation 19:6 MEV)

Lord Jesus Christ, Lord of Shining Greatness

> My Christian brothers, our Lord Jesus Christ is the Lord of Shining-Greatness. Since your trust is in Him, do not look on one person as more important than another. (James 2:1 NLV)

Great and Glorious Lord

> None of the rulers of this world understood this wisdom. If they had understood it, they would not have killed our Great and Glorious Lord on a cross. (1 Corinthians 2:8 ERV)

Lord of the Harvest

> Ask the Lord of the Harvest, therefore, to send out workers into His harvest field. (Matthew 9:38 NIV)

Lord of Lords

> Which God will bring about in His own time—God, the blessed and only Ruler, the King of Kings and Lord of Lords. (1 Timothy 6:15 NIV)

Living Water

> Whoever believes in Me, as the Scripture says, "out of his innermost being will flow rivers of Living Water." (John 7:38 TLV)

> Jesus answered her, "If you knew [about] God's gift [of eternal life], and who it is who says, 'Give Me a drink,' if you would have asked Him [instead], and He would have given you Living Water (eternal life)." (John 4:10 AMP)

Lamp, Light to My Path

> Your Word is a Lamp to my feet and a Light to my Path. (Psalm 119:105 AMP)

Look, Lord

> Look for the Lord while He may be found. Call upon Him while He is near. (Isaiah 55:6 NLV)

Love for God

> I will give you one heart and a new spirit; I will take from you your hearts of stone and give you tender hearts of Love for God. (Ezekiel 11:19 TLB)

Life-Giving

> This is the fresh, new, Life-Giving way that Christ has opened up for us by tearing the curtain—His human body—to let us into the holy presence of God. (Hebrews 10:20 TLB)

Leader

> Church Leaders, I am writing to encourage you. I too am a Leader, as well as a witness to Christ's suffering, and I will share in His glory when it is shown to us. (1 Peter 5:1 CEV)

Leads Us

> We must keep our eyes on Jesus, who Leads Us and makes our faith complete. He endured the shame of being nailed to a cross, because He knew later on, He would be glad He did. Now He is seated at the right side of God's throne! (Hebrews 12:2 CEV)

> But the wisdom that comes from above Leads Us to be pure, friendly, gentle, sensible, kind, helpful, genuine, and sincere. (James 3:17 CEV)

> Wisdom makes life pleasant and Leads us safely along. (Proverbs 3:17 CEV)

Darkness to Light

> To open their eyes and to turn them from Darkness to Light, and from the power of Satan to God, that they may receive forgiveness of sins and an inheritance among those who are sanctified by faith that is in Me. (Acts 26:18 KJ21)

His Wonderful Light

> But you are not like that, for you have been chosen by God Himself—you are priests of the King, you are holy and pure, you are God's very own—all this so that you may show to others how God called you out of the darkness into His Wonderful Light. (1 Peter 2:9 TLB)

Let Your Light Shine, Lord

> Arise, my people! Let Your Light Shine for all the nations to see! For the glory of the Lord is streaming from you. Darkness as black as night shall cover all the peoples of the earth, but the glory of the Lord will shine from you. All nations will come to your Light; mighty kings will come to see the glory of the Lord upon you. (Isaiah 60:1–3 TLB)

Lift Up, One Who Leads them

> Lift Up your eyes and see. Who has made these stars? It is the One Who Leads them out by number. He calls them all by name. Because of the greatness of His strength, and because He is strong in power, not one of them is missing. (Isaiah 40:26 NLV)

Lift up my Eyes

> I will Lift up my Eyes to the mountains. Where will my help come from? (Psalm 121:1 NLV)

> I Lift Up My Eyes to You, O You Whose throne is in the heavens. (Psalm 123:1 NLV)

179

Long as I Live, Lift Up My Hands

> I will praise You as Long as I Live, and in Your name, I will Lift Up My Hands. (Psalm 63:4 NIV)

Limitless Joy

> Then my fears will dissolve into Limitless Joy; my whole being will overflow with gladness because of your mighty deliverance. (Psalm 35:9 TPT)

Lord, Love is Limitless

> But You, O Lord, Your mercy-seat Love is Limitless, reaching higher than the highest heavens. Your great faithfulness is infinite, stretching over the whole earth. (Psalm 36:5 TPT)

Lavish, Limitless Power

> They will tell the world of the Lavish splendor of Your kingdom and preach about Your Limitless Power. (Psalm 145:11 TPT)

Lord, Great and Limitless Power

> We give thanks to You, Lord God Almighty, who is, and who was, because You have established Your Great and Limitless Power and begun to reign! (Revelation 11:17 TPT)

Praise the Lord, His Loyal Love Endures

> Praise the Lord. Give thanks to the Lord, for He is good, and His Loyal Love Endures. (Psalm 106:1 NET)

PRAYERS (USING L WORDS)

We praise You, **Lord** Jesus that we are in the **Lambs** Book of **Life**. You are the **Lamb of God** who takes away the sins of the world and we **love** You for that. You are the **Light** of the world and a **Lamp** unto our feet. We are in awe, God, in **learning** just how amazing Your **love** is. You have given us Your **Living Water**, and we are grateful. You are our **Lord of Lords** and King of Kings. We have received Your **Living Bread**, and we will **live** forever. Your gift of **Eternal Life** is such a blessing. Our **lives** are in Your hands, **Lord**, and we glorify You, God. We thank You Father God for **leading** us into the **luscious land** of the free! Your Spirit **lives** inside us. Thank You for helping me **lift** my head, eyes, and hands to praise You as **long** as I **live**. We praise You, Our **Lord of Lords!** We want to be **loyal** to you and **let** our **lights** shine forever.

In Your **loving** name, Jesus, we pray.

Amen.

M

One Mediator between God and Men, Man Jesus

> For there is one God, and one Mediator between God and Men, the Man Christ Jesus. (1 Timothy 2:5 KJ21)

Messiah

> We have found the Messiah (that is, the Christ). (John 1:41b NIV)

> Then Jesus told her, "I am the Messiah!" (John 4:26 TLB)

> "Yes, Lord," she replied, "I believe that you are the Messiah, the Son of God, who is to come into the world." (John 11:27 NIV)

> Therefore, let all Israel be assured of this: God has Made this Jesus, whom you crucified, both Lord and Messiah. (Acts 2:36 NIV)

Mighty One

> Then you will know that I, the Lord, am your Savior, your Redeemer, the Mighty One of Jacob. (Isaiah 60:16b NIV)

Meek

> Blessed are the Meek, for they shall inherit the earth. (Matthew 5:5 KJ21)

The Meek shall eat and be satisfied; they shall praise the Lord that seek Him. Your hearts shall live forever. (Psalm 22:26 KJ21)

The Meek will He guide in judgment, and the Meek He will teach His way. (Psalm 25:9 KJ21)

But the Meek shall inherit the earth, and shall delight themselves in the abundance of peace. (Psalm 37:11 KJ21)

The Meek also shall increase their joy in the Lord, and the poor among Men shall rejoice in the Holy One of Israel. (Isaiah 29:19 KJ21)

I will leave a Meek and humble people among you, and they will take refuge in the name of the Lord. (Zephaniah 3:12 CSB)

Take My yoke upon you, and learn of Me. For I am Meek and lowly in heart, and ye shall find rest unto your souls. (Matthew 11:29 KJ21)

God loves you and has chosen you as His own special people. So be gentle, kind, humble, Meek, and patient. (Colossians 3:12 CEV)

Manner, Meekness

Walk in a Manner worthy of the calling with which you were called. With all humility, Meekness, and patience, bearing with one another in love. (Ephesians 4:1b–2 MEV)

Meekness

Who is wise and understanding among you? By His good conduct let Him show His works in the Meekness of wisdom. (James 3:13 ESV)

Mercies, Gracious and Merciful God

> Nevertheless, in Your great Mercies You did not make an end of them or forsake them, for You are a Gracious and Merciful God. (Nehemiah 9:31 ESV)

Merciful and Gracious

> The Lord is Merciful and Gracious, slow to anger and abounding in steadfast love. (Psalm 103:8 ESV)

Merciful

> Be Merciful, even as your Father is Merciful. (Luke 6:36 ESV)

> For His Merciful kindness is great toward us, and the truth of the Lord endureth forever. Praise ye the Lord! (Psalm 117:2 KJ21)

> I seek Your favor with my whole heart; be Merciful to me according to Your word. (Psalm 119:58 MEV)

> For I will be Merciful toward their iniquities, and their sins I will remember no more. (Hebrews 8:12 ESV)

> Look upon me, and be Merciful to me, as You are for those who love Your name. (Psalm 119:132 MEV)

Merciful, My Memory

> I will be Merciful when they fail, and I will erase their sins and wicked acts out of My Memory as though they had never existed. (Hebrews 8:12 VOICE)

Mercy

> But—When God our Savior revealed His kindness and love, He saved us, not because of the righteous things we had done, but because of His Mercy. He washed away our sins, giving us a new birth and new life through the Holy Spirit. (Titus 3:4–5 NLT)

Praise the Lord! For He has heard my cry for Mercy. (Psalm 28:6 NLT)

"O Lord," I prayed, "have Mercy on me. Heal me, for I have sinned against You." (Psalm 41:4 NLT)

Have Mercy on me, O God, because of Your unfailing love. Because of Your great compassion, blot out the stain of my sins. (Psalm 51:1 NLT)

Answer my prayers, O Lord, for your unfailing love is wonderful. Take care of me, for Your Mercy is so plentiful. (Psalm 69:16 NLT)

But You, O Lord, are a God of compassion and Mercy, slow to get angry and filled with unfailing love and faithfulness. (Psalm 86:15 NLT)

People who conceal their sins will not prosper, but if they confess and turn from them, they will receive Mercy. (Proverbs 28:13 NLT)

I will tell of the Lord's unfailing love. I will praise the Lord for all He has done. I will rejoice in His great goodness to Israel, which He has granted according to His Mercy and love. (Isaiah 63:7 NLT)

Hate what is evil, love what is right, and see that justice prevails in the courts. Perhaps the Lord will be Merciful to the people of this nation who are still left alive. (Amos 5:15 GNT)

No, O people, the Lord has told you what is good, and this is what He requires of you: to do what is right, to love Mercy, and to walk humbly with your God. (Micah 6:8 NLT)

He shows Mercy from generation to generation to all who fear Him. (Luke 1:50 NLT)

Grace, Mercy, and Peace, which come from God the Father and from Jesus Christ—the Son of the Father—will continue to be with us who live in truth and love. (2 John 1:3 NLT)

Moses, Mercy

The Lord passed in front of Moses, calling out, "Yahweh! The Lord! The God of compassion and Mercy! I am slow to anger and filled with unfailing love and faithfulness." (Exodus 34:6 NLT)

Merciful, Mercy

God blesses those who are Merciful, for they will be shown Mercy. (Matthew 5:7 NLT)

Meaning, Meditate

Help me understand the Meaning of your commandments, and I will Meditate on your wonderful deeds. (Psalm 119:27 NLT)

Meditate on Book of Instruction

Study this Book of Instruction continually. Meditate on it day and night so you will be sure to obey everything written in it. Only then will you prosper and succeed in all you do. (Joshua 1:8 NLT)

Meditate On Your Work and All Your Deeds

I will Meditate On all Your Work and I will ponder all Your Deeds. (Psalm 77:12 EHV)

Man Meditates Day and Night in the Law of the Lord

Blessed is the Man who walks not in the counsel of the ungodly, nor stands in the path of sinners, nor sits in the seat of scoffers; but his delight is in the Law of the Lord, and in His Law, he Meditates Day and Night. (Psalm 1:1–2 MEV)

My Words, My Thoughts, My Mighty Rock

> Let My Words and My Thoughts be pleasing to You, Lord, because You are My Mighty Rock and My protector. (Psalm 19:14 CEV)

Your Law is My Meditation

> Oh, how I love Your Law! It is My Meditation all the day. (Psalm 119:97 MEV)

Majesty, Meditate

> On the glorious splendor of Your Majesty, and on Your wonderful works, I will Meditate. (Psalm 145:5 AMP)

Hearts and Minds Made New

> Your Hearts and Minds must be Made completely New. (Ephesians 4:23 GNT)

Set Minds on Things of the Spirit

> For those who live according to the flesh have their Minds set on the things of the flesh, but those who live according to the Spirit have their Minds Set on the Things of the Spirit. (Romans 8:5 CSB)

Mind Is Stayed on You

> You will keep Him in perfect peace, whose Mind Is Stayed on You, because he trusts in You. (Isaiah 26:3 MEV)

Make a New Agreement, Write My Laws on Hearts and Minds

> Here is the new agreement that I, the Lord, will Make with the people of Israel: "I will write My Laws on their Hearts and Minds. I will be their God, and they will be my people." (Jeremiah 31:33 CEV)

Mind, Minds

> Set your Mind on the things that are above, not on the things that are upon the earth. (Colossians 3:2 ASV)

> The god of this age has blinded the Minds of unbelievers, so that they cannot see the light of the gospel that displays the glory of Christ, who is the image of God. (2 Corinthians 4:4 NIV)

> So then, have your Minds ready for action. Keep alert and set your hope completely on the blessing which will be given you when Jesus Christ is revealed. (1 Peter 1:13 GNT)

Love of Money, Many Sorrows

> For the Love of Money is the first step toward all kinds of sin. Some people have even turned away from God because of their love for it, and as a result have pierced themselves with Many sorrows. (1 Timothy 6:10 TLB)

Formed the Mountains, Made the Winds, Morning to Darkness

> For you are dealing with the One who formed the Mountains, Made the winds, and knows your every thought; He turns the Morning to darkness and crushes down the Mountains underneath His feet: Jehovah, the Lord, the Lord Almighty, is His name. (Amos 4:13 TLB)

Mountains May Move, Mercy

> "For the Mountains May Move and the hills disappear, but even then, my faithful love for you will remain. My covenant of blessing will never be broken," says the Lord, who has Mercy on you. (Isaiah 54:10 NLT)

Mountains, Messenger

> How beautiful on the Mountains are the feet of the Messenger who brings good news, the good news of peace and salvation, the news that the God of Israel reigns! (Isaiah 52:7 NLT)

Lord Our Maker

> Come, let us worship and bow down. Let us kneel before the Lord Our Maker. (Psalm 95:6 NLT)

Man of Sorrows

> He was despised and rejected—a Man of Sorrows, acquainted with deepest grief. We turned our backs on Him and looked the other way. He was despised, and we did not care. (Isaiah 53:3 NLT)

Make Clean from Evil, Made Holy, Master

> All who Make themselves Clean from Evil will be used for special purposes. They will be Made Holy, useful to the Master, ready to do any good work. (2 Timothy 2:21 NCV)

The Master You Serve

> Remember that the Lord will give you as a reward what He has kept for His people. For Christ is the real Master You Serve. (Colossians 3:24 GNT)

Cannot Serve Two Masters, God and Money

> You Cannot Serve Two Masters at the same time. You will hate one and love the other, or you will be loyal to one and not care about the other. You cannot serve God and Money at the same time. (Matthew 6:24 ERV)

Mind of the Lord, Mind of Christ

> For "who has known the Mind of the Lord that He may instruct Him?" But we have the Mind of Christ. (1 Corinthians 2:16 KJV)

Majesty, Might

> To the only God our Savior, through Jesus Christ our Lord, be glory, Majesty, Might, and authority, from all ages past, and now, and forever and ever! Amen. (Jude 1:25 GNT)

Majesty on High

> He is the radiance of the glory of God and the exact imprint of His nature, and He upholds the universe by the word of His power. After making purification for sins, He sat down at the right hand of the Majesty on High. (Hebrews 1:3 ESV)

Majesty, Meekness

> In your Majesty ride out victoriously for the cause of truth and Meekness and righteousness; let your right hand teach you awesome deeds! (Psalm 45:4 ESV)

Majesty

> Bless the Lord, O my soul! O Lord my God, You are very great! You are clothed with splendor and Majesty. (Psalm 104:1 ESV)

> I will speak of the glorious honor of Thy Majesty and of Thy wondrous works. (Psalm 145:5 KJ21)

> Yours, O Lord, is the greatness, and the power, and the glory, and the victory, and the Majesty, for all that is in the heavens and in the earth is Yours. Yours is the kingdom, O Lord, and You are exalted as head above all. (1 Chronicles 29:11 ESV)

Majesty, Most High God

> Listen, Your Majesty: The Most High God gave kingship, power, glory, and Majesty to your father Nebuchadnezzar. (Daniel 5:18 CEB)

Magnify the Lord

> Oh, Magnify the Lord with me, and let us exalt His name together. (Psalm 34:3 KJ21)

Mystery

> But we speak the wisdom of God in a Mystery, even the hidden wisdom which God ordained before the world for our glory. (1 Corinthians 2:7 KJ21)

> To them God would make known what is the glorious riches of this Mystery among the nations. It is Christ in you, the hope of glory. (Colossians 1:27 MEV)

> That their hearts may be comforted, being knit together in love, and receive all the riches and assurance of full understanding, and knowledge of the Mystery of God, both of the Father and of Christ, in whom are hidden all the treasures of wisdom and knowledge. (Colossians 2:2–3 MEV)

Magnificent, Unfailing Love

> In keeping with your Magnificent, Unfailing Love, please pardon the sins of this people, just as you have forgiven them ever since they left Egypt. (Numbers 14:19 NLT)

Marvelous Kindness

> Blessed be the Lord, for He hath shown me His Marvelous Kindness in a stronghold city! (Psalm 31:21 KJ21)

Moses, Marvelous

> They sang the song of Moses, the servant of God, and the song of the Lamb, saying: "Great and Marvelous are Your works, Lord God Almighty! Just and true are Your ways, O King of saints!" (Revelation 15:3 MEV)

Ministry

> When He began His Ministry, Jesus Himself was about thirty years of age, being, as was supposed, the son of Joseph, the son of Eli. (Luke 3:23 NASB)

> How will the Ministry of the Spirit not be more glorious? (2 Corinthians 3:8 CSB)

Ministry, Meditates

> But now Jesus, our High Priest, has been given a Ministry that is far superior to the old priesthood, for He is the one who Mediates for us a far better covenant with God, based on better promises. (Hebrews 8:6 NLT)

Make the Way Ready, Make the Road

> A voice is calling, "Make the Way Ready for the Lord in the desert. Make the Road in the desert straight for our God." (Isaiah 40:3 NLV)

Making a Path

> I am the Lord, who opened a way through the waters, Making a Path right through the sea. (Isaiah 43:16 TLB)

Make a Way

> Behold, I am doing a new thing; now it springs forth, do you not perceive it? I will Make a Way in the wilderness and rivers in the desert. (Isaiah 43:19 ESV)

Mankind

> No temptation has overtaken you except what is common to Mankind. And God is faithful; He will not let you be tempted beyond what you can bear. But when you are tempted, He will also provide a way out so that you can endure it. (1 Corinthians 10:13 NIV)

More Than Enough

> For just as Christ's sufferings are ours in abundance [as they overflow to His followers], so also our comfort [our reassurance, our encouragement, our consolation] is abundant through Christ [it is truly More Than Enough to endure what we must]. (2 Corinthians 1:5 AMP)

> God has the power to provide you with More Than Enough of every kind of grace. That way, you will have everything you need always and in everything to provide More Than Enough for every kind of good work. (2 Corinthians 9:8 CEB)

Mustard Seed, Mountain, Move

> He said to them, "Because of your little faith. For truly, I say to you, if you have faith like a grain of Mustard Seed, you will say to this Mountain, 'Move from here to there,' and it will Move, and nothing will be impossible for you." (Matthew 17:20 ESV)

Mustard Seed, Mulberry Tree

> And the Lord said, "If you had faith like a grain of Mustard Seed, you could say to this Mulberry Tree, 'Be uprooted and planted in the sea,' and it would obey you." (Luke 17:6 ESV)

My Heart and My Portion Forever

> My flesh and my heart may fail, but God is the strength of My Heart and My Portion Forever. (Psalm 73:26 ESV)

My Portion

> You are My Portion, Lord; I have promised to obey your words. (Psalm 119:57 NIV)

> I cry to you, Lord; I say, "You are my refuge, My Portion in the land of the living." (Psalm 142:5 NIV)

> "The Lord is My Portion," saith my soul, "therefore I will hope in Him." (Lamentations 3:24 KJ21)

Man's, Motives

> A Man's conscience is the Lord's searchlight exposing his hidden Motives. (Proverbs 20:27 TLB)

Motives

> We can justify our every deed, but God looks at our Motives. (Proverbs 21:2 TLB)

Men, Motives

> End all wickedness, O Lord, and bless all who truly worship God; for you, the righteous God, look deep within the hearts of Men and examine all their Motives and their thoughts. (Psalm 7:9 TLB)

Motives

> Only the Lord knows! He searches all hearts and examines deepest Motives so He can give to each person his right reward, according to his deeds—how He has lived. (Jeremiah 17:10 TLB)

> The day will surely come when at God's command Jesus Christ will judge the secret lives of everyone, their inmost thoughts and Motives; this is all part of God's great plan, which I proclaim. (Romans 2:16 TLB)

Mature

> Yet when I am among Mature believers, I do speak with words of wisdom, but not the kind of wisdom that belongs to this world or to the rulers of this world, who are soon forgotten. (1 Corinthians 2:6 NLT)

Mature, Measured

> Until we all reach the unity of faith and knowledge of God's Son. God's goal is for us to become Mature adults—to be fully grown, Measured by the standard of the fullness of Christ. (Ephesians 4:13 CEB)

Spiritually Mature

> Of course, my friends, I really do not think that I have already won it; the one thing I do, however, is to forget what is behind me and do my best to reach what is ahead. So, I run straight toward the goal in order to win the prize, which is God's call through Christ Jesus to the life above. All of us who are Spiritually Mature should have this same attitude. But if some of you have a different attitude; God will make this clear to you. (Philippians 3:13–15 GNT)

Mature, Heavenly Matters

> But solid food is for the Mature, whose spiritual senses perceive Heavenly Matters. And they have been adequately trained by what they've experienced to emerge with understanding of the difference between what is truly excellent and what is evil and harmful. (Hebrews 5:14 TPT)

Messiah, Maturity

> Therefore, leaving behind the elementary teachings about the Messiah, let us continue to be carried along to Maturity. (Hebrews 6:1a ISV)

Mature

> I have written to you who are God's children because you know the Father. I have written to you who are Mature in the faith because you know Christ, who existed from the beginning. (1 John 2:14a NLT)

Miraculous

> This Miraculous sign at Cana in Galilee was the first time Jesus revealed His glory. And His disciples believed in Him. (John 2:11 NLT)

Manifest

> But all things that are reproved are made Manifest by the light, for whatsoever doth make Manifest is light. (Ephesians 5:13 KJ21)

Manifestation of the Spirit

> But the Manifestation of the Spirit is given to each one for the profit of all. (1 Corinthians 12:7 NKJV)

Manifested

> And ye know that He was Manifested to take away our sins, and in Him is no sin. (1 John 3:5 KJ21)

> In this was Manifested the love of God toward us: that God sent His only begotten Son into the world, that we might live through Him. (1 John 4:9 KJ21)

Members

> And let the peace that comes from Christ rule in your hearts. For as Members of one body, you are called to live in peace. And always be thankful. (Colossians 3:15 NLT)

> And we are Members of His body. (Ephesians 5:30 NLT)

That there may be no division in the body, but that the Members may have the same care for one another. (1 Corinthians 12:25 ESV)

Memory

The Memory of the righteous is a blessing, but the name of the wicked rots. (Proverbs 10:7 CEB)

Merry Heart, Medicine

A Merry Heart does good like a Medicine, but a broken spirit dries the bones. (Proverbs 17:22 MEV)

Mourn

Blessed are those who Mourn, for they shall be comforted. (Matthew 5:4 ESV)

<u>PRAYERS</u> (USING M WORDS)

Father God, we are in awe of Your glorious riches of this *mystery*, which is Christ in *me*. Thank You for *making* a way, and You are *more* than enough. You are *marvelous*, Lord, and we *magnify* Your name. We are grateful that You help us keep our *minds* on things above, and we *meditate* on Your *mercy, meekness, miracles,* and *majesty*. We are so blessed to have *marvelous memories* of Your *miraculous* love. We are *members* of Your body, Jesus. We love the beautiful *mountains* that you have created. We are grateful that you have given us faith the size of a grain of a *mustard* seed, and we learned that You can *move mountains* because nothing is impossible for You. Thank You, Lord, for *making* and creating us in our *mothers'* wombs. Babies are *magnificent!*

We pray this in the *mighty* name of Jesus.

Amen.

N

Name

Your Name, O Lord, endures forever; Your fame, O Lord, is known to every generation. (Psalm 135:13 NLT)

Let them praise Your great and awesome Name! Holy is He! (Psalm 99:3 ESV)

As your Name deserves, O God, You will be praised to the ends of the earth. Your strong right hand is filled with victory. (Psalm 48:10 NLT)

All day long we talk about how great God is. We will praise Your Name forever. (Psalm 44:8 NIRV)

Give unto the Lord the glory due unto His Name; worship the Lord in the beauty of holiness. (Psalm 29:2 KJ21)

He restores my soul; He leads me in paths of righteousness for His Name's sake. (Psalm 23:3 ESV)

And those who know Your Name put their trust in You, for You, O Lord, have Not forsaken those who seek You. (Psalm 9:10 ESV)

O Lord, our Lord, how majestic and glorious and excellent is Your Name in all the earth! You have displayed Your splendor above the heavens. (Psalm 8:1 AMP)

Lord, you are my God. I honor You and praise Your Name, because You did amazing things. The words You said long ago are completely true; everything happened exactly as You said it would. (Isaiah 25:1 ERV)

You are loyal and kind to thousands of people, but You also bring punishment to children for their fathers' sins. Great and powerful God, Your Name is the Lord All-Powerful. (Jeremiah 32:18 ERV)

And the Lord will be king over all the earth. On that day there will be one Lord—His Name alone will be worshiped. (Zechariah 14:9 NLT)

He said, "Praise God's Name forever and ever! Power and wisdom belong to Him." (Daniel 2:20 ERV)

For all people walk each in the name of his god, But we will walk in the Name of the Lord our God forever and ever. (Micah 4:5 NKJV)

But for you who fear My Name, the Sun of Righteousness will rise with healing in His wings. And you will go free, leaping with joy like calves let out to pasture. (Malachi 4:2 TLB)

For where two or three are gathered together in My Name, there am I in the midst of them. (Matthew 18:20 KJ21)

And He said unto them, When ye pray, say, Father, Hallowed be thy Name. Thy kingdom come. (Luke 11:2 ASV)

He said to the followers, "Whoever receives this child in My Name, receives Me. Whoever receives Me, receives Him Who sent Me. The one who is least among you is the one who is great." (Luke 9:48 NLV)

But these are written so that you may believe that Jesus is the Christ, the Son of God. Then, by believing, you may have life through His Name. (John 20:31 NCV)

Until Now you have Not asked for anything in My Name. Ask and you will receive, so that your joy may be made complete. (John 16:24 EHV)

And if you ask for anything in My Name, I will do it for you. Then the Father's glory will be shown through the Son. (John 14:13 ERV)

But whoever did receive Him, those trusting in His Name, to these He gave the right to become children of God. (John 1:12 TLV)

Peter said to them, "Repent and be baptized, every one of you, in the Name of Jesus Christ for the forgiveness of sins, and you shall receive the gift of the Holy Spirit." (Acts 2:38 MEV)

And whoever calls on the Name of the Lord shall be saved. (Acts 2:21 MEV)

Such were some of you. But you were washed, you were sanctified, and you were justified in the Name of the Lord Jesus by the Spirit of our God. (1 Corinthians 6:11 MEV)

Through Him, then, let us continually offer to God the sacrifice of praise, which is the fruit of our lips, giving thanks to His Name. (Hebrews 13:15 MEV)

For this reason, also God highly exalted Him, and bestowed on Him the Name which is above every Name. (Philippians 2:9 NASB)

By doing this the Name of our Lord Jesus will be glorified in you, and you will be glorified in Him, by the marvelous grace of our God and the Lord Jesus Christ. (2 Thessalonians 1:12 TPT)

But the firm foundation of God has written upon it these two inscriptions: "The Lord God recognizes those who are truly His!" and, "Everyone who worships the Name of the Lord Jesus must forsake wickedness!" (2 Timothy 2:19 TPT)

I am writing to you, little children, because your sins are forgiven for His Name's sake. (1 John 2:12 ESV)

And this is His commandment: that we should believe in the Name of His Son Jesus Christ and love one another, as He gave us commandment. (1 John 3:23 KJ21)

I have written these things to you who believe in the Name of the Son of God, that you may know that you have eternal life, and that you may continue to believe in the Name of the Son of God. (1 John 5:13 MEV)

You have endured, and have been patient, and for My Name's sake have labored and have not grown weary. (Revelation 2:3 MEV)

On His robe and on His thigh, He has a Name written: "KING OF KINGS AND LORD OF LORDS." (Revelation 19:16 MEV)

Anyone whose Name was Not found written in the Book of Life was cast into the lake of fire. (Revelation 20:15 MEV)

Name, Never

Then you will have plenty to eat. You will be full. You will praise the Name of the Lord Your God. He has done wonderful things for you. My people will Never again be ashamed. (Joel 2:26 ERV)

Name of the Lord

Our help is in the Name of the Lord, who made heaven and earth. (Psalm 124:8 MEV)

Those who are left will be the poor and the humble, and they will trust in the Name of the Lord. (Zephaniah 3:12 TLB)

And those who went before, and those who followed, cried out, saying, "Hosanna! Blessed is He who comes in the Name of the Lord!" (Mark 11:9 MEV)

Blessed be the Name of the Lord from this time forth and forevermore! From the rising of the sun to its setting, the Name of the Lord is to be Praised! (Psalm 113:2–3 ESV)

No One Like You, Your Name

Lord, there is No One Like You. You are great; Your Name is great in power. (Jeremiah 10:6 CSB)

No One Else, One Name, Name of Jesus

There is No One Else who has the power to save us, for there is only One Name to whom God has given authority by which we must experience salvation: the Name of Jesus. (Acts 4:12 TPT)

Name Is the Word of God

His eyes were like a flame of fire, and He wore many crowns on His head. He had a Name written on Him, but No one except Himself knows what it is. The robe He wore was covered with blood. His Name Is "The Word of God." (Revelation 19:12–13 GNT)

Believes in Him Is Not Condemned, Does Not Believe Stands Condemned

Whoever Believes in Him Is Not Condemned, but whoever Does Not Believe Stands Condemned already because they have Not believed in the Name of God's one and only Son. (John 3:18 ESV)

Nation, Name

> Through Him we have received God's kindness and the privilege of being apostles who bring people from every Nation to the obedience that is associated with faith. This is for the honor of His Name. (Romans 1:5 GW)

Praise Your Name, Nations Worship You

> Lord, who won't fear and Praise Your Name? You are the only holy one, and all the Nations will come to Worship You because they know about Your fair judgments. (Revelation 15:4 GW)

His Holy Name

> Glory in His Holy Name; let the hearts of those who seek the Lord rejoice! (Psalm 105:3 ESV)

Bless His Name

> Enter into His gates with thanksgiving, and into His courts with praise; Give thanks to Him; Bless His Name. (Psalm 100:4 ESV)

Praise His Name

> Sing to the Lord and Praise His Name! Tell the Good News every day about how He saves us! (Psalm 96:2 ERV)

Revere and Honor Your Name

> Teach me Your ways, Lord, that I may walk in Your truth; let me wholeheartedly Revere Your Name. I will praise You, Lord my God, with my whole being; and I will Honor Your Name continuously. (Psalm 86:11–12 ISV)

Praise His Glorious Name

>Praise His Glorious Name forever! Let the whole earth be filled with His glory. Amen and Amen! (Psalm 72:19 NLT)

King's Name, Nations Be Blessed

>May the King's Name endure forever; may it continue as long as the sun shines. May all Nations Be Blessed through Him and bring Him praise. (Psalm 72:17 NLT)

Meet All Your Needs

>And my God will Meet All Your Needs according to the riches of His glory in Christ Jesus. (Philippians 4:19 NIV)

Satisfy Your Needs

>The Lord will always lead you and Satisfy Your Needs in dry lands. He will give strength to your bones. You will be like a garden that has plenty of water, like a spring that Never goes dry. (Isaiah 58:11 ERV)

Love Never Fails

>Love Never fails. But if there are prophecies, they shall fail; if there are tongues, they shall cease; and if there is knowledge, it shall vanish. (1 Corinthians 13:8 MEV)

Love Never Ends, Mercies Never Cease

>The faithful Love of the Lord Never Ends! His Mercies Never Cease. (Lamentations 3:22 NLT)

Righteousness Will Never Fail

>Lift up your eyes to the heavens, look at the earth beneath; the heavens will vanish like smoke, the earth

will wear out like a garment and its inhabitants die like flies. But my salvation will last forever, my Righteousness Will Never Fail. (Isaiah 51:6 NIV)

Covenant Will Never Fail

I will maintain my love to Him forever, and my Covenant with Him Will Never Fail. (Psalm 89:28 NIV)

Word of God Will Never Fail

For the Word of God Will Never Fail. (Luke 1:37 NLT)

Nazareth, Nazarene

He went to a town called Nazareth and lived there. This gave full meaning to what God said through the prophets. God said the Messiah would be called a Nazarene. (Matthew 2:23 ERV)

Lord Is Near, Honor His Holy Name

The Lord Is Near to all who call on Him, to all who call on Him in truth. He will fill the desire of those who fear Him. He will also hear their cry and will save them. The Lord takes care of all who love Him. But He will destroy all the sinful. My mouth will speak the praise of the Lord. And all flesh will Honor His Holy Name forever and ever. (Psalm 145:18–21 NLV)

Nation, God Is Near to Us

For what great Nation has a God as Near to them as the Lord our God is Near to Us whenever we call on Him? (Deuteronomy 4:7 NLT)

Always Near, Not Far Away

This message is from the Lord. "I am God, and I am Always Near. I am Not Far Away." (Jeremiah 23:23 ERV)

None Besides You, No Rock Like Our God

> There is None Holy like the Lord: there is None Besides You; there is No Rock Like Our God. (1 Samuel 2:2 AMPC)

None Like Him

> And Samuel said to all the people, "Do you see Him whom the Lord has chosen? There is None Like Him among all the people." And all the people shouted, "Long live the king!" (1 Samuel 10:24 ESV)

None Like You, No God Besides You

> Therefore, You are great, O Lord God. For there is None Like You, and there is No God Besides You, according to all that we have heard with our ears. (2 Samuel 7:22 AMP)

None Like You, Name Is Great

> There is None Like You, O Lord; You are Great, and Great is Your mighty and powerful Name. (Jeremiah 10:6 AMP)

Lord Is Near, Nations

> The day of the Lord is Near for all Nations. As you have done, it will be done to you. (Obadiah 1:15a NIV)

Never Heard

> How can people have faith in the Lord and ask Him to save them, if they have Never Heard about Him? And how can they hear, unless someone tells them? (Romans 10:14 CEV)

Nailed to the Cross with Jesus

> We know that the persons we used to be were Nailed to the Cross with Jesus. This was done, so our sinful bodies would no longer be the slaves of sin. (Romans 6:6 CEV)

New Heavens, New Earth

> I am creating New Heavens and a New Earth; everything of the past will be forgotten. (Isaiah 65:17 CEV)

> But God has promised us a New Heaven and a New Earth, where justice will rule. We are really looking forward to this! (2 Peter 3:13 CEV)

New Creature, all things have become New

> Therefore, if any man be in Christ, he is a New Creature; old things are passed away; behold, all things have become New. (2 Corinthians 5:17 KJ21)

New Life

> It gives us New Life to know that you are standing firm in the Lord. (1 Thessalonians 3:8 NLT)

> For you have been born again, but not to a life that will quickly end. Your New Life will last forever because it comes from the eternal, living Word of God. (1 Peter 1:23 NLT)

> He died for everyone so that those who receive His New Life will no longer live for themselves. Instead, they will live for Christ, who died and was raised for them. (2 Corinthians 5:15 NLT)

> Yes, Adam's one sin brings condemnation for everyone, but Christ's one act of righteousness brings a right relationship with God and New Life for everyone. (Romans 5:18 NLT)

New Creation, New Way of Living

>Whoever is a believer in Christ is a New Creation. The old way of living has disappeared. A New Way of Living has come into existence. (2 Corinthians 5:17 GW)

Nothing Can Separate Us

>Yes, I am sure that Nothing Can Separate Us from God's love—Not death, life, angels, or ruling spirits. I am sure that Nothing now, Nothing in the future, No powers, Nothing above us or Nothing below us—Nothing in the whole created world—will ever be able to separate us from the love God has shown us in Christ Jesus our Lord. (Romans 8:38–39 ERV)

Not, Nurture

>And ye fathers, provoke Not your children to wrath, but bring them up in the Nurture and admonition of the Lord. (Ephesians 6:4 KJ21)

Narrow Gate

>Enter through the Narrow Gate. For wide is the gate and broad is the road that leads to destruction, and many enter through it. (Matthew 7:13 NIV)

Narrow Door

>Make every effort to enter through the Narrow Door, because I tell you, many will try to enter and won't be able. (Luke 13:24 CSB)

Divine Nature

>By which He has granted to us His precious and very great promises, so that through them you may become partakers of the Divine Nature, having escaped from the corruption that is in the world because of sinful desire. (2 Peter 1:4 ESV)

Numbered

> But even the hairs of your head are all Numbered. (Matthew 10:30 ESV)

Needy

> But you are a tower of refuge to the poor, O Lord, a tower of refuge to the Needy in distress. You are a refuge from the storm and a shelter from the heat. For the oppressive acts of ruthless people are like a storm beating against a wall. (Isaiah 25:4 NLT)

Needy, Not Steep, Glorify Your Name

> Trust in the Lord always, for the Lord God is the eternal Rock. He humbles the proud and brings down the arrogant city. He brings it down to the dust. The poor and oppressed trample it underfoot, and the Needy walk all over it. But for those who are righteous, the way is Not Steep and rough. You are a God who does what is right, and you smooth out the path ahead of them. Lord, we show our trust in you by obeying your laws; our heart's desire is to Glorify Your Name. (Isaiah 26:4–8 NLT)

Needy

> "He gave justice and help to the poor and Needy, and everything went well for Him. Isn't that what it means to know me?" says the Lord. (Jeremiah 22:16 NLT)

Those in Need, Not be Forgotten, Not be Lost

> But Those in Need will Not always be Forgotten. The hope of the poor will Not be Lost forever. (Psalm 9:18 NLV)

In Need

> But I am poor and In Need. Hurry to me, O God! You are my help and the One Who takes me out of trouble. O Lord, do not wait. (Psalm 70:5 NLV)

<u>PRAYERS</u> (Using N Words)

We are in awe of Your *name*, Lord. We know that it is a *name* above all *names*, and we surely love You, Jesus. You meet all of our *needs*, and Your love *never* fails. Thank You for always being *nearby*. There is *no one* like You. We are grateful that You were *nailed* to the cross so that we are *no* longer living in sin. We love our *new* life in You, and we look forward to Your *new* heaven and *new* earth. *Nothing* can separate us from Your love. We thank You, Father God, for the *nourishment* You feed our hearts and bodies daily. Jesus, You are *noble* due to Your high qualities of being dignified. We *notice* how You transform others and that is so *nice* and wonderful. Your miracles are too *numerous* to count.

We will praise Your holy *name* forever, Jesus!

Amen.

NAMES OF GOD

Adonai: Lord or Master

> The Maker of the universe rules over us from a big picture and personally. God is Lord, and we are His servants. We want to be quick to do God's will. Our powerful Lord uses His power on our behalf.

El-Olam: The Everlasting and/or Eternal God

> God has been here since the beginning and will be here for all eternity. God has no beginning and no end. God's love endures forever. A day is like a thousand years, and a thousand years are like a day.

El-Roi: The God Who Sees All

> God watches us and sees our joys and tears. It gives us comfort to know that God oversees our lives.

Jehovah-Rapha: The Lord Our Healer

> God plans to redeem our souls, our spirits, and our bodies in heaven.

El-Deah: The God of Knowledge

> Scripture reveals God as the ultimate source of knowledge. He knows all—every detail about us. This can affect our trust in Him.

Jehovah-Jireh: The God Who Provides

> In amazing and ordinary ways, God always provides. If you need something, talk to God about it. God provided for His people in the Bible.

El-Chuwl: The God Who Gave You Birth

> Your existence is not by coincidence. Even before you were born, God knew everything about you. He has given us life, and our lives have a purpose.

El-Gibhor: Mighty God

> God is all-powerful. He is able to help us overcome challenges in our lives.

Jehovah-Tsidkenu: The Lord Our Righteousness

> Sin makes our lives impure and impairs our reasoning and judgment. God is pure, perfect, and just, and we can live in righteousness because of Him.

Jehovah-Nissi: The Lord Our Banner

> God is our banner as we face spiritual battles. He covers us and fights for us. We can trust Him in our challenges. A banner is a flag that goes before an army or group to be identified.

Jehovah-Shalom: The Lord Is Peace

> The unsaved world calls for peace. God promises an eternity of peace to believers. We can be in the midst of chaos and turn to God for peace. His Son, Jesus, is called the Prince of Peace. Live in harmony with God.

Jehovah-Rohi: The Lord Our Shepherd

> Sheep can't do much on their own. Shepherds are needed to meet their needs, guide them, protect them, bind their wounds, and groom them. God watches over us day and night, and He feeds us and guides us.

El Shadday: God Almighty

> He is a refuge from all storms. No matter how tough life is, no power in heaven or earth can change His plan for us as long as we follow Him.

Yahweh: The God of Your Fathers, the God of Abraham, Isaac, and Jacob

> This is the name that is most closely linked to God's redeeming acts in the history of His chosen people. God draws near to us to save us from sin.

Esh Oklah, El Kanna: Consuming Fire, Jealous God

> The Lord will ultimately destroy whatever is opposed to His holiness. We need to have a great desire to honor and exalt His name.

Qedosh Yisrael: Holy One of Israel

> We are to be set apart for God and to be holy because He is holy.

Yahweh Tsebaoth: The Lord of Hosts

> God is so magnificent that all creation serves His purposes. This means great power. When the battle is at its worst, the Lord is able to do more than we can ask or imagine.

Yahweh Tsuri: The Lord My Rock

> God gives us protection, and He can always be counted on. He is our stronghold and our refuge. He is faithful.

O

OUR GOD'S ATTRIBUTES

Our God is Omniscient and all-knowing. He has complete knowledge.

> Our Lord is great and powerful! He understands everything. (Psalm 147:5 CEV)

Our God is Omnipotent, has unlimited power, and is able to do anything.

> Sovereign Lord, You made the earth and the sky by Your great power and might; nothing is too difficult for You. (Jeremiah 32:17 GNT)

> "I am the Lord, the God of all people. Nothing is too difficult for Me." (Jeremiah 32:27 GNT)

Our God is Omnipresent. He is able to be everywhere at the same time. He is always present.

> Where can I go from Your Spirit? Where can I flee from Your presence? If I go up to the heavens, You are there; if I make my bed in the depths, You are there. If I rise on the wings of the dawn, if I settle on the far side of the sea, even there Your hand will guide me, Your right hand will hold me fast. (Psalm 139:7–10 NIV)

Our God is Infinite.

> God has no limits, eternal and everlasting. He is limitless and immeasurable.

> Did any of you measure the ocean by yourself or stretch out the sky with your own hands? Did you put the soil of the earth in a bucket or weigh the hills and mountains on balance scales? Has anyone told the Lord what He must do or given Him advice? (Isaiah 40:12–13 CEV)

Our God is Sovereign. He has no limits on anyone's authority. He rules and reigns.

> To Him the nations are far less than nothing; God controls the stars in the sky and everyone on this earth. When God does something, we cannot change it or even ask why. (Daniel 4:35 CEV)

Our God is Incomprehensible. He cannot be fully known. He has infinite mystery, and He is beyond human reasoning.

> Can you understand the mysteries surrounding God All-Powerful? They are higher than the heavens and deeper than the grave. So, what can you do when you know so little, and these mysteries outreach the earth and the ocean? (Job 11:7–9 CEV)

Our God is Existent. God creates something from nothing, God is uncreated, He created all.

> The Son is the image of the invisible God, the firstborn over all creation. For in Him all things were created: things in heaven and on earth, visible and invisible, whether thrones or powers or rulers or authorities; all things have been created through Him and for Him. He is before all things, and in Him all things hold together. (Colossians 1:15–17 NIV)

Our God is Self-Sufficient. He has no needs. He is a God of Infinite provision.

> He made the world and everything in it, and since He is Lord of heaven and earth, He doesn't live in man-made temples; and human hands can't minister to His needs— for He has no needs! He Himself gives life and breath to everything, and satisfies every need there is. (Acts 17:24–25 TLB)

Our God is Eternal. He has no end and is Everlasting. He is a God of Infinite days.

> He has made everything beautiful in its time. He has also set eternity in the human heart; yet no one can fathom what God has done from beginning to end. I know that there is nothing better for people than to be happy and to do good while they live. That each of them may eat and drink, and find satisfaction in all their toil—this is the gift of God. I know that everything God does will endure forever; nothing can be added to it and nothing taken from it. God does it so that people will fear Him. (Ecclesiastes 3:11–14 NIV)

Our God is Immutable. God is the same yesterday, today, and forever. He is a God of Infinite sameness.

> Jesus Christ is the same yesterday and today and forever. (Hebrews 13:8 NIV)

Obey

> The Lord God has told us what is right and what He demands: "See that justice is done, let mercy be your first concern, and humbly Obey Your God." (Micah 6:8 CEV)

> The Lord watches over those who Obey Him, those who trust in His constant love. (Psalm 33:18 GNT)

Obey the Lord's teachings and you will live—disobey and you will die. (Proverbs 19:16 CEV)

You Obeyed my message and endured. So, I will protect you from the time of testing that everyone in all the world must go through. (Revelation 3:10 CEV)

You show that you are my intimate friends when you Obey all that I command you. (John 15:14 TPT)

Be strong and very courageous. Be careful to Obey all the instructions Moses gave you. Do not deviate from them, turning either to the right or to the left. Then you will be successful in everything you do. (Joshua 1:7 NLT)

Be careful to Obey all these commands I am giving you. Show love to the Lord your God by walking in His ways and holding tightly to Him. (Deuteronomy 11:22 NLT)

The Lord is your God, so you must always love Him and Obey His laws and teachings. (Deuteronomy 11:1 CEV)

Look, today I am giving you the choice between a blessing and a curse! You will be blessed if you Obey the commands of the Lord your God that I am giving you today. (Deuteronomy 11:26–27 NLT)

Like the nations the Lord is about to destroy before you, you will perish if you do not Obey the Lord your God. (Deuteronomy 8:20 CSB)

That's why the Lord our God demands that we Obey His laws and worship Him with fear and trembling. And if we do, He will protect us and help us be successful. (Deuteronomy 6:24 CEV)

Thus, you will remember and Obey all My commandments and be holy to your God. (Numbers 15:40 NET)

You must Obey my rules and follow my laws. Be sure to follow my rules because I am the Lord your God.

You must Obey my rules and my laws, because whoever Obeys them will live. I am the Lord. (Leviticus 18:4–5 ERV)

Be careful to Obey all these things I command you, so that you and your children after you may prosper forever, because you will be doing what is good and right in the sight of the Lord your God. (Deuteronomy 12:28 CSB)

You must definitely Obey the Lord your God's voice, keeping all His commandments that I am giving you right now, by doing what is right in the Lord your God's eyes! (Deuteronomy 13:18 CEB)

Obey the Lord your God and follow His commands and decrees that I give you today. (Deuteronomy 27:10 NIV)

If you fully Obey the Lord your God and carefully keep all His commands that I am giving you today, the Lord your God will set you high above all the nations of the world. You will experience all these blessings if you Obey the Lord your God. (Deuteronomy 28:1–2 NLT)

He said, "Always remember this song I have taught you today. And let it be a warning that you must teach your children to Obey everything written in The Book of God's Law." (Deuteronomy 32:46 CEV)

Be strong and very courageous. Be careful to Obey all the law my servant Moses gave you; do not turn from it to the right or to the left, that you may be successful wherever you go. (Joshua 1:7–8 NIV)

All will go well with you if you honor the Lord your God, serve Him, listen to Him, and Obey His commands, and if you and your king follow Him. (1 Samuel 12:14 GNT)

Your written instructions are miraculous. That is why I Obey them. (Psalm 119:129 GW)

Save me from those who want to hurt me, and I will Obey your instructions. (Psalm 119:134 ERV)

I have cried a river of tears because people don't Obey your teachings. (Psalm 119:136 ERV)

I love and Obey your laws with all my heart. (Psalm 119:167 CEV)

However, I did give them this command: "Obey me, and then I will be your God, and you will be my people. Follow every way I command you so that it may go well with you." (Jeremiah 7:23 CSB)

Jesus replied, "Rather, how blessed are those who hear and Obey God's Word." (Luke 11:28 GW)

Therefore, never let sin rule your physical body so that you Obey its desires. (Romans 6:12 GW)

Jesus answered Him, "Those who love Me will Obey my teaching. My Father will love them, and my Father and I will come to them and live with them." (John 14:23 GNT)

Slaves, Obey your earthly masters with respect and fear, and with sincerity of heart, just as you would Obey Christ. Obey them not only to win their favor when their eye is on you, but as slaves of Christ, doing the will of God from your heart. (Ephesians 6:5–6 NIV)

But Peter and the apostles answered, "We must Obey God rather than men." (Acts 5:29 ESV)

Bless You Only, Obey

He will bless you Only if you listen carefully to the Lord your God and faithfully Obey all these commands, I'm giving you today. (Deuteronomy 15:5 GW)

Only the Lord, Obey

> Serve Only the Lord your God and fear Him alone. Obey His commands, listen to His voice, and cling to Him. (Deuteronomy 13:4 NLT)

Obey, Ones Who Love Me

> Those who accept my commandments and Obey them are the Ones Who Love Me. And because they love me, my Father will love them. And I will love them and reveal myself to each of them. (John 14:21 NLT)

Obey, Take Over the Land

> Therefore, be careful to Obey every command I am giving you today, so you may have strength to go in and Take Over the Land you are about to enter. If you Obey, you will enjoy a long life in the land the Lord swore to give to your ancestors and to you, their descendants—a land flowing with milk and honey! (Deuteronomy 11:8–9 NLT)

Obey Your Parents

> Children, Obey Your Parents because you belong to the Lord, for this is the right thing to do. "Honor your father and mother." This is the first commandment with a promise: If you honor your father and mother, "things will go well for you, and you will have a long life on the earth." (Ephesians 6:1–3 NLT)

Obey, My Own Special Treasure

> Now if you will Obey me and keep my covenant, you will be My Own Special Treasure from among all the peoples on earth; for all the earth belongs to Me. (Exodus 19:5 NLT)

Obey, Oath

> But if you seek the Lord your God from there, you will find Him, if, indeed, you seek Him with all your heart and soul. In your distress when all these things happen to you in future days, if you return to the Lord your God and Obey Him (for He is a merciful God), He will not let you down or destroy you, for He cannot forget the covenant with your ancestors that He confirmed by Oath to them. (Deuteronomy 4:29–31 NET)

Obey, Ordinance

> Obey these instructions as a lasting Ordinance for you and your descendants. (Exodus 12:24 NIV)

Obstacle, Obey

> We destroy every proud Obstacle that keeps people from knowing God. We capture their rebellious thoughts and teach them to Obey Christ. (2 Corinthians 10:5 NLT)

Offspring, Obey

> And through your Offspring all nations on earth will be blessed, because you have Obeyed Me. (Genesis 22:18 NIV)

Outcome, Obey

> For the time has come for judgment to begin with the household of God. And if it begins with us, what will be the Outcome for those who refuse to Obey the Gospel of God? (1 Peter 4:17 ISV)

Obedient

> Then He took the Book of the Covenant and read it as the people listened; and they said, "All that the Lord has spoken we will do, and we will be Obedient!" (Exodus 24:7 NASB)

I have refused to walk the paths of evil, for I will remain Obedient to Your Word. (Psalm 119:101 TLB)

Obedience, Love Each Other

Now that your Obedience to the truth has purified your souls, you can have true love for your Christian brothers and sisters. So, Love Each Other deeply with all your heart. (1 Peter 1:22 NCV)

Obeying

May you, His people, always be faithful to the Lord Our God, Obeying all His laws and commands as you do today. (1 Kings 8:61 GNT)

But if you stop your sinning and begin Obeying the Lord your God, He will cancel all the punishment He has announced against you. (Jeremiah 26:13 TLB)

Obeys

Who among you fears the Lord and Obeys the voice of His servant? Let him who walks in darkness and has no light trust in the name of the Lord and rely on His God. (Isaiah 50:10 ESV)

I am telling you the truth: whoever Obeys my teaching will never die. (John 8:51 GNT)

Offer, Obedient, One You Obey, Obedience, Once Slaves of Sin

Don't you know that when you Offer yourselves to someone as Obedient slaves, you are slaves of the One You Obey—either of sin, which leads to death, or of Obedience, which leads to righteousness? But thank God that, though you were Once Slaves of Sin, you became Obedient from your hearts to that form of teaching with which you were entrusted! (Romans 6:16–17 ISV)

Overflow, Others

> My prayer for you is that you will Overflow more and more with love for Others, and at the same time keep on growing in spiritual knowledge and insight. (Philippians 1:9 TLB)

On Earth, Of All Nations, Observe

> Then Jesus came and spoke to them, saying, "All authority has been given to Me in heaven and On Earth. Go therefore and make disciples Of All Nations, baptizing them in the name Of the Father and Of the Son and Of the Holy Spirit, teaching them to Observe all things I have commanded you. And remember, I am with you always, even to the end of the age." Amen. (Matthew 28:18–20 MEV)

One Who Saves, Our Lord, Our Hope

> This letter is from Paul, a missionary of Jesus Christ. I am sent by God, the One Who Saves, and by Our Lord Jesus Christ Who is Our Hope. (1 Timothy 1:1 NLV)

Our Hope, Our Help, Our Shield

> We put Our Hope in the Lord. He is Our Help and Our Shield. (Psalm 33:20 CEB)

Our Hope

> Let Your unfailing love surround us, Lord, for Our Hope is in You alone. (Psalm 33:22 NLT)

Only Help, Our Best, Our Hope, One Who Would Save All Men

> Growing strong in body is all right but growing in God-like living is more important. It will not Only Help you in this life now but in the next life also. These words are true and they can be trusted. Because of this, we work

hard and do Our Best because Our Hope is in the living God, the One Who Would Save All Men. He saves those who believe in Him. (1 Timothy 4:8–10 NLV)

Opposes the Proud

But He gives more grace. Therefore, it says, "God Opposes the Proud but gives grace to the humble." (James 4:6 ESV)

Only One God, Only One

There is Only One God, and Christ Jesus is the Only One who can bring us to God. Jesus was truly human, and He gave Himself to rescue all of us. (1 Timothy 2:5 CEV)

Only Wise God

Now unto the King eternal, immortal, invisible, the Only Wise God, be honor and glory for ever and ever. Amen. (1 Timothy 1:17 KJ21)

One God, Over All

One God and Father of all, who is Over All, and through all and in all. (Ephesians 4:6 ASV)

Only One God, Eliminates Our Guilt

Since there is Only One God, He will treat us all the same— He Eliminates Our Guilt and makes us right with Him by faith no matter who we are. (Romans 3:30 TPT)

One True God

You can believe all you want that there is One True God, that's wonderful! But even the demons know this and tremble with fear before Him, yet they're unchanged— they remain demons. (James 2:19 TPT)

Only True God

> And this is life eternal: that they might know Thee, the Only True God, and Jesus Christ whom Thou hast sent. (John 17:3 KJ21)

One, Our God is the One and Only God

> Jesus replied, "The One that says, 'Hear, O Israel! The Lord Our God is the One and Only God.'" (Mark 12:29 TLB)

Only Begotten Son

> In this was manifested the love of God toward us: that God sent His Only Begotten Son into the world, that we might live through Him. (1 John 4:9 KJ21)

Oppressed

> The Lord is a refuge for the Oppressed, a place of safety in times of trouble. (Psalm 9:9 GNT)

Our Redeemer, Holy One

> Our Redeemer, whose name is the Lord of Heaven's Armies, is the Holy One of Israel. (Isaiah 47:4 NLT)

Alpha and Omega, Overcomes

> He said to me, "It is done. I am the Alpha and the Omega, the Beginning and the End. I will give of the spring of the water of life to Him who thirsts. He who Overcomes shall inherit all things, and I will be His God and He shall be My son." (Revelation 21:6–7 MEV)

Overcome

> Do not be Overcome by evil, but Overcome evil with good. (Romans 12:21 MEV)

Opened the Doors of Heaven

> Yet He had commanded the skies above and Opened the Doors of Heaven. (Psalm 78:23 MEV)

Overwhelming Greatness of God's Power

> And what is the Overwhelming Greatness of God's Power that is working among us believers. This power is conferred by the energy of God's powerful strength. (Ephesians 1:19 CEB)

One Who Lives Forever

> For the high and honored One Who Lives Forever, whose name is Holy, says, "I live in the high and holy place. And I also live with those who are sorry for their sins and have turned from them and are not proud. I give new strength to the spirit of those without pride, and also to those whose hearts are sorry for their sins." (Isaiah 57:15 NLV)

<u>PRAYERS</u> (USING O WORDS)

We praise You, God, for being all-knowing, all-powerful, and always present. We know You are *our* Helper and *our* Redeemer. You are *our one* and *only* true God. We want to *obey* You and Your Word, God. Thank You for *opening* the doors of heaven. We worship Your *only* begotten Son, the Holy *One*. We are *overcoming* sin because *of* Your *overwhelming* greatness and power to forgive *our* sins. We want to be *obedient* to You, Jesus, and love *others*. We are in awe. You are *our one* and *only* hope. We praise You, God, for being *Omnipotent, Omniscient,* and *Omnipresent*.

You are the *one* and *only* Son, Jesus, and we pray in Your name!

Amen.

P

Praise

Let them all Praise the Name of the Lord. For His name is very great; His glory towers over the earth and heaven! (Psalm 148:13 NLT)

I will Praise You every day; yes, I will Praise You forever. (Psalm 145:2 NLT)

Sing to the Lord and Praise His name. Every day tell how He saves us. (Psalm 96:2 ICB)

For the Lord is great and certainly worthy of Praise; He is more awesome than all gods. (Psalm 96:4 NET)

Praise the Lord, O my soul. And all that is within me, Praise His holy name. (Psalm 103:1 NLV)

Everything the Lord has made should Praise Him throughout the world that He rules! My soul, Praise the Lord! (Psalm 103:22 ERV)

I Praise You, Lord God, with all my heart. You are glorious and majestic, dressed in royal robes. (Psalm 104:1 CEV)

I will sing to the Lord as long as I live. I will Praise God to my last breath! (Psalm 104:33 TLB)

Praise the Lord! Give thanks to the Lord, for He is good! His faithful love endures forever. Who can list the glorious miracles of the Lord? Who can ever Praise him enough? (Psalm 106:1–2 NLT)

Praise His glorious name forever! Let the whole earth be filled with His glory. Amen and amen! (Psalm 72:19 NLT)

Our Lord, let the heavens now Praise your miracles, and let all of your angels Praise your faithfulness. (Psalm 89:5 CEV)

Our God, You are the one who rides on the clouds, and we Praise You. Your name is the Lord, and we celebrate as we worship you. (Psalm 68:4 CEV)

Praise the God and Father of our Lord Jesus Christ for the spiritual blessings that Christ has brought us from heaven! (Ephesians 1:3 CEV)

Great men of God were your fathers, and Christ Himself was one of you, a Jew so far as His human nature is concerned, He who now rules over all things. Praise God Forever! (Romans 9:5 TLB)

Let the whole world glorify the Lord; let it sing His Praise. (Isaiah 42:12 NLT)

The Lord lives! Praise to my Rock! May the God of my salvation be exalted! (Psalm 18:46 NLT)

Praise be to the Lord, the God of Israel, from everlasting to everlasting. Amen and Amen. (Psalm 41:13 NIV)

Again, and again their voices rang, "Praise the Lord! The smoke from her burning ascends forever and forever!" Then the twenty-four Elders and four Living Beings fell down and worshiped God, who was sitting upon the throne, and said, "Amen! Hallelujah! Praise the Lord!"

And out of the throne came a voice that said, "Praise Our God, all you His servants, small and great, who fear Him." (Revelation 19:3–5 TLB)

Praises

No wonder my heart is glad, and my tongue shouts His Praises! My body rests in hope. (Acts 2:26 NLT)

My lips shall shout for joy when I sing Praises to You, and my inner being, which You have redeemed. (Psalm 71:23 AMPC)

Praised

It is better to be criticized by the wise than Praised by the foolish. (Ecclesiastes 7:5 ERV)

Great is the Lord, and greatly to be Praised in the city of our God, on the mountain of His holiness. (Psalm 48:1 KJ21)

Praise, Praises

Praise the Lord, for the Lord is good. Sing Praises to His name, for it is gracious and lovely. (Psalm 135:3 AMP)

I will Praise the Lord at all times. I will constantly speak His Praises. (Psalm 34:1 NLT)

It is good to Praise the Lord, to sing Praises to God Most High. (Psalm 92:1 ICB)

Then I will Praise God's name with singing, and I will honor Him with thanksgiving. (Psalm 69:30 NLT)

I will Praise You, Lord, with all my heart; I will tell of all the marvelous things You have done. I will be filled with joy because of You. I will sing Praises to your name, O Most High. (Psalm 9:1–2 NLT)

Praise, Power

> Praise the Lord! Praise God in His holy place! Praise Him in the heavens of His Power! Praise Him for His great works! Praise Him for all His greatness! Praise Him with the sound of a horn. Praise Him with harps. Praise Him with timbrels and dancing. Praise Him with strings and horns. Praise Him with loud sounds. Praise Him with loud and clear sounds. Let everything that has breath Praise the Lord. Praise the Lord! (Psalm 150:1–6 NLV)

> After this, I heard what sounded like a vast crowd in heaven shouting, Praise the Lord! Salvation and glory and Power belong to our God. (Revelation 19:1 NLT)

> He said, "Praise the Name of God Forever and ever, for He has all Wisdom and Power." (Daniel 2:20 NLT)

Praise, Poured

> So, we Praise God for the glorious grace He has Poured out on us who belong to His dear Son. (Ephesians 1:6 NLT)

Praise God, Privilege

> But it is no shame to suffer for being a Christian. Praise God for the Privilege of being in Christ's family and being called by His wonderful name! (1 Peter 4:16 TLB)

Planned, Praise

> He Planned all of this so that we who had already focused our hope on Christ would Praise Him and give Him glory. (Ephesians 1:12 GW)

Poor, Praise

> The Poor will eat and be satisfied. All who seek the Lord will Praise Him. Their hearts will rejoice with everlasting joy. (Psalm 22:26 NLT)

Pure, Praise

> Let the godly sing for joy to the Lord; it is fitting for the Pure to Praise Him. (Psalm 33:1 NLT)

Put Your Hope, Praise

> Why, my soul, are you so dejected? Why are you in such turmoil? Put Your Hope in God, for I will still Praise Him, my Savior and my God. (Psalm 42:5 CSB)

People, Praise

> God, Your name is known everywhere. Everywhere on earth People Praise You. Your right hand is full of goodness. (Psalm 48:10 ICB)

People, Praising

> With Praise and thanks, they sang this song to the Lord: "He is so good! His faithful love for Israel endures forever!" Then all the People gave a great shout, Praising the Lord because the foundation of the Lord's Temple had been laid. (Ezra 3:11 NLT)

Praise, Promises

> I Praise Your Promises! I trust You and am not afraid. No one can harm me. (Psalm 56:4 CEV)

Praise, Prayer

> Your unfailing love is better than life itself; how I Praise You! I will Praise You as long as I live, lifting up my hands to You in Prayer. (Psalm 63:3–4 NLT)

Praying, Praises

> Is anyone among you suffering? He should keep on Praying about it. And those who have reason to be thankful should continually be singing Praises to the Lord. (James 5:13 TLB)

Passed, Praised

> After this time had Passed, I, Nebuchadnezzar, looked up to heaven. My sanity returned, and I Praised and worshiped the Most High and honored the one who lives forever. His rule is everlasting, and His kingdom is eternal. (Daniel 4:34 NLT)

Power, People, Praise

> God is awesome in His sanctuary. The God of Israel gives Power and strength to His People. Praise be to God! (Psalm 68:35 NLT)

Praise, Presence, People

> I will Praise You forever, O God, for what You have done. I will trust in Your good name in the Presence of your faithful People. (Psalm 52:9 NLT)

People, Praise Our God, Sing His Praise

> You People, Praise Our God. Loudly Sing His Praise. (Psalm 66:8 ICB)

Praised God, Prophet, People

> Great fear swept the crowd, and they Praised God, saying, "A mighty Prophet has risen among us," and "God has visited His People today." (Luke 7:16 NLT)

Pure, Purifies, Precious to God, Praise

> These trials are only to test your faith, to see whether or not it is strong and Pure. It is being tested as fire tests gold and Purifies it—and your faith is far more Precious

to God than mere gold; so, if your faith remains strong after being tried in the test tube of fiery trials, it will bring you much Praise and glory and honor on the day of His return. (1 Peter 1:7 TLB)

Promised, Purchased, People, Praise

The Spirit is God's guarantee that He will give us the inheritance He Promised and that He has Purchased us to be His own People. He did this so we would Praise and glorify Him. (Ephesians 1:14 NLT)

Passover, Palm Branches, Praise God, Prophecy, People

The next day, the news that Jesus was on the way to Jerusalem swept through the city. A large crowd of Passover visitors took Palm Branches and went down the road to meet Him. They shouted, "Praise God! Blessings on the one who comes in the name of the Lord! Hail to the King of Israel!" Jesus found a young donkey and rode on it, fulfilling the Prophecy that said: "Don't be afraid, People of Jerusalem. Look, your King is coming, riding on a donkey's colt." (John 12:12–15 NLT)

Proclaim, Praise, People

For He said to God, "I will Proclaim your name to my brothers and sisters. I will Praise you among your assembled People." (Hebrews 2:12 NLT)

Peace

Then you will experience God's Peace, which exceeds anything we can understand. His Peace will guard your hearts and minds as you live in Christ Jesus. (Philippians 4:7 NLT)

I have told you all this so that you may have Peace in Me. Here on earth, you will have many trials and sorrows. But take heart, because I have overcome the world. (John 16:33 NLT)

You are joined together with Peace through the Spirit. Do all you can to continue as you are, letting Peace hold you together. (Ephesians 4:3 ERV)

Now may the Lord of Peace Himself give you His Peace at all times and in every situation. The Lord be with you all. (2 Thessalonians 3:16 NLT)

So, letting your sinful nature control your mind leads to death. But letting the Spirit control your mind leads to life and Peace. (Romans 8:6 NLT)

Do all that you can to live in Peace with everyone. (Romans 12:18 NLT)

Look at those who are honest and good, for a wonderful future awaits those who love Peace. (Psalm 37:37 NLT)

Those who love Your laws have great Peace of heart and mind and do not stumble. (Psalm 119:165 TLB)

Yes, the king will give us Peace again. I know that you are like an angel of God and can discern good from evil. May God be with you. (2 Samuel 14:17 TLB)

I will lie down and sleep in Peace. O Lord, You alone keep me safe. (Psalm 4:8 NLV)

How beautiful is the person who comes over the mountains to bring good news. How beautiful is the one who announces Peace. He brings good news and announces salvation. How beautiful are the feet of the one who says to Jerusalem, "Your God is King." (Isaiah 52:7 ICB)

You will live in joy and Peace. The mountains and hills, the trees of the field—all the world around you—will rejoice. (Isaiah 55:12 TLB)

Glory to God in the highest, and on earth Peace, good will toward men. (Luke 2:14 KJ21)

And now may our God, who gives Peace, be with you all. Amen. (Romans 15:33 TLB)

Peace I leave with you. My Peace I give to you. Not as the world gives do I give to you. Do not let your heart be troubled, and do not let it be afraid. (John 14:27 EHV)

Finally, brothers and sisters, rejoice. Become mature, be encouraged, be of the same mind, be at Peace, and the God of love and Peace will be with you. (2 Corinthians 13:11 CSB)

Peace, Part

Let your heart be always guided by the Peace of the Anointed One, who called you to Peace as Part of His one body. And always be thankful. (Colossians 3:15 TPT)

Protect, Peace

May the Lord bless you and Protect you. May the Lord smile on you and be gracious to you. May the Lord show you His favor and give you, His Peace. (Numbers 6:24–26 NLT)

Priest, Peace

And the Priest said to them, "Go in Peace. The journey on which you go is under the eye of the Lord." (Judges 18:6 ESV)

Peace, Prosperity

Submit to God and be at Peace with Him; in this way Prosperity will come to you. (Job 22:21 NIV)

People, Peace

The Lord will give strength unto His People. The Lord will bless His People with Peace. (Psalm 29:11 KJ21)

I will listen to what God the Lord says. For He will make Peace with His People, His faithful followers. Yet they must not return to their foolish ways. (Psalm 85:8 NET)

I offer Peace to all, both near and far! I will heal my People. (Isaiah 57:19 GNT)

For Christ Himself has brought Peace to us. He united Jews and Gentiles into one People when, in His own body on the cross, He broke down the wall of hostility that separated us. (Ephesians 2:14 NLT)

Peace, Pursue

Depart from evil and do good; seek Peace and Pursue it. (Psalm 34:14 KJ21)

Peacemakers

Blessed are the Peacemakers, for they shall be called the children of God. (Matthew 5:9 KJ21)

Power, Peace, High Places

Power and fear belong to God. He keeps Peace in His High Places. (Job 25:2 NLV)

Perfect Peace

You will keep in Perfect Peace all who trust in You, all whose thoughts are fixed on You! (Isaiah 26:3 NLT)

Plot Evil, Promote Peace

Deceit is in the hearts of those who Plot Evil, but those who Promote Peace have joy. (Proverbs 12:20 CSB)

Peace, Performed

Lord, You will establish Peace for us, Since You have also Performed for us all that we have done. (Isaiah 26:12 AMP)

Precious to God, Peace, Please Speak

"Don't be afraid," He said, "for you are very Precious to God. Peace! Be encouraged! Be strong!" As He spoke these words to me, I suddenly felt stronger and said to Him, "Please Speak to me, my Lord, for You have strengthened me." (Daniel 10:19 NLT)

Follow Godly Paths, Peace

For those who Follow Godly Paths will rest in Peace when they die. (Isaiah 57:2 NLT)

Putting Our Trust in Him, Peace

Now that we have been made right with God by Putting Our Trust in Him, we have Peace with Him. It is because of what our Lord Jesus Christ did for us. (Romans 5:1 NLV)

Pleasing God, Living in Peace

God's kingdom isn't about eating and drinking. It is about Pleasing God, about Living in Peace, and about true happiness. All this comes from the Holy Spirit. (Romans 14:17 CEV)

Pray, Peace, Power

I Pray that God, who gives hope, will bless you with complete happiness and Peace because of your faith. And may the Power of the Holy Spirit fill you with hope. (Romans 15:13 CEV)

Prayer, Peace

My Prayer is that God our Father and the Lord Jesus Christ will be kind to you and will bless you with Peace! (1 Corinthians 1:3 CEV)

Peace, People

> Try to live in Peace with all People. And try to live lives free from sin. If anyone's life is not holy, He will never see the Lord. (Hebrews 12:14 ICB)

New Person, People, Peace

> All that matters is that you are a New Person. If you follow this rule, you will belong to God's true People. God will treat you with undeserved kindness and will bless you with Peace. (Galatians 6:15b–16 CEV)

Pursuit, Peace, Pure Hearts

> Run as fast as you can from all the ambitions and lusts of youth; and chase after all that is Pure. Whatever builds up your faith and deepens your love must become your holy Pursuit. And live in Peace with all those who worship our Lord Jesus with Pure Hearts. (2 Timothy 2:22 TPT)

People, Peace, Peaceful

> People who work for Peace in a Peaceful way get the blessings that come from right living. (James 3:18 ERV)

Patient Spirit, Proud Spirit

> The end of a matter is better than its beginning; a Patient Spirit is better than a Proud Spirit. (Ecclesiastes 7:8 CSB)

Patience of People, God's Patience

> Isaiah replied, "Listen, now, descendants of King David. It's bad enough for you to wear out the Patience of People—do you have to wear out God's Patience too?" (Isaiah 7:13 GNT)

Patient, Pray He will Help you Live at Peace

> God is the one who makes us Patient and cheerful. I Pray that He will Help you Live at Peace with each other, as you follow Christ. (Romans 15:5 CEV)

Pure Lives, Patience

> We show that we are God's servants by our Pure Lives, by our understanding, by our Patience, and by our kindness. We show it by the Holy Spirit, by genuine love. (2 Corinthians 6:6 ERV)

Pleases Him, Produce, Great Power, Be Patient

> That this will help you live in a way that brings honor to the Lord and Pleases Him in every way; that your life will Produce good works of every kind & that you will grow in your knowledge of God; that God will strengthen you with His own Great Power, so that you will Be Patient and not give up when troubles come. Then you will be happy. (Colossians 1:10–11 ERV)

Holy People, Patient

> God has chosen you and made you His Holy People. He loves you. So, your new life should be like this: Show mercy to others. Be kind, humble, gentle, and Patient. (Colossians 3:12 ERV)

Purpose, Patience

> But you have observed my teaching, my way of life, my Purpose, my faith, my Patience, my love, my endurance. (2 Timothy 3:10 ISV)

Pure Joy, Produces Perseverance

> Consider it Pure Joy, my brothers and sisters, whenever you face trials of many kinds, because you know that the testing of your faith Produces Perseverance. Let Perseverance finish its work so that you may be mature and complete, not lacking anything. (James 1:2–4 NIV)

Perseveres, Person, Promised

> Blessed is the one who Perseveres under trial because, having stood the test, that Person will receive the crown of life that the Lord has Promised to those who love Him. (James 1:12 NIV)

Plans to Prosper You

> "For I know the Plans I have for you," declares the Lord, "Plans to Prosper You and not to harm you, Plans to give you hope and a future." (Jeremiah 29:11 NIV)

Prophet, Prepare, Paths

> This is just as it was written in the scroll of the words of (Isaiah the Prophet, A voice crying out in the wilderness: "Prepare the way for the Lord; make His Paths straight." (Luke 3:4 CEB)

Pure

> Blessed are the Pure in heart, for they shall see God. (Matthew 5:8 KJ21)

Praise, Pure

> Brothers and sisters, continue to think about what is good and worthy of Praise. Think about what is true and honorable and right and Pure and beautiful and respected. (Philippians 4:8 ERV)

Purpose, Promote Love, Pure

> My Purpose in telling you to do this is to Promote Love—the kind of love shown by those whose thoughts are Pure, who do what they know is right, and whose faith in God is real. (1 Timothy 1:5 ERV)

Part, Keep Yourself Pure

> Do not be hasty in the laying on of hands, nor take Part in the sins of others; Keep Yourself Pure. (1 Timothy 5:22 ESV)

Make Your Thinking Pure

> Come near to God and He will come near to you. You are sinners, so clean sin out of your lives. You are trying to follow God and the world at the same time. Make Your Thinking Pure. (James 4:8 ERV)

Prudence

> Strike a scoffer, and the simple will learn Prudence; reprove a man of understanding, and he will increase in knowledge. (Proverbs 19:25 AMPC)

> *(Prudence is being careful in the way you make decisions.)*

Promised, Perfectly Sure, Plans

> God also bound Himself with an oath, so that those He Promised to help would be Perfectly Sure and never need to wonder whether He might change His Plans. (Hebrews 6:17 TLB)

Purest Gold, Highest Purposes

> If you stay away from sin, you will be like one of these dishes made of Purest Gold—the very best in the house—so that Christ Himself can use you for His Highest Purposes. (2 Timothy 2:21 TLB)

Passions, Pursue, Peace, Pure Heart

> Flee from youthful Passions. Instead, Pursue righteousness, faithfulness, love, and Peace together with those who call on the Lord with a Pure Heart. (2 Timothy 2:22 ISV)

Power, Preserves

> The Lord made the earth by His Power, and He Preserves it by His wisdom. With His own understanding He stretched out the heavens. (Jeremiah 51:15 NLT)

Precious Promises, Participate

> Through these He has given us His very great and Precious Promises, so that through them you may Participate in the divine nature, having escaped the corruption in the world caused by evil desires. (2 Peter 1:4 NIV)

Perfect, Promises Prove True, Protection

> God's way is Perfect. All the Lord's Promises Prove True. He is a shield for all who look to Him for Protection. (Psalm 18:30 NLT)

My People, Pray

> If My People, who are called by My name, shall humble themselves and Pray, and seek My face and turn from their wicked ways, then will I hear from heaven, and will forgive their sin and will heal their land. (2 Chronicles 7:14 KJ21)

Personal Account

> Yes, each of us will give a Personal Account to God. (Romans 14:12 NLT)

Patience

> May God, who gives this Patience and encouragement, help you live in complete harmony with each other, as is fitting for followers of Christ Jesus. (Romans 15:5 NLT)

Protect

> But all who find safety in You will rejoice; they can always sing for joy. Protect those who love You; because of You they are truly happy. (Psalm 5:11 GNT)

Protect, Present, Presence

> To the one who is able to Protect you from falling, and to Present you blameless and rejoicing before His glorious Presence. (Jude 1:24 CEB)

Presence

> Because of Christ and our faith in Him, we can now come boldly and confidently into God's Presence. (Ephesians 3:12 NLT)

> You have shown me the way of life, and You will fill me with the joy of Your Presence. (Acts 2:28 NLT)

Be Persistent in Prayer, Pray

> Be Persistent in Prayer, and keep alert as you Pray, giving thanks to God. (Colossians 4:2 GNT)

Pray for Each Other, Earnest Prayer, a Righteous Person has Great Power, Produces Results

> Confess your sins to each other and Pray for Each Other so that you may be healed. The Earnest Prayer of a Righteous Person Has Great Power and Produces wonderful Results. (James 5:16 NLT)

People, Powerful God, Prince of Peace

> This will happen when the special child is born. God will give us a son who will be responsible for leading the People. His name will be "Wonderful Counselor, Powerful God, Father Who Lives Forever, Prince of Peace." (Isaiah 9:6 ERV)

Potter

> But, Lord, you are Our Father. We are like clay, and you are the Potter. Your hands made us all. (Isaiah 64:8 ERV)

Pray, Power

> In this manner therefore Pray ye: Our Father who art in Heaven, hallowed be Thy Name, Thy kingdom come. Thy will be done, on earth, as it is in Heaven. Give us this day our daily bread. And forgive us our debts, as we forgive our debtors. And lead us not into temptation, but deliver us from evil. For Thine is the Kingdom, and the Power and the glory forever. Amen. (Matthew 6:9–13 KJ21)

With God, All Things Are Possible

> Jesus looked at them and said, "With man this is impossible, but With God All Things Are Possible." (Matthew 19:26 CSB)

Provide Rest, Persecuted

> And God will Provide Rest for you who are being Persecuted and also for us when the Lord Jesus appears from heaven. He will come with His mighty angels. (2 Thessalonians 1:7 NLT)

The Son Paid the Price

> The Son Paid the Price to make us free. In Him we have forgiveness of our sins. (Colossians 1:14 ERV)

Perfect High Priest, Provides the Way

> This made Him the Perfect High Priest, who Provides the Way for everyone who obeys Him to be saved forever. (Hebrews 5:9 ERV)

Provide Plants

> You make the grass grow to feed the animals. You Provide Plants for the crops we grow—the Plants that give us food from the earth. (Psalm 104:14 ERV)

Provides Food

> He Provides Food for all living things. His faithful love will last forever. (Psalm 136:25 ERV)

Passions

> Those who belong to Christ Jesus have nailed the Passions and desires of their sinful nature to His cross and crucified them there. (Galatians 5:24 NLT)

<u>PRAYERS</u> (USING P WORDS)

We are in awe of Your *presence, peace,* and *power*. We *praise* Your holy name! Thank You, *Prince of Peace,* for teaching us how to *pray*. You are the *Potter*, and we are the clay. With You, God, all things are *possible*. We are grateful for Your *protection*, Your *provision*, and Your many wonderful *promises*. It is a *privilege* to *participate* in *praising* and worshipping You, Jesus. We continue to *persevere* in our *pursuit* of You. Our lives are *pure* joy. We are *passionate* in seeking You, the *Perfect* One, and we have the *passion* to *plant* seeds in the lives of Your *people*. We *praise* You that we have a *purpose* in life. Thank You for teaching us *patience*. We love that You are guiding and directing us with Your *plans*.

We *praise* You in the highest, Father God, and we *pray* this in Your *powerful* name.

Amen.

Q

Quickened

> And you hath He Quickened, who were dead in trespasses and sins. (Ephesians 2:1 KJ21)

Not be Quarrelsome

> God's people must not be Quarrelsome; they must be gentle, patient teachers of those who are wrong. (2 Timothy 2:24 TLB)

Nor Quarrel

> They must not speak evil of anyone, Nor Quarrel, but be gentle and truly courteous to all. (Titus 3:2 TLB)

Quake

> God is our refuge and strength, a very ready help in trouble. Therefore, we will not fear, though the earth shakes and the mountains slip into the heart of the sea, though its waters roar and foam, Though the mountains Quake at its swelling pride. (Psalm 46:1–3 NASB)

Cannot Quench Love

> Surging waters Cannot Quench Love; floodwaters cannot overflow it. If someone were to offer all his possessions to buy love, the offer would be utterly despised. (Song of Solomon 8:7 NET)

Quench

>Do not Quench the Spirit. (1 Thessalonians 5:19 ESV)

Qualified

>In this way, God Qualified Him as a perfect High Priest, and He became the source of eternal salvation for all those who obey Him. (Hebrews 5:9 NLT)

Quiet Lives

>Pray this way for kings and all who are in authority so that we can live peaceful and Quiet Lives marked by godliness and dignity. (1 Timothy 2:2 NLT)

Quiet Spirit

>Rather, it should be that of your inner self, the unfading beauty of a gentle and Quiet Spirit, which is of great worth in God's sight. (1 Peter 3:4 NIV)

Quietly

>It is good that one waits Quietly for the salvation of the Lord. (Lamentations 3:26 AMP)

>My soul rests Quietly in God alone. My salvation is from Him. (Psalm 62:1 EHV)

>Let all that I am wait Quietly before God, for my hope is in Him. (Psalm 62:5 NLT)

>Now stand here Quietly before the Lord as I remind you of all the good things, He has done for you and for your ancestors. (1 Samuel 12:7 TLB)

>Also, make it your goal to live Quietly, do your work, and earn your own living, as we ordered you. (1 Thessalonians 4:11 GW)

Quietly, Quiet

Instead, I am content and at peace. As a child lies Quietly in its mother's arms, so my heart is Quiet within me. (Psalm 131:2 GNT)

Quiet Pools

He lets me rest in fields of green grass and leads me to Quiet Pools of fresh water. (Psalm 23:2 GNT)

Quiet Streams

Now this is what the Lord says: "Sing with joy for Israel. Shout for the greatest of nations! Shout out with praise and joy: 'Save your people, O Lord, the remnant of Israel!' Tears of joy will stream down their faces, and I will lead them home with great care. They will walk beside Quiet Streams and on smooth paths where they will not stumble. For I am Israel's father, and Ephraim is my oldest child." (Jeremiah 31:7, 9 NLT)

Quiet

But now, the whole country rests and is Quiet. Now the people begin to celebrate. (Isaiah 14:7 ERV)

This is what the Lord says to me: "I will remain Quiet and will look on from my dwelling place, like shimmering heat in the sunshine, like a cloud of dew in the heat of harvest." (Isaiah 18:4 NIV)

They found good, rich pasture, and the land was spacious, Quiet, and peaceful. (1 Chronicles 4:40a EHV)

My people will live in a peaceful place, in safe homes and Quiet places of rest. (Isaiah 32:18 GW)

Teach me, and I will keep Quiet. Show me what I have done wrong. (Job 6:24 NLT)

There is a time to tear apart, and a time to sew together; a time to be Quiet, and a time to speak. (Ecclesiastes 3:7 NLV)

Quietness

And the effect of righteousness will be peace, And the result of righteousness will be Quietness and confident trust forever. (Isaiah 32:17 AMP)

Wait Quietly, Quietness

This is what the Lord God, the Holy One of Israel, says: If you repent and Wait Quietly, you will be saved. Your strength will depend on Quietness and trust. But you refused. (Isaiah 30:15 EHV)

Quit, Quiet Spirit

If the boss is angry with you, don't Quit! A Quiet Spirit will Quiet his bad temper. (Ecclesiastes 10:4 TLB)

Obey Quickly, Quietly

He must have a well-behaved family, with children who Obey Quickly and Quietly. (1 Timothy 3:4 TLB)

Quickly

For you have been born again, but not to a life that will Quickly end. Your new life will last forever because it comes from the eternal, living Word of God. (1 Peter 1:23 NLT)

"It was not because of his sins or his parents' sins," Jesus answered. "This happened so the power of God could be seen in him. We must Quickly carry out the tasks assigned us by the One who sent us. The night is coming, and then no one can work. But while I am here in the world, I am the light of the world." (John 9:3–5 NLT)

The seeds on the rocky soil represent those who hear the message and receive it with joy. But since they don't have deep roots, they believe for a while, then they fall away when they face temptation. The seeds that fell among the thorns represent those who hear the message, but all too Quickly the message is crowded out by the cares and riches and pleasures of this life. And so, they never grow into maturity. And the seeds that fell on the good soil represent honest, good-hearted people who hear God's Word, cling to it, and patiently produce a huge harvest. (Luke 8:13–15 NLT)

Because the Lord does what he says completely and Quickly. (Romans 9:28 CEB)

Quick to Listen

Understand this, my dear brothers and sisters: You must all be Quick to Listen, slow to speak, and slow to get angry. (James 1:19 NLT)

Quick-Tempered

A church leader is a manager of God's household, so he must live a blameless life. He must not be arrogant or Quick-Tempered; he must not be a heavy drinker, violent, or dishonest with money. (Titus 1:7 NLT)

Quit Quarreling with God

Quit Quarreling with God! Agree with him and you will have peace at last! His favor will surround you if you will only admit that you were wrong. (Job 22:21 TLB)

<u>PRAYERS</u> (USING Q WORDS)

Thank You, God, for giving us *quiet* time with You. You are teaching us how to have a *quiet* spirit and a *quiet* mind. You have *quieted* our thinking and put our thoughts on You. We don't want to *quench* Your Holy Spirit because we are on fire for You, Jesus. You have chosen and *qualified* us to be in Your kingdom. You are *quick* to hear our prayers and to *quiet* and calm our hearts, dear Lord. Thank You for allowing us to be a part of Your royalty and for making us feel like *queens*. We are in awe because You protect us from *quarrelsome* people and situations.

We praise You, God, for being *quick* to show us love! In Your name, we pray.

Amen.

R

Reverence

> Reverence for the Lord gives confidence and security to a man, and his family. (Proverbs 14:26 GNT)

Reconciled

> For if, while we were enemies, we were Reconciled to God by the death of His Son, it is even more certain that, since we have been Reconciled, we will be saved by His life. (Romans 5:10 CEV)

Redeemer

> But as for me, I know that my Redeemer lives, and He will stand upon the earth at last. (Job 19:25 TLB)

> This is what the Lord says—your Redeemer, the Holy One of Israel: "I am the Lord your God, who teaches you what is good for you and leads you along the paths you should follow." (Isaiah 48:17 NLT)

> This is what the Lord, the King of Israel and its Redeemer, the Lord of Armies, says: I am the first and I am the last. There is no God but Me. (Isaiah 44:6 CSB)

> This is what the Lord, your Redeemer who formed you from the womb, says: I am the Lord, who made everything; who stretched out the heavens by myself; who alone spread out the earth. (Isaiah 44:24 CSB)

As for our Redeemer, the Lord of the hosts is His name, the Holy One of Israel. (Isaiah 47:4 KJ21)

For thy Maker is thine husband; the Lord of hosts is His name; and thy Redeemer the Holy One of Israel; The God of the whole earth shall He be called. (Isaiah 54:5 KJV)

Redeemed

Praise the Lord, the God of Israel, because He has visited and Redeemed His people. (Luke 1:68 NLT)

Now this is what the Lord says—the one who created you, Jacob, and the one who formed you, Israel "Do not fear, for I have Redeemed you; I have called you by your name; you are mine." (Isaiah 43:1 CSB)

Return, Redeemed

I have swept away your transgressions like a cloud, and your sins like a mist. Return to me, for I have Redeemed you. (Isaiah 44:22 CSB)

Rock, Redeemer

May the words of my mouth and the meditation of my heart be pleasing to you, O Lord, my Rock and my Redeemer. (Psalm 19:14 NLT)

Remembered, Rock, Redeemer

Then they Remembered that God was their Rock, that God Most High was their Redeemer. (Psalm 78:35 EHV)

Rock

And all drank the same spiritual drink; for they drank of that spiritual Rock that followed them, and that Rock was Christ. (1 Corinthians 10:4 KJ21)

There is no one holy like the Lord. Yes, there is no one but You, and there is no Rock like our God. (1 Samuel 2:2 EHV)

Therefore, everyone who hears these words of mine and acts on them will be like a wise man who built his house on the Rock. (Matthew 7:24 CSB)

The Lord is my Rock, and my fortress, and my deliverer; my God, my strength, in whom I will trust; my buckler, and the horn of my salvation, and my high tower. (Psalm 18:2 KJ21)

Trust in the Lord forever, because in the Lord, the Lord Himself, is an everlasting Rock! (Isaiah 26:4 CSB)

Raised from the Dead

Let it be known to all of you and to all the people of Israel that by the name of Jesus Christ the Nazarene, whom you crucified, whom God Raised from the Dead! By Him this man stands before you healed. (Acts 4:10 EHV)

Christ died for everyone so that they would live for Him. They should not live to please themselves but for Christ Who died on a cross and was Raised from the Dead for them. (2 Corinthians 5:15 NLV)

And He was shown to be the Son of God when He was Raised from the Dead by the power of the Holy Spirit. He is Jesus Christ our Lord. (Romans 1:4 NLT)

Raised to Life, Ruin, Raised

It will be the same when those who have died are Raised to Life. The body that is "planted" in the grave will Ruin and decay, but it will be Raised to a life that cannot be destroyed. (1 Corinthians 15:42 ERV)

Resurrection and the Life

> Jesus said to her, "I am the Resurrection and the Life. The one who believes in Me, even if he dies, will live." (John 11:25 CSB)

Really Raised from Death, Resurrection

> But Christ Really has been Raised from Death—the first one of all those who will be Raised. Death comes to people because of what one man did. But now there is Resurrection from death because of another man. I mean that in Adam all of us die. And in the same way, in Christ all of us will be made alive again. (1 Corinthians 15:20–22 ERV)

Responsibility

> Now these are the gifts Christ gave to the church: the apostles, the prophets, the evangelists, and the pastors and teachers. Their Responsibility is to equip God's people to do His work and build up the church, the Body of Christ. (Ephesians 4:11– 12 NLT)

Rejoicing in the Lord

> The lovers of God will be glad, Rejoicing in the Lord. They will be found in His glorious wraparound presence, singing songs of praise to God! (Psalm 64:10 TPT)

Restore, Revive, Repentant

> The high and lofty one who lives in eternity, the Holy One, says this: "I live in the high and holy place with those whose spirits are contrite and humble. I Restore the crushed spirit of the humble and Revive the courage of those with Repentant hearts." (Isaiah 57:15 NLT)

Rescue Me

> I must calm down and turn to God; only He can Rescue Me. (Psalm 62:1 ERV)

The Lord will Rescue Me from every evil work and will bring me safely into His heavenly kingdom. To Him be the glory forever and ever! Amen. (2 Timothy 4:18 CSB)

Rescued Us

For He has Rescued Us and has drawn us to Himself from the dominion of darkness, and has transferred us to the kingdom of His beloved Son. (Colossians 1:13 AMP)

He gave Himself for our sins to Rescue Us from this present evil age, according to the will of our God and Father. (Galatians 1:4 EHV)

Rescue, Redeem, Ruthless

I will Rescue you from the power of evil people and Redeem you from the grasp of the Ruthless. (Jeremiah 15:21 CSB)

Return to the Lord Your God, He Relents

Return To the Lord Your God, for He is gracious and merciful, slow to anger, and abounding in steadfast love; and He Relents from punishing. (Joel 2:13b MEV)

Refuge

The Lord is good, a strong Refuge when trouble comes. He is close to those who trust in Him. (Nahum 1:7 NLT)

He will cover you with His feathers, and under His wings you will find Refuge. His truth is your shield and armor. (Psalm 91:4 GW)

Every word of God is pure; He is a shield to those who take Refuge in Him. (Proverbs 30:5 CSB)

The Lord also will be a Refuge for the oppressed, a Refuge in times of trouble. (Psalm 9:9 KJ21)

God—His way is perfect; the word of the Lord is pure. He is a shield to all who take Refuge in Him. (Psalm 18:30 CSB)

Oh, taste and see that the Lord is good! Blessed is the man who takes Refuge in Him! (Psalm 34:8 CSB)

How priceless your faithful love is, God! People take Refuge in the shadow of your wings. (Psalm 36:7 ESV)

Rescue, Refuge

Protect my life, and Rescue me! Do not let me be put to shame. I have taken Refuge in you. (Psalm 25:20 GW)

Rock, Refuge

On God, my salvation and my glory is the Rock of my strength. My Refuge is in God. (Psalm 62:8 TLV)

Refuge, Rock

But the Lord has been my Refuge, And my God the Rock of my Refuge. (Psalm 94:22 NASB)

Righteous, Refuge

But the salvation of the Righteous is from the Lord; He is their Refuge and stronghold in the time of trouble. (Psalm 37:39 AMP)

Right Hand, Refuge, Rise Up

Perform wonders through your mercy. By your Right Hand save those who seek Refuge from those who Rise Up against them. (Psalm 17:7 EHV)

Refuge, Rejoice

But let all who take Refuge in You Rejoice; let them sing joyful praises forever. Spread Your protection over them, that all who love Your Name may be filled with joy. (Psalm 5:11 NLT)

Refuge, Reward

> May the Lord, the God of Israel, under whose wings you have come to take Refuge, Reward you fully for what you have done. (Ruth 2:12 NLT)

Rest

> "Yes, I will feed my flock and I will lead them to a place of Rest." This is what the Lord God said. (Ezekiel 34:15 ERV)

> Then Jesus said, "Come to me, all of you who are weary and carry heavy burdens, and I will give you Rest. Take my yoke upon you. Let me teach you, because I am humble and gentle at heart, and you will find Rest for your souls." (Matthew 11:28–29 NLT)

Rest Quietly in God

> My soul, Rest Quietly in God alone, for my hope comes from Him. (Psalm 62:5 EHV)

My Soul Rejoices, My Body Rests

> That is why my heart is glad and My Soul Rejoices. My Body Rests securely. (Psalm 16:9 GW)

Ridiculed, Rests

> If you are Ridiculed for the Name of Christ, you are blessed, because the Spirit of glory and of God Rests on you. (1 Peter 4:14 CSB)

Restore

> And after you have suffered a little while, the God of all grace, who has called you to His eternal glory in Christ, will Himself Restore, confirm, strengthen, and establish you. (1 Peter 5:10 ESV)

Restore the joy of your salvation to me, and provide me with a spirit of willing obedience. (Psalm 51:12 GW)

Renewed

And be Renewed in the spirit of your mind. (Ephesians 4:23 KJ21)

And have put on the new self. You are being Renewed in knowledge according to the image of your Creator. (Colossians 3:10 CSB)

Therefore, we do not give up. Even though our outer person is being destroyed, our inner person is being Renewed day by day. (2 Corinthians 4:16 CSB)

Righteous One

From the ends of the earth, we hear songs, "Glory and Honor to the Righteous One." (Isaiah 24:16a AMP)

Radiates, Right Hand

The Son Radiates God's own glory and expresses the very character of God, and He sustains everything by the mighty power of His command. When He had cleansed us from our sins, He sat down in the place of honor at the Right Hand of the majestic God in heaven. (Hebrews 1:3 NLT)

Right Hand

The joyful songs I now sing will be sung again in the hearts and homes of all your devoted lovers. My loud shouts of victory will echo throughout the land. For Yahweh's Right Hand conquers valiantly! (Psalm 118:15 TPT)

The Right Hand of Yahweh exalts! The Right Hand of Yahweh will never fail. (Psalm 118:16 TPT)

Representative

> And whatever you do or say, do it as a Representative of the Lord Jesus, giving thanks through Him to God the Father. (Colossians 3:17 NLT)

Righteous Acts Revealed

> Lord, who will not fear and glorify Your Name? For You alone are holy. All the nations will come and worship before You because Your Righteous Acts have been Revealed. (Revelation 15:4 CSB)

Righteousness

> With the mighty deeds of the Lord God I will come, I will praise thy Righteousness, thine alone. (Psalm 71:16 RSV)

> The Sovereign Lord will show His justice to the nations of the world. Everyone will praise Him! His Righteousness will be like a garden in early spring, with plants springing up everywhere. (Isaiah 61:11 NLT)

> But in keeping with His promise we are looking forward to a new heaven and a new earth, where Righteousness dwells. (2 Peter 3:13 NIV)

> For human anger does not accomplish God's Righteousness. (James 1:20 CSB)

> And we are instructed to turn from godless living and sinful pleasures. We should live in this evil world with wisdom, Righteousness, and devotion to God. (Titus 2:12 NLT)

> But you, O man of God, flee these things and pursue Righteousness, godliness, faith, love, patience, gentleness. (1 Timothy 6:11 NKJV)

> And be found in Him. In Christ I have a Righteousness that is not my own and that does not come from the

Law but rather from the faithfulness of Christ. It is the Righteousness of God that is based on faith. (Philippians 3:9 CEB)

Don't team up with those who are unbelievers. How can Righteousness be a partner with wickedness? How can light live with darkness? (2 Corinthians 6:14 NLT)

And when He comes, He will convict the world of its sin, and of God's Righteousness, and of the coming judgment. (John 16:8 NLT)

Those who are wise will shine as bright as the sky, and those who lead many to Righteousness will shine like the stars forever. (Daniel 12:3 NLT)

Open up, O heavens, and pour out your Righteousness. Let the earth open wide so salvation and Righteousness can sprout up together. I, the Lord, created them. (Isaiah 45:8 NLT)

I am overwhelmed with joy in the Lord my God! For He has dressed me with the clothing of salvation and draped me in a Robe of Righteousness. I am like a bridegroom dressed for his wedding or a bride with her jewels. (Isaiah 61:10 NLT)

Whoever pursues Righteousness & unfailing love will find life, Righteousness, and honor. (Proverbs 21:21 NLT)

Your Righteousness is like the mighty mountains, your justice like the ocean depths. You care for people and animals alike, O Lord. (Psalm 36:6 NLT)

Result, Noah Received Righteousness

It was faith that made Noah hear God's warnings about things in the future that He could not see. He obeyed God and built a boat in which He and his family were saved. As a Result, the world was condemned, and Noah Received from God the Righteousness that comes by faith. (Hebrews 11:7 GNT)

But we who live by the Spirit eagerly wait to Receive by faith the Righteousness God has promised to us. (Galatians 5:5 NLT)

Reap a Harvest of Righteousness

And those who are peacemakers will plant seeds of peace and Reap a Harvest of Righteousness. (James 3:18 NLT)

Righteousness, Reap, Rain

Sow Righteousness for yourselves and Reap faithful love; break up your unplowed ground. It is time to seek the Lord until He comes and sends Righteousness on you like the Rain. (Hosea 10:12 CSB)

Righteousness, Reject

It would be better if they had never known the way to Righteousness than to know it and then Reject the command, they were given to live a holy life. (2 Peter 2:21 NLT)

Righteous People, Righteousness, Remembered

When I tell Righteous People that they will live, but then they sin, expecting their past Righteousness to save them, then none of their Righteous acts will be Remembered. I will destroy them for their sins. (Ezekiel 33:13 NLT)

Crown of Righteousness, Righteous Judge, His Return

And now the prize awaits me—the Crown of Righteousness, which the Lord, the Righteous Judge, will give me on the day of His Return. And the prize is not just for me but for all who eagerly look forward to His appearing. (2 Timothy 4:8 NLT)

Rule, Gift of Righteousness, Receive, Christ's One Act of Righteousness brings a Right Relationship with God

> For the sin of this one man, Adam, caused death to Rule over many. But even greater is God's wonderful grace and His Gift of Righteousness, for all who Receive it will live in triumph over sin and death through this one man, Jesus Christ. Yes, Adam's one sin brings condemnation for everyone, but Christ's One Act of Righteousness brings a Right Relationship with God and new life for everyone. (Romans 5:17–18 NLT)

Reveals His Glory and Majesty, His Righteousness Never Fails

> Everything He does Reveals His Glory and Majesty. His Righteousness Never Fails. (Psalm 111:3 NLT)

Remember, Day of Redemption

> And do not bring sorrow to God's Holy Spirit by the way you live. Remember, He has identified you as His own, guaranteeing that you will be saved on the Day of Redemption. (Ephesians 4:30 NLT)

Eternal Redemption

> Not with the blood of goats and calves, but with His own blood He went into the Most Holy Place once for all and secured our Eternal Redemption. (Hebrews 9:12 ISV)

Repent

> Now Repent of your sins and turn to God, so that your sins may be wiped away. (Acts 3:19 NLT)

> But if you warn them to Repent and they don't Repent, they will die in their sins, but you will have saved yourself. (Ezekiel 33:9 NLT)

> And saying, "The time is fulfilled, and the Kingdom of God is at hand; Repent and believe in the gospel." (Mark 1:15 ESV)

From that time Jesus began to preach and to say, "Repent, for the Kingdom of Heaven is at hand." (Matthew 4:17 KJ21)

But unless you Repent you will all likewise perish. (Luke 13:5b ESV)

Rebuke, Repents

Be on your guard. If your brother sins, Rebuke him; and if he Repents, forgive him. (Luke 17:3 CSB)

Repents, Righteous, Repentance

Just so, I tell you, there will be more joy in heaven over one sinner who Repents than over ninety-nine Righteous persons who need no Repentance. (Luke 15:7 ESV)

Repentance

The Lord does not delay His promise, as some understand delay, but is patient with you, not wanting any to perish but all to come to Repentance. (2 Peter 3:9 CSB)

Repentance, Regret

For [godly] sorrow that is in accord with the will of God produces a Repentance without Regret, leading to salvation; but worldly sorrow [the hopeless sorrow of those who do not believe] produces death. (2 Corinthians 7:10 AMP)

Repentance, Rejecting the Son of God

And who then turn away from God. It is impossible to bring such people back to Repentance; by Rejecting the Son of God, they themselves are nailing Him to the cross once again and holding Him up to public shame. (Hebrews 6:6 NLT)

Did What Is Right

> Christ also suffered once for sins. The One who Did What Is Right suffered for those who don't do Right. He suffered to bring you to God. His Body was put to death. But the Holy Spirit brought him back to life. (1 Peter 3:18 NIRV)

Return to God, Receive Holy Spirit

> And Peter replied, "Each one of you must turn from sin, Return to God, and be baptized in the name of Jesus Christ for the forgiveness of your sins; then you also shall Receive this gift, the Holy Spirit." (Acts 2:38 TLB)

Reveals

> He Reveals deep and mysterious things and knows what lies hidden in darkness, though He is surrounded by light. (Daniel 2:22 NLT)

Revelations

> I must go on boasting, although there is nothing to be gained. So, I will go on to visions and Revelations from the Lord. (2 Corinthians 12:1 EHV)

Rid of, Run the Race

> Since we are surrounded by so many examples of faith, we must get Rid Of everything that slows us down, especially sin that distracts us. We must Run the Race that lies ahead of us and never give up. (Hebrews 12:1 GW)

Christ's Return, Did Not Run the Race in Vain

> Hold firmly to the word of life; then, on the day of Christ's Return, I will be proud that I Did Not Run the Race in Vain and that my work was not useless. (Philippians 2:16 NLT)

Not Return Void

> So shall my word be that goeth forth out of my mouth: it shall Not Return unto me Void, but it shall accomplish that which I please, and it shall prosper in the thing whereto I sent it. (Isaiah 55:11 KJ21)

Open Rebuke

> Better is Open Rebuke than love that is hidden. (Proverbs 27:5 ASV)

Royal Priests, Result

> But you are not like that, for you are a chosen people. You are Royal Priests, a holy nation, God's very own possession. As a Result, you can show others the goodness of God, for He called you out of the darkness into His wonderful light. (1 Peter 2:9 NLT)

PRAYERS (Using R Words)

We praise You, God, for *rescuing, restoring,* and *redeeming* us. You are our *Refuge* and our *Rock*. We *rejoice* and *rest* in You, Lord. We *receive* Your *righteousness*. Thank You for leading us to *repentance*, and as a *result*, we look forward to Your *return* someday. Thank You for *revealing* Your *reassuring* Word to us as we *run* the *race* ahead of us. We are in awe of You, God, and are *ready* to continue our *respectful reverence* of You. We can have a *right relationship* with You and because of You, we have received the Holy Spirit. Your *radiant* light shines in our hearts. We are grateful that You *renew* and *reconcile* us to You day by day.

Father God, we love the *results* that we *receive* from knowing You! We pray this in Your *righteous* name!

Amen.

S

Saves, Splendor, Keep you from Slipping, Sinless, Mighty Shouts

> And now—all glory to Him who alone is God, who Saves us through Jesus Christ our Lord; yes, Splendor and majesty, all power and authority are His from the beginning; His they are and His they evermore shall be. And He is able to Keep you from Slipping and falling away, and to bring you, Sinless and perfect, into His glorious presence with Mighty Shouts of everlasting joy. Amen. (Jude 1:24–25 TLB)

Eternal Salvation

> For the free gift of Eternal Salvation is now being offered to everyone. (Titus 2:11 TLB)

Salvation

> He shall receive the blessing from the Lord, and righteousness from the God of His Salvation. (Psalm 24:5 KJ21)

> May you always be filled with the fruit of your Salvation—the righteous character produced in your life by Jesus Christ—for this will bring much glory and praise to God. (Philippians 1:11 NLT)

For God says, "At just the right time, I heard you. On the day of Salvation, I helped you." Indeed, the "right time" is now. Today is the day of Salvation. (2 Corinthians 6:2 NLT)

Salvation, Saved

There is Salvation in no one else! God has given no other name under heaven by which we must be Saved. (Acts 4:12 NLT)

Salvation of your Souls

The reward for trusting Him will be the Salvation of your Souls. (1 Peter 1:9 NLT)

Holy Scriptures, Salvation

You have known the Holy Scriptures since you were a child. These Scriptures are able to make you wise. And that wisdom leads to Salvation through faith in Christ Jesus. (2 Timothy 3:15 ERV)

Salvation, Spirit

But we always must thank God for you, brothers and sisters who are loved by God. This is because He chose you from the beginning to be the first crop of the harvest. This brought Salvation, through your dedication to God by the Spirit and through your belief in the truth. (2 Thessalonians 2:13 CEB)

Saying Hallelujah, Salvation and Glory and Power to God— After this I heard what seemed to be the roar of a great multitude of voices, saying: "Hallelujah! Salvation and Glory and Power to our God!" (Revelation 19:1 TPT)

Sacrifices, Songs of Praise, Salvation

> But I will offer Sacrifices to you with Songs of Praise, and I will fulfill all my vows. For my Salvation comes from the Lord alone. (Jonah 2:9 NLT)

Sent His Son, Sacrifice for Our Sins

> This is love: not that we loved God, but that He loved us and Sent His Son to be the atoning Sacrifice for Our Sins. (1 John 4:10 EHV)

Good Shepherd, Sacrifices His Life, Sheep

> I am the Good Shepherd. The Good Shepherd Sacrifices His Life for the Sheep. (John 10:11 NLT)

Sacrifice That Atones Sins

> He Himself is the Sacrifice That Atones for our Sins— and not only our Sins but the Sins of all the world. (1 John 2:2 NLT)

Sacrifice, Sitting, Right Side

> But Christ offered Himself as a Sacrifice that is good forever. Now He is Sitting at God's Right Side. (Hebrews 10:12 CEV)

Sacrifice for Sin, Jesus Sacrificed His Life, Shedding His Blood, Shows, Sinned

> For God presented Jesus as the Sacrifice for Sin. People are made right with God when they believe that Jesus Sacrificed His Life, Shedding His Blood. This Sacrifice Shows that God was being fair when He held back and did not punish those who Sinned in times past. (Romans 3:25 NLT)

Sinful Deeds, Eternal Spirit, Perfect Sacrifice, Sins

> Just think how much more the blood of Christ will purify our consciences from Sinful Deeds so that we can worship the living God. For by the power of the Eternal Spirit, Christ offered Himself to God as a Perfect Sacrifice for our Sins. (Hebrews 9:14 NLT)

Sacrifice to Take Away Sins, Salvation

> So also, Christ was offered once for all time as a Sacrifice to Take Away the Sins of many people. He will come again, not to deal with our Sins, but to bring Salvation to all who are eagerly waiting for Him. (Hebrews 9:28 NLT)

Shouting, Salvation, Sits on the Throne

> And they were Shouting with a great roar, "Salvation comes from our God who Sits on the Throne and from the Lamb!" (Revelation 7:10 NLT)

Sanctified, Sacrifice

> By God's will we have been Sanctified once and for all through the Sacrifice of the body of Jesus, the Messiah. (Hebrews 10:10 ISV)

Our Savior

> To the only God Our Savior through Jesus the Messiah, our Lord, be glory, majesty, power, and authority, before all time, and now, and for all eternity! Amen. (Jude 1:25 ISV)

A Savior is Born

> For unto you Is Born this day in the city of David a Savior, who is Christ the Lord. (Luke 2:11 KJ21)

Savior Jesus Christ

> Rather, you must grow in the grace and knowledge of our Lord and Savior Jesus Christ. All glory to Him, both now and forever! Amen. (2 Peter 3:18 NLT)

Our Savior

> Praise the Lord; Praise God Our Savior! For each day He carries us in His arms. (Psalm 68:19 NLT)

> But we are citizens of heaven, where the Lord Jesus Christ lives. And we are eagerly waiting for Him to return as Our Savior. (Philippians 3:20 NLT)

Spirit, Our Savior

> He poured out His Spirit on us abundantly through Jesus Christ Our Savior. (Titus 3:6 CSB)

My Spirit, My Savior

> My Spirit, My Savior How My Spirit rejoices in God My Savior! (Luke 1:47 NLT)

Mighty Savior, Joyful Songs

> For the Lord Your God is living among you. He is a Mighty Savior. He will take delight in you with gladness. With His love, He will calm all your fears. He will rejoice over you with Joyful Songs. (Zephaniah 3:17 NLT)

My Shield, Power Saves Me, My Place of Safety, My Savior, Saves Me from Violence

> My God is my rock, in whom I find protection. He is My Shield, the Power that Saves Me, and My Place of Safety. He is my refuge, My Savior, the one who Saves Me from Violence. (2 Samuel 22:3 NLT)

Your Strength Shall Be My Song of Joy, Sunrise, Stronghold

> But as for me, Your Strength Shall Be My Song of Joy. At each and every Sunrise, my lyrics of Your love will fill the air! For You have been my glory-fortress, a Stronghold in my day of distress. (Psalm 59:16 TPT)

Soul

> Instead, I have kept my Soul calm and quiet. My Soul is content as a weaned child is content in its mother's arms. (Psalm 131:2 GW)

Soul, Silence, Salvation

> For God alone my Soul waits in Silence; from Him comes my Salvation. (Psalm 62:1 AMP)

Servant

> Instead, He emptied Himself of His outward glory by reducing Himself to the form of a lowly Servant. He became human! (Philippians 2:7 TPT)

Supported Me, Success

> It was You who Supported me from the day I was born, loving me, helping me through my life's journey. You've made me into a miracle; no wonder I trust You and praise You forever! Many marvel at my Success, but I know it is all because of You, my mighty protector! (Psalm 71:6–7 TPT)

Suffered for Our Sins, Never Sinned, Died for Sinners, Safely Home to God, Spirit

> Christ Suffered for Our Sins once for all time. He Never Sinned, but He Died for Sinners to bring you Safely Home to God. He Suffered physical death, but He was raised to life in the Spirit. (1 Peter 3:18 NLT)

Suffer for Christ, I Am Strong

> Each time He said, "My grace is all you need. My power works best in weakness." So now I am glad to boast about my weaknesses, so that the power of Christ can work through me. That's why I take pleasure in my weaknesses, and in the insults, hardships, persecutions, and troubles that I Suffer for Christ. For when I am weak, then I Am Strong. (2 Corinthians 12:9–10 NLT)

Stay Away

> Stay Away from every kind of evil. (1 Thessalonians 5:22 CSB)

Sovereign

> And when they heard it, they raised their voices together to God and said, "O Sovereign Lord [having complete power and authority], it is You who made the heaven and the earth and the sea, and everything that is in them. (Acts 4:24 AMP)

Sovereign Lord, Strength, Sure-Footed, Keeps Me Safe

> The Sovereign Lord gives me Strength. He makes me Sure- Footed as a deer and Keeps Me Safe on the mountains. (Habakkuk 3:19 GNT)

Our God Saves, Sovereign Lord Rescues Us

> Our God is a God who Saves! The Sovereign Lord Rescues Us from death. (Psalm 68:20 NLT)

Sovereign Lord, Strong Hand

> O Sovereign Lord! You made the heavens and earth by Your Strong Hand and powerful arm. Nothing is too hard for you! (Jeremiah 32:17 NLT)

Strong

> So be made Strong even in your weakness by lifting up your tired hands in prayer and worship. (Hebrews 12:12a TPT)

Sovereignty, Should Serve Him

> Dominion, glory and Sovereignty were given to Him that all peoples, nations, and languages Should Serve Him. His dominion is an everlasting dominion that will never pass away, and His kingdom is one that will not be destroyed. (Daniel 7:14 TLV)

Sincerely

> Trust the Lord and Sincerely worship Him; think of all the tremendous things He has done for you. (1 Samuel 12:24 TLB)

Sins, Show Sincere Love as Brothers and Sisters

> You were cleansed from your Sins when you obeyed the truth, so now you must Show Sincere Love to each other as Brothers and Sisters. Love each other deeply with all your heart. (1 Peter 1:22 NLT)

Sing to Our God

> Hallelujah! How good it is to Sing to Our God, for praise is pleasant and lovely. (Psalm 147:1 CSB)

Sing

> Sing to God, Sing praises to Him, dwell on all His wondrous works. (1 Chronicles 16:9 CEB)

> Sing to the Lord, all you godly ones! Praise His holy name. (Psalm 30:4 NLT)

Sing praises to God and to His name! Sing loud praises to Him who rides the clouds. His name is the Lord—rejoice in His presence! (Psalm 68:4 NLT)

Strength

Honor and great power are with Him. Strength and beauty are in His holy place. (Psalm 96:6 NLV)

Strength, I Will Sing Praises, Strong, Shows Me Loving-Kindness

O my Strength, I Will Sing Praises to You. For God is my Strong place and the God Who Shows Me Loving-Kindness. (Psalm 59:17 NLV)

Sending His Son, Sacrificial Offering

This is love. He loved us long before we loved Him. It was His love, not ours. He proved it by Sending His Son to be the pleasing Sacrificial Offering to take away our sins. (1 John 4:10 TPT)

Son of Man, Seek and Save the Lost

For the Son of Man came to Seek and to Save that which was Lost. (Luke 19:10 ASV)

Spare, Son

Since He did not Spare even His own Son but gave Him up for us all, won't He also give us everything else? (Romans 8:32 NLT)

Spend Your Energy, Seeking, Son of Man, Seal of His Approval

But don't be so concerned about perishable things like food. Spend Your Energy Seeking the eternal life that the Son of Man can give you. For God the Father has given me the Seal of His Approval. (John 6:27 NLT)

Son of the Highest

> He shall be great and shall be called the Son of The Highest; and The Lord God shall give unto Him the throne of His father David. (Luke 1:32 KJ21)

Strengtheneth Me

> I can do all things through Christ who Strengtheneth Me. (Philippians 4:13 KJ21)

Sovereign Lord, Strong Deliverer, Shield

> O Sovereign Lord, my Strong Deliverer, You Shield my head in the day of battle. (Psalm 140:7 NET)

Strength and Stronghold

> The Lord is good, a Strength and Stronghold in the day of trouble; He knows (recognizes, has knowledge of, and understands) those who take refuge and trust in Him. (Nahum 1:7 AMPC)

Spiritual Gifts, Serve Another

> God has given each of you a gift from His great variety of Spiritual Gifts. Use them well to Serve one Another. (1 Peter 4:10 NLT)

Sin, Spirit of God, Same Spirit

> And Christ lives within you, so even though your body will die because of Sin, the Spirit gives you life because you have been made right with God. The Spirit of God, who raised Jesus from the dead, lives in you. And just as God raised Christ Jesus from the dead, He will give life to your mortal bodies by this Same Spirit living within you. (Romans 8:10–11 NLT)

Sheep Wandered Away, Turned to Your Shepherd, Souls

> Once you were like Sheep who Wandered Away. But now you have Turned to Your Shepherd, the Guardian of your Souls. (1 Peter 2:25 NLT)

Satan

> Satan, who is the god of this world, has blinded the minds of those who don't believe. They are unable to see the glorious light of the Good News. They don't understand this message about the glory of Christ, who is the exact likeness of God. (2 Corinthians 4:4 NLT)

Satan Disguises Himself

> But I am not surprised! Even Satan Disguises Himself as an angel of light. (2 Corinthians 11:14 NLT)

Defeat Satan

> The God who brings peace will soon Defeat Satan and give you power over him. The grace of our Lord Jesus be with you. (Romans 16:20 ERV)

Outsmarted by Satan

> A further reason for forgiveness is to keep from being Outsmarted by Satan, for we know what he is trying to do. (2 Corinthians 2:11 TLB)

Get Away, Satan!

> Jesus said to the devil, "Get away, Satan. It is written, 'You must worship the Lord Your God. You must obey Him only.'" (Matthew 4:10 NLV)

Satan, Sins Forgiven, Set Apart for God

> You are to open their eyes. You are to turn them from darkness to light. You are to turn them from the power of Satan to the power of God. In this way, they may

have their Sins Forgiven. They may have what is given to them, along with all those who are Set Apart for God by having faith in Me. (Acts 26:18 NLV)

Satan, Stumbling Block, Setting Your Mind

But Jesus turned and said to Peter, "Get behind Me, Satan! You are a Stumbling Block to Me; for you are not Setting Your Mind on things of God, but on things of man." (Matthew 16:23 AMP)

Get Behind Me, Satan, God Only Shalt Thou Serve

And Jesus answered and said unto him, Get thee Behind Me, Satan; for it is written, Thou Shalt worship the Lord thy God, and Him Only Shalt Thou Serve. (Luke 4:8 KJ21)

Stand, Speaks

You are of your father the devil, and you want to carry out your father's desires. He was a murderer from the beginning and does not Stand in the truth, because there is no truth in him. When he tells a lie, he Speaks from His own nature, because he is a liar and the father of lies. (John 8:44 CSB)

Submit to God

Submit yourselves therefore to God. Resist the devil, and he will flee from you. (James 4:7 KJ21)

Sin

Sin will not be your master, because you are not under law. You now live under God's grace. (Romans 6:14 ERV)

Showed, Sending Christ, Still Sinners

But God Showed His great love for us by Sending Christ to die for us while we were Still Sinners. (Romans 5:8 NLT)

Won't Step with the Wicked, Nor Share the Sinner's Way, Nor Sitting in the Scorner's Seat

> What delight comes to the one who follows God's ways! He won't walk in Step with the Wicked, Nor Share the Sinner's Way, Nor be found Sitting in the Scorner's Seat. (Psalm 1:1 TPT)

Sinners

> Let not your heart envy Sinners, but continue in the reverent and worshipful fear of the Lord all the day long. (Proverbs 23:17 AMPC)

> I have not come to call the righteous, but Sinners to repentance. (Luke 5:32 CSB)

> Adam caused many to be Sinners because he disobeyed God, and Christ caused many to be made acceptable to God because He obeyed. (Romans 5:19 TLB)

Sinful Self, Spiritual Death, Spirit

> If your thinking is controlled by your Sinful Self, there is Spiritual Death. But if your thinking is controlled by the Spirit, there is life and peace. (Romans 8:6 ERV)

Love for Sinners, Save

> For when the time was right, the Anointed One came and died to demonstrate His Love for Sinners who were entirely helpless, weak, and powerless to Save themselves. (Romans 5:6 TPT)

Saved, Sinners, His Sight, Save from God's Wrath

> But didn't He earn His right to heaven by all the good things He did? No, for being Saved is a gift; if a person could earn it by being good, then it wouldn't be free— but it is! It is given to those who do not work for it. For

God declares Sinners to be good in His Sight if they have faith in Christ to Save them from God's Wrath. (Romans 4:5 TLB)

Still, Say, Sight, Sacrifice of Jesus

And there is Still much more to Say of His unfailing love for us! For through the blood of Jesus we have heard the powerful declaration, "You are now righteous in my Sight." And because of the Sacrifice of Jesus, you will never experience the wrath of God. (Romans 5:9 TPT)

Scripture

All Scripture is inspired by God and is useful to teach us what is true and to make us realize what is wrong in our lives. It corrects us when we are wrong and teaches us to do what is right. God uses it to prepare and equip His people to do every good work. (2 Timothy 3:16–17 NLT)

Self-Control

Everyone who enters an athletic contest practices Self-Control in everything. They do it to win a wreath that withers away, but we run to win a prize that never fades. (1 Corinthians 9:25 ISV)

Self-Control, Brothers and Sisters in Christ

Because you have these blessings, do all you can to add to your life these things: to your faith add goodness; to your goodness add knowledge; to your knowledge add Self-Control; to your Self-Control add patience; to your patience add devotion to God; to your devotion add kindness toward your Brothers and Sisters in Christ, and to this kindness add love. (2 Peter 1:5–7 ERV)

Spirit, Sound Mind

> For God hath not given us the Spirit of fear, but of power, and of love, and of a Sound Mind. (2 Timothy 1:7 KJ21)

Be Still

> God says, "Be Still and know that I am God. I will be praised in all the nations. I will be praised throughout the earth." (Psalm 46:10 ICB)

Supreme Son

> And when He brought His Supreme Son into the world, God said, "Let all of God's angels worship Him." (Hebrews 1:6 NLT)

Supreme Over All Creation

> Christ is the visible image of the invisible God. He existed before anything was created and is Supreme Over All Creation. (Colossians 1:15 NLT)

Supreme Over All Earth

> For You, O Lord, are Supreme Over All the Earth; you are exalted far above all gods. (Psalm 97:9 NLT)

Sow or Reap, Storeroom

> Consider the ravens: They don't Sow or Reap; they don't have a Storeroom or a barn; yet God feeds them. Aren't you worth much more than the birds? (Luke 12:24 CSB)

Son, Sustaining All Things, Sins, Sat Down

> The Son is the radiance of God's glory and the exact expression of His nature, Sustaining All Things by His powerful word. After making purification for Sins, He Sat Down at the right hand of the Majesty on high. (Hebrews 1:3 CSB)

Snaps the Spear, Burns the Shields

> He causes wars to end throughout the earth. He breaks the bow and Snaps the Spear; He Burns the Shields with fire. (Psalm 46:9 NLT)

Shield of Faith

> And above all, taking the Shield of Faith, with which you will be able to extinguish all the fiery arrows of the evil one. (Ephesians 6:16 MEV)

Ask, Seek, Knock

> Ask and it will be given to you; Seek and you will find; Knock and the door will be opened to you. (Matthew 7:7 CSB)

Shelter, Shadow of Your Wings

> How precious is Your unfailing love, O God! All humanity finds Shelter in the Shadow of Your Wings. (Psalm 36:7 NLT)

Find Shelter in Him

> The godly will rejoice in the Lord and Find Shelter in Him. And those who do what is right will praise Him. (Psalm 64:10 NLT)

Shelter, Shadow of the Almighty

> He who dwells in the Shelter of the Most High will abide in the Shadow of the Almighty. (Psalm 91:1 ESV)

Sanctuary, Safe, Shelter of Your Wings

> Let me live forever in Your Sanctuary, Safe beneath the Shelter of Your Wings! (Psalm 61:4 NLT)

Shelter

He will cover you with His feathers. He will Shelter you with His wings. His faithful promises are your armor and protection. (Psalm 91:4 NLT)

Simon Peter, Son of the Living God

Simon Peter replied, "You are the Christ, the Son of the Living God." (Matthew 16:16 AMPC)

We have believed and have come to know that You are the Christ, the Son of The Living God. (John 6:69 MEV)

Search Scriptures

You Search the Scriptures because you think they give you eternal life. But the Scriptures point to Me! (John 5:39 NLT)

Shine in Our Hearts, Seen

For God, who said, "Let there be light in the darkness," has made this light Shine in Our Hearts so we could know the glory of God that is Seen in the face of Jesus Christ. (2 Corinthians 4:6 NLT)

My Grace Is Sufficient

But He said to me, "My Grace is Sufficient for you, for My power is made perfect in weakness." Therefore, I will boast all the more gladly about my weaknesses, so that Christ's power may rest on me. (2 Corinthians 12:9 NIV)

With His Stripes, We Are Healed

But He was wounded for our transgressions; He was bruised for our iniquities. The chastisement of our peace was upon Him, and with His Stripes We Are Healed. (Isaiah 53:5 KJ21)

Christ Set Us Free, Stand Firm, Don't Submit to Slavery

> For freedom, Christ Set Us Free. Stand Firm, then, and Don't Submit again to a yoke of Slavery. (Galatians 5:1 CSB)

Set Free from Sin

> So, Christ brings a new agreement from God to His people. Those who are called by God can now receive the blessings that God has promised. These blessings will last forever. They can have those things because Christ died so that the people who lived under the first agreement could be Set Free from Sin. (Hebrews 9:15 ICB)

Serve, He Satisfies Every Need

> And human hands can't Serve His needs—for He has no needs. He Himself gives life and breath to everything, and He Satisfies Every Need. (Acts 17:25 NLT)

Signs and Wonders, Holy Spirit

> And God confirmed the message by giving Signs and Wonders and various miracles and gifts of the Holy Spirit whenever He chose. (Hebrews 2:4 NLT)

Signs and Wonders, God's Spirit

> They were convinced by the power of miraculous Signs and Wonders and by the power of God's Spirit. (Romans 15:19a NLT)

Speak

> Don't you believe that I am in the Father and the Father is in me? The words I Speak are not my own, but my Father who lives in Me does His work through Me. (John 14:10 NLT)

Surround, Surrounds His People

> Just as the mountains Surround Jerusalem, so the Lord Surrounds His People, both now and forever. (Psalm 125:2 NLT)

Swift to Hear, Slow to Speak, Slow to Anger

> Therefore, my beloved brothers, let every man be Swift to Hear, Slow to Speak, and Slow to Anger. (James 1:19 MEV)

Supplieth Seed, Sower, Shall Supply, Seed for Sowing

> And he that Supplieth Seed to the Sower and bread for food, Shall Supply and multiply your Seed for Sowing, and increase the fruits of your righteousness. (2 Corinthians 9:10 ASV)

Speaks, Speaking, Serves, Serving, Strength, Supplies

> If anyone Speaks, let him do it as one Speaking the messages of God. If anyone Serves, let him do it as one Serving with the Strength God Supplies so that God may be glorified in every way through Jesus Christ. To Him belong the glory and the power forever and ever. Amen. (1 Peter 4:11 EHV)

PRAYERS (USING S WORDS)

Father God, we pray for all to receive You as their **Savior** and come to the knowledge of Your **Son**, Jesus Christ! The **Salvation** Prayer is on the very next page. Please guide the hearts of all who need You for their **salvation**. You are **significant** with Your **signs** and wonders. We love You, **Holy Spirit**, for living inside of us. Thank You for **speaking** Your Word to us. You **surround** us with Your **spectacular** creation. You are very **special** to us. We love having Your **shield** of faith and the **sword** of the **Spirit** that we receive from Your armor. You bless us with **safety**, **shelter**, and **strength**. You are **supreme** over all and **satisfy** all our needs. We **sing songs** of praise to You, Father God, for helping us **succeed** in life. We praise You, Jesus, for being the **solution** to all our problems!

We pray, Father God, in Your **Son's** name. Jesus is our beautiful **Savior**.

Amen.

THE PRAYER OF SALVATION

If you are ready to receive this free gift, pray this prayer:

Lord Jesus, I confess my sins and ask for Your forgiveness. Please come into my heart as my Lord and Savior. Take complete control of my life and help me to walk in Your footsteps daily by the power of the Holy Spirit. Thank You, Lord, for saving me and answering my prayers. In Jesus's name, Amen.

The ABCs to Salvation: **A**ccept, **B**elieve, **C**onfess

> For all have sinned and fall short of the glory of God. (Romans 3:23 CSB)

> For God so loved the world that He gave His only Son, that whoever believes in Him should not perish but have eternal life. (John 3:16 ESV)

> He who believes in the Son has everlasting life; and he who does not believe the Son shall not see life, but the wrath of God abides on him. (John 3:36 NKJV)

> For whoever calls on the name of the Lord shall be saved. (Romans 10:13 NKJV)

You can use the next section to sign your name and date if you prayed this prayer. This way, you will always remember your date of salvation.

Name:

Date:

T

Truth, Teach

> Make them holy by Your Truth; Teach them Your Word, which is Truth. (John 17:17 NLT)

Truth

> But you have had the Holy Spirit poured out on you by Christ, and so all of you know the Truth. (1 John 2:20 GNT)

> The Lord is close to all who call on Him, yes, to all who call on Him in Truth. (Psalm 145:18 NLT)

Turn to Him, Truth

> Be humble when you correct people who oppose you. Maybe God will lead them to Turn to Him and learn the Truth. (2 Timothy 2:25 CEV)

Love and Truth

> But Lord, You are a God full of compassion, generous in grace, slow to anger, and boundless in loyal Love and Truth. (Psalm 86:15 VOICE)

The Way, Truth, Life, Through Me

> Jesus answered, "I am the Way, the Truth and the Life. No one comes to the Father except Through Me." (John 14:6 CEB)

The Truth Will Set You Free

> And you will know the Truth, and the Truth Will Set You Free. (John 8:32 NLT)

Those, Living Truth

> I love you all as Those who are in the Truth. And I'm not the only one, for all who come to know the Truth share my love for you because of the Living Truth that has a permanent home in us and will be with us forever. (2 John 1:1b–2 TPT)

Talk, True Love, Way of Truth

> My children, our love should not be only words and Talk. Our love must be True Love. And we should show that love by what we do. This is the way we know that we belong to the Way of Truth. When our hearts make us feel guilty, we can still have peace before God. God is greater than our hearts, and He knows everything. (1 John 3:18–20 ICB)

Spirit of Truth

> We belong to God, and anyone who knows God listens to us, while anyone who does not belong to God refuses to hear us. This is how we know the Spirit of Truth and the spirit of deceit. (1 John 4:6 NABRE)

Those God Has Chosen, Teach Them Truth

> I have been sent to proclaim faith to Those God Has Chosen and to Teach Them to know the Truth that shows them how to live godly lives. (Titus 1:1b NLT)

This Truth, That They Have Eternal Life

> This Truth gives them confidence That They Have Eternal Life, which God—who does not lie—promised them before the world began. (Titus 1:2 NLT)

Through the Power, Guard the Precious Truth

> Through the Power of the Holy Spirit who lives within us, carefully Guard the Precious Truth that has been entrusted to you. (2 Timothy 1:14 NLT)

Teach Those Things, Teach These Great Truths to Trustworthy Men

> For you must Teach others Those Things you and many others have heard me speak about. Teach These Great Truths to Trustworthy men who will, in Turn, pass them on to others. (2 Timothy 2:2 TLB)

Teach Me, Truth

> Teach Me Your ways, O Lord, that I may live according to Your Truth! Grant me purity of heart, so that I may honor You. (Psalm 86:11 NLT)

Teach, Truth

> So, Jesus responded, "I don't Teach my own ideas, but the Truth revealed to me by the One who sent me." (John 7:16 TPT)

God's Truth, Knows Those, Turn away

> But God's Truth stands firm like a foundation stone with This inscription: "The Lord Knows Those who are His," and "All who belong to the Lord must Turn away from evil." (2 Timothy 2:19 NLT)

Grace and Truth

> And the Word became flesh and dwelt among us, full of Grace and Truth; we have beheld His glory, glory as of the only Son from the Father. (John 1:14 RSV)

Truth, Taught, Thankfulness

> And now, just as you accepted Christ Jesus as your Lord, you must continue to follow Him. Let your roots grow

down into Him, and let your lives be built on Him. Then your faith will grow Strong in the Truth you were Taught, and you will overflow with Thankfulness. (Colossians 2:6–7 NLT)

Truth, Triumph

Put on Truth as a belt to strengthen you to stand in Triumph. Put on holiness as the protective armor that covers your heart. (Ephesians 6:14 TPT)

Truths, Teaching, Triumphantly

He continued to proclaim to all the Truths of God's kingdom realm, Teaching them about the Lord Jesus, the Anointed One, speaking Triumphantly and without any restriction. (Acts 28:31 TPT)

Teach, True, Spirit Teaches You, What He Teaches Is True, Taught

But you have received the Holy Spirit, and He lives within you, so you don't need anyone to Teach you what is True. For the Spirit Teaches You everything you need to know, and What He Teaches Is True—it is not a lie. So just as He has Taught you, remain in Fellowship with Christ. (1 John 2:27 NLT)

The Door

I am The Door; by Me if any man enter in, he shall be saved and shall go in and out, and find pasture. (John 10:9 KJ21)

Thanks

Thanks be unto God for His unspeakable gift! (2 Corinthians 9:15 KJ21)

O Lord my God, I will give Thanks to You with all my heart. I will bring honor to Your name forever. (Psalm 86:12 NLV)

Thankful

> Be Thankful in all circumstances, for this is God's will for you who belong to Christ Jesus. (1 Thessalonians 5:18 NLT)

Talk, Always Give Thanks for Everything

> Talk with each other much about the Lord, quoting psalms and hymns and singing sacred songs, making music in your hearts to the Lord. Always Give Thanks for Everything to our God and Father in the name of our Lord Jesus Christ. (Ephesians 5:19–20 TLB)

Thanks To Our God, Throne

> Again, They said, "Thanks To Our God. The smoke from her burning goes up forever." The twenty-four leaders and the four living beings got down and worshiped God who was sitting on the Throne. They said, "Let it be so. Thanks To Our God!" A voice came from the Throne, saying, "Give Thanks To Our God, you servants who are owned by Him. Give Thanks To Our God, you who honor Him with love and fear, both small and great." (Revelation 19:3–5 NLV)

Thanksgiving, Thankful

> Enter into His gates with Thanksgiving; and into His courts with praise. Be Thankful unto Him and bless His name! (Psalm 100:4 KJ21)

Thanksgiving

> Then I will praise God's name with singing, and I will honor Him with Thanksgiving. (Psalm 69:30 NLT)

> They sang, "Amen! Blessing and glory and wisdom and Thanksgiving and honor and power and strength belong to our God forever and ever! Amen." (Revelation 7:12 NLT)

Only True God

> And we know that the Son of God has come, and He has given us understanding so that we can know the True God. And now we live in Fellowship with the True God because we live in Fellowship with His Son, Jesus Christ. He is the Only True God, and He is eternal life. (1 John 5:20 NLT)

Thoughts

> "For my Thoughts are not your Thoughts, neither are your ways my ways," declares the Lord. "As the heavens are higher than the earth, so are my ways higher than your ways and my Thoughts than your Thoughts." (Isaiah 55:8–9 NIV)

> The Lord—knows the Thoughts of man, that they are but a breath. (Psalm 94:11 ESV)

> O Lord, what great works you do! And how deep are your Thoughts. (Psalm 92:5 NLT)

> For the Word of God is alive and powerful. It is sharper than the sharpest Two-edged sword, cutting between soul and spirit, between joint and marrow. It exposes our innermost Thoughts and desires. (Hebrews 4:12 NLT)

Thing, Fix Your Thoughts, True, Think about Things

> And now, dear brothers and sisters, one final Thing. Fix your Thoughts on what is True, and honorable, and right, and pure, and lovely, and admirable. Think about Things that are excellent and worthy of praise. (Philippians 4:8 NLT)

Thoughts, Fall to Their Knees, God Is Truly Here

> As they listen, their secret Thoughts will be exposed, and They will Fall to Their Knees and worship God, declaring, "God is Truly here among you." (1 Corinthians 14:25 NLT)

True Vine

> I am the True Vine, and My Father is the Vinedresser. (John 15:1 AMPC)

Trust in the Lord

> All of you that honor the Lord and obey the words of His servant, the path you walk may be dark indeed, but Trust in the Lord, rely on Your God. (Isaiah 50:10 GNT)

Trust in His Love

> We know how much God loves us, and we have put our Trust in His Love. God is love, and all who live in love live in God, and God lives in Them. (1 John 4:16 NLT)

Trust in the Lord, Path to Take

> Trust in the Lord with all your heart; do not depend on your own understanding. Seek His will in all you do, and He will show you which Path to Take. (Proverbs 3:5–6 NLT)

Trusting Him

> The reward for Trusting Him will be the salvation of your souls. (1 Peter 1:9 NLT)

Trust

> So, if you are suffering in a manner that pleases God, keep on doing what is right, and Trust your lives to the God who created you, for He will never fail you. (1 Peter 4:19 NLT)

Then Christ will make His home in your hearts as you Trust in Him. Your roots will grow down into God's love and keep you strong. (Ephesians 3:17 NLT)

Your Commands Can Be Trusted

But you are near me, Lord, and all Your Commands Can Be Trusted. (Psalm 119:151 ERV)

Trustworthy Anchor, Leads Us Through

This hope is a strong and Trustworthy Anchor for our souls. It Leads Us Through the curtain into God's inner sanctuary. (Hebrews 6:19 NLT)

Throw, Trust in the Lord

So do not Throw away this confident Trust in the Lord. Remember the great reward it brings you! (Hebrews 10:35 NLT)

Trust in Him, Through the Power

I pray that God, the source of hope, will fill you completely with joy and peace because you Trust in Him. Then you will overflow with confident hope Through the Power of the Holy Spirit. (Romans 15:13 NLT)

Tongue

My lips will speak no evil, and my Tongue will speak no lies. (Job 27:4 NLT)

And that every Tongue should confess that Jesus Christ is Lord to the glory of God the Father. (Philippians 2:11 KJ21)

Your awe-inspiring deeds will be on every Tongue; I will proclaim Your greatness. (Psalm 145:6 NLT)

Those who control their Tongue will have a long life; opening your mouth can ruin everything. (Proverbs 13:3 NLT)

Tame the Tongue

But no one can Tame the Tongue. It is a restless evil, full of deadly poison. (James 3:8 NLT)

Tell, Every Tongue Will Confess, Truth

Just as it is written: "As surely as I am the Living God, I Tell you: 'Every knee will bow before Me and Every Tongue Will Confess the Truth and glorify Me!'" (Romans 14:11 TPT)

Temptation, Tempted

No Temptation has overtaken you that is not common to man. God is faithful, and He will not let you be Tempted beyond your ability, but with the Temptation He will also provide the way of escape, that you may be able to endure it. (1 Corinthians 10:13 ESV)

Trials, Testing

Consider it pure joy, my brothers and sisters, whenever you face Trials of many kinds, because you know that the Testing of your faith produces perseverance. (James 1:2–3 NIV)

Times of Trouble

God is our protection and our strength. He always helps in Times of Trouble. (Psalm 46:1 NCV)

Do Not Be Terrified

Be strong and courageous. Do Not Be afraid or Terrified because of them, for the Lord Your God goes with you; He will never leave you nor forsake you. (Deuteronomy 31:6 NIV)

These Words, His Teaching

> When Jesus had finished saying These things, the crowds were astonished at His Teaching. (Matthew 7:28 CSB)

Teach Me

> Teach Me and I will be silent. Help me understand what I have done wrong. (Job 6:24 EHV)

Baptize Them, Teach Them, Things I Have Told You

> Go and make followers of all the nations. Baptize Them in the name of the Father and of the Son and of the Holy Spirit. Teach Them to do all the Things I Have Told You. And I am with you always, even to the end of the world. (Matthew 28:19–20 NLV)

Teachings, Christ Taught

> Anyone who goes too far and does not live by the Teachings of Christ does not have God. If you live by what Christ Taught, you have both the Father and the Son. (2 John 1:9 NLV)

Teach

> So, Teach us to number our days, that we may apply our hearts unto wisdom. (Psalm 90:12 KJ21)

Grace Teaches, Turn

> This same grace Teaches us how to live each day as we Turn our backs on ungodliness and indulgent lifestyles, and it equips us to live self-controlled, upright, godly lives in this present age. (Titus 2:12 TPT)

Thoroughly Equipped

> So that the servant of God may be Thoroughly Equipped for every good work. (2 Timothy 3:17 NIV)

Promises Thoroughly Tested, Love Them

> Your Promises have been Thoroughly Tested; That is why I Love Them so much. (Psalm 119:140 NLT)

Time Has Come

> "Fear God," He shouted. "Give glory to Him. For the Time Has Come when He will sit as judge. Worship Him who made the heavens, the earth, the sea, and all the springs of water." (Revelation 14:7 NLT)

Trusting, Time

> By Trusting, you are being protected by God's power for a salvation ready to be revealed in the last Time. (1 Peter 1:5 TLV)

Latter Times, Turn, Teaching

> The Spirit clearly says that in Latter Times some people will Turn away from the faith. They will pay attention to spirits that deceive and to the Teaching of demons. (1 Timothy 4:1 CEB)

Time Is Right, Bring Together

> Then when the Time Is Right, God will do all He has planned, and Christ will Bring Together everything in heaven and on earth. (Ephesians 1:10 CEV)

Same Time, Take Delight, Thought

> We live with a joyful confidence, yet at the Same Time we Take Delight in the Thought of leaving our bodies behind to be at home with the Lord. (2 Corinthians 5:8 TPT)

Right Time

> For while we were still weak, at the Right Time Christ died for the ungodly. (Romans 5:6 ESV)

The Time Has Come

> Jesus answered them, "The Time Has Come for the Son of Man to be glorified. (John 12:23 EHV)

Trusted, Turn Away from Foolish Talk, Those Who Think

> Timothy, keep safe what God has Trusted you with. Turn Away from Foolish Talk. Do not argue with Those Who Think they know so much. They know less than They Think They do. (1 Timothy 6:20 NLV)

Trouble

> Make sure that no one falls short of the grace of God and that no root of bitterness springs up, causing Trouble and by it, defiling many. (Hebrews 12:15 HCSB)

Take Every Thought Captive

> We destroy arguments and every lofty opinion raised against the knowledge of God, and Take Every Thought Captive to obey Christ. (2 Corinthians 10:5 ESV)

Transformed

> And we all, who with unveiled faces contemplate the Lord's glory, are being Transformed into His image with ever-increasing glory, which comes from the Lord, who is the Spirit. (2 Corinthians 3:18 NIV)

Tranquil Spirit

> A Tranquil Spirit revives the body, but envy is rottenness to the bones. (Proverbs 14:30 NET)

Shout in Triumph

> I will be glad and Shout in Triumph. I will sing praise to Your exalted name, O Most High. (Psalm 9:2 TPT)

Day of Trouble, Treasure, His Tent, Triumphant

> In the Day of Trouble, He will Treasure me in His shelter, under the cover of His Tent. He will lift me high upon a rock, out of reach from all my enemies who surround me. Triumphant now, I'll bring Him my offerings of praise, singing and shouting with ecstatic joy! Yes, I will sing praises to Yahweh! (Psalm 27:5–6 TPT)

Treasure

> For where your Treasure is, there will your heart be also. (Matthew 6:21 KJ21)

Treasure Your Law, Throughout the Day

> O how I love and Treasure Your Law; Throughout the Day I fill my heart with its light! (Psalm 119:97 TPT)

Rarest Treasures, His Truth

> The Rarest Treasures of life are found in His Truth. That's why God's Word is prized like others prize the finest gold. Sweeter also than honey are His living words—sweet words dripping from the honeycomb! (Psalm 19:10 TPT)

Good Things, Treasure Chest, Those Who Turn and Hide Themselves in You

> Lord, how wonderful You are! You have stored up so many Good Things for us, like a Treasure Chest heaped up and spilling over with blessings—all for Those who honor and worship You! Everybody knows what You can do for Those Who Turn and Hide Themselves in You. (Psalm 31:19 TPT)

Greatest Treasure, Treason

> I consider Your Word to be my Greatest Treasure, and I Treasure it in my heart to keep me from committing sin's Treason against you. (Psalm 119:11 TPT)

Throughout, Think, Treasure Your Word to Me

> Throughout the night I Think of You, dear God; I Treasure Your every Word to Me. (Psalm 119:55 TPT)

Joyous Treasure

> Everything you speak to me is like Joyous Treasure, filling my life with gladness. (Psalm 119:111 TPT)

Thrills, Hidden Treasure

> Your promises are the source of my bubbling joy; the revelation of Your Word Thrills me like one who has discovered Hidden Treasure. (Psalm 119:162 TPT)

Times, This Treasure

> He will be your constant source of stability in changing Times, and out of His abundant love He gives you the riches of salvation, wisdom, and knowledge. Yes, the fear of the Lord is the key to This Treasure! (Isaiah 33:6 TPT)

Treasure

> Treasure My instructions, and cherish them within your heart. (Proverbs 7:3 TPT)

Treasure My Teaching, Troubled

> So, listen to Me, you who care for what is right, who Treasure My Teaching in your hearts: Do not fear the insults of others; do not be Troubled when they revile you. (Isaiah 51:7 TPT)

Treasures, Thieves

> Don't store up for yourselves Treasures on earth, where moth and rust destroy and where Thieves break in and steal. But store up for yourselves Treasures in heaven, where neither moth nor rust destroys, and where Thieves don't break in and steal. (Matthew 6:19–20 CSB)

Treasures of Redemption

Since we are now joined to Christ, we have been given the Treasures of Redemption by His blood—the total cancellation of our sins—all because of the cascading riches of His grace. (Ephesians 1:7 TPT)

Treasures, True Gospel, Today, Truth

Your faith and love rise within you as you access all the Treasures of your inheritance stored up in the heavenly realm. For the revelation of the True Gospel is as real Today as the day you first heard of our glorious hope, now that you have believed in the Truth of the gospel. (Colossians 1:5 TPT)

God's Chosen Treasure, Throughout

But you are God's Chosen Treasure—priests who are kings, a spiritual "nation" set apart as God's devoted ones. He called you out of darkness to experience His marvelous light, and now He claims you as His very own. He did this so that you would broadcast His glorious wonders Throughout the world. (1 Peter 2:9 TPT)

Triumphant King

For God is the Triumphant King; all the powers of the earth are His. So, sing your celebration songs of highest praise to the glorious Enlightened One! (Psalm 47:7 TPT)

Through You, Trouble, Triumphed

Through You I'm saved—rescued from every Trouble. I've seen with my eyes the defeat of my enemies. I've Triumphed over them all! (Psalm 54:7 TPT)

Triumph, Trample

> The godly will celebrate in the Triumph of good over evil, and the lovers of God will Trample the wickedness of the wicked under their feet! (Psalm 58:10 TPT)

Triumphal Processions, Toward the Holy Place

> O God, my King, your Triumphal Processions keep moving onward in holiness; you're moving onward Toward the Holy Place! (Psalm 68:24 TPT)

Triumphant Shout

> O Lord, how blessed are the people who know the Triumphant Shout, for They walk in the radiance of Your presence. (Psalm 89:15 TPT)

Truths, Teaching, Speaking Triumphantly

> He continued to proclaim to all the Truths of God's kingdom realm, Teaching them about the Lord Jesus, the Anointed One, Speaking Triumphantly and without any restriction. (Acts 28:31 TPT)

Through, Travel, Only for Those Who Walk in God's Ways, There

> And a great road will go Through that once deserted land. It will be named the Highway of Holiness. Evil-minded people will never Travel on it. It will be Only for Those Who Walk in God's Ways; fools will never walk There. (Isaiah 35:8 NLT)

Triumphant Power

> But as the mighty Son of God, He was raised from the dead and miraculously set apart with a display of Triumphant Power supplied by the Spirit of Holiness. And now Jesus is our Lord and our Messiah. (Romans 1:4 TPT)

Triumphant Joy

> With Triumphant Joy you will drink deeply from the wells of salvation. (Isaiah 12:3 TPT)

Triumph

> Who then is left to condemn us? Certainly not Jesus, the Anointed One! For He gave His life for us, and even more than that, He has conquered death and is now risen, exalted, and enthroned by God at His right hand. So how could He possibly condemn us since He is continually praying for our Triumph? (Romans 8:34 TPT)

Endless Triumph, Through

> God always makes His grace visible in Christ, who includes us as partners of His Endless Triumph. Through our yielded lives He spreads the fragrance of the knowledge of God everywhere we go. (2 Corinthians 2:14 TPT)

These Things, Triumph

> Yet even in the midst of all These Things, we Triumph over Them all, for God has made us to be more than conquerors and His demonstrated love is our glorious victory over everything! (Romans 8:37 TPT)

God's Triumphant Power Together

> For although He was crucified as a "weakling," now He lives robed with God's power. And we also are "weak ones" in our co-crucifixion with Him, but now we live in God's Triumphant Power Together with Him, which is demonstrated on your behalf. (2 Corinthians 13:4 TPT)

Then Reign Together, His Triumph

> If we are joined with Him in His sufferings, Then we will Reign Together with Him in His Triumph. But if we disregard Him, Then He will also disregard us. (2 Timothy 2:12 TPT)

Triumphant Voice

> Then I heard a Triumphant Voice in heaven proclaiming: "Now salvation and power are set in place, and the kingdom reign of our God and the ruling authority of His Anointed One are established." (Revelation 12:10a TPT)

Transformed

> And be not conformed to this world, but be ye Transformed by the renewing of your mind, that ye may prove what is that good and acceptable and perfect will of God. (Romans 12:2 KJ21)

> We all, with unveiled faces, are looking as in a mirror at the glory of the Lord and are being Transformed into the same image from glory to glory; This is from the Lord who is the Spirit. (2 Corinthians 3:18 CSB)

> As the men watched, Jesus' appearance was Transformed so That His face shone like the sun, and his clothes became as white as light. (Matthew 17:2 NLT)

> The Spirit of the Lord will control you, you will prophesy with them, and you will be Transformed into a different person. (1 Samuel 10:6 HCSB)

> For our earthly bodies, the ones we have now that can die, must be Transformed into heavenly bodies that cannot perish but will live forever. (1 Corinthians 15:53 TLB)

All Things, Transform

> By the power that enables Him to subject all Things to Himself, He will Transform our humble bodies to be like His glorious body. (Philippians 3:21 EHV)

These Commandments, Today, Transform

> If you fully obey all of These Commandments of the Lord your God, the laws I am declaring to you Today, God will Transform you into the greatest nation in the world. (Deuteronomy 28:1 TLB)

Think, Transform

> Just Think how much more surely the blood of Christ will Transform our lives and hearts. His sacrifice frees us from the worry of having to obey the old rules and makes us want to serve the living God. For by the help of the eternal Holy Spirit, Christ willingly gave Himself to God to die for our sins—He being perfect, without a single sin or fault. (Hebrews 9:14 TLB)

Testimony

> Listen to my Testimony: I cried to God in my distress and He answered me. He freed me from all my fears! (Psalm 34:4 TPT)

> And if you will swear by Me alone, the living God, and begin to live good, honest, clean lives, then you will be a Testimony to the nations of the world, and They will come to Me and glorify My name. (Jeremiah 4:2 TLB)

<u>PRAYERS</u> (Using T Words)

Thank You for your glorious *truth that teaches* us about our *true* God. God, we are not *terrified* in *times* of *trouble* because we can *turn to* You in all our *tests* and *trials*. We are in awe because we are Your chosen *treasure*. We take delight in Your *triumphant* joy and power. You have given us beautiful *testimonies*. You have *transformed* our lives and given us *tranquil* spirits. *Through* Your precious *truth*, we have learned to *take* every *thought* captive. *Thank* You, Jesus, for *taming* our *tongues* and helping us control our words and *thoughts*. We are grateful, God, that You *taught* us about *temptation* and will provide a way of escape. You have *taught* us that the *testing* of our faith produces perseverance. We praise You, Father God, and we love You because we can put our *total* and complete *trust* in You.

We pray these *things* in Your *triumphant* power, Jesus.

Amen.

U

Understanding

> Trust in the Lord with all your heart; do not lean on your own Understanding. (Proverbs 3:5 ESV)

> Then He said to mankind: Listen carefully. The fear of the Lord—that is wisdom, and to turn away from evil is Understanding. (Job 28:28 EHV)

> I will eagerly pursue Your commandments because you continue to increase my Understanding. (Psalm 119:32 GW)

> If you refuse to be corrected, you are only hurting yourself. Listen to criticism, and you will gain Understanding. (Proverbs 15:32 ERV)

> But God made the earth by His power; He founded the world by His wisdom and stretched out the heavens by His Understanding. (Jeremiah 10:12 NIV)

> How great is our God! There's absolutely nothing His power cannot accomplish, and He has infinite Understanding of everything. (Psalm 147:5 TPT)

> Wisdom is a gift from a generous God, and every word He speaks is full of revelation and becomes a fountain of Understanding within you. (Proverbs 2:6 TPT)

Wise and Understanding Heart

> I will give you what you asked for! I will give you a Wise and Understanding Heart such as no one else has had or ever will have! (1 Kings 3:12 NLT)

Gives Guidance and Understanding

> But wisdom and power are with God. He Gives Guidance and Understanding. (Job 12:13 EHV)

Perfect in His Understanding

> Yes, God is mighty, but He despises no one; He Understands all things. (Job 36:5 CSB)

Spiritual Understanding

> All my words are clear and straightforward to everyone who possesses Spiritual Understanding. If you have an open mind, you will receive revelation-knowledge. (Proverbs 8:9 TPT)

Understand

> Be a friend to yourself; do all you can to be wise. Try hard to Understand, and you will be rewarded. (Proverbs 19:8 ERV)

Unending, Unfailing Love

> I will live enthroned with you forever! Guard me, God, with your Unending, Unfailing love. Let me live my days walking in grace and truth before you. (Psalm 61:7 TPT)

Your Unfailing Love

> But I trust in Your Unfailing Love; my heart rejoices in Your salvation. (Psalm 13:5 NIV)

> Let the dawning day bring me revelation of Your tender, Unfailing Love. Give me light for my path and teach me, for I trust in You. (Psalm 143:8 TPT)

With Your Unfailing Love You lead the people You have redeemed. In Your might, You guide them to Your sacred home. (Exodus 15:13 NLT)

The Lord loves righteousness and justice; the earth is full of His Unfailing Love. (Psalm 33:5 NIV)

But the eyes of the Lord are on those who fear Him, on those whose hope is in His Unfailing Love. (Psalm 33:18 NIV)

Satisfy us in the morning with Your Unfailing Love, that we may sing for joy and be glad all our days. (Psalm 90:14 NIV)

I bow before Your holy Temple as I worship. I praise your name for Your Unfailing Love and faithfulness; for Your promises are backed by all the honor of Your name. (Psalm 138:2 NLT)

The Lord delights in those who fear him, who put their hope in His Unfailing Love. (Psalm 147:11 NIV)

"Though the mountains be shaken and the hills be removed, yet My Unfailing Love for you will not be shaken nor my covenant of peace be removed," says the Lord, who has compassion on you. (Isaiah 54:10 NIV)

Remember O Lord, Your compassion and Unfailing Love, which You have shown from long ages past. (Psalm 25:6 NLT)

I will tell of the Lord's Unfailing Love. I will praise the Lord for all He has done. I will rejoice in His great goodness to Israel, which He has granted according to His mercy and love. (Isaiah 63:7 NLT)

Let them give thanks to the Lord for His Unfailing Love and His wonderful deeds for mankind. (Psalm 107:8 NIV)

So, the Word became human and made His home among us. He was full of Unfailing Love and faithfulness. And we have seen His glory, the glory of the Father's one and only Son. (John 1:14 NLT)

Built Up, Until, Unity in the Faith

To equip His people for works of service, so that the body of Christ may be Built Up Until we all reach Unity in the Faith and in the knowledge of the Son of God and become mature, attaining to the whole measure of the fullness of Christ. (Ephesians 4:12–13 NIV)

Unity of the Spirit

Make every effort to keep the Unity of the Spirit through the bond of peace. (Ephesians 4:3 NIV)

Perfect Unity

For the very glory you have given to Me I have given them so that they will be joined together as one and experience the same Unity that we enjoy. You live fully in Me and now I live fully in them so that they will experience Perfect Unity, and the world will be convinced that You have sent Me, for they will see that you love each one of them with the same passionate love that you have for Me. (John 17:22–23 TPT)

Finally, beloved friends, be cheerful! Repair whatever is broken among you, as your hearts are being knit together in Perfect Unity. Live continually in peace, and God, the source of love and peace, will mingle with you. (2 Corinthians 13:11 TPT)

Sweet Unity

How truly wonderful and delightful it is to see brothers and sisters living together in Sweet Unity. (Psalm 133:1 TPT)

Unity, Created the Universe

> When the believers heard their report, they raised their voices in Unity and prayed, "Lord Yahweh, You are the Lord of all! You Created the Universe—the earth, the sky, the sea, and everything that is in them." (Acts 4:24 TPT)

United, Understanding

> Now I urge you, brothers and sisters, in the name of our Lord Jesus Christ, that all of you agree in what you say, that there be no divisions among you, and that you be United with the same Understanding and the same conviction. (1 Corinthians 1:10 CSB)

United

> I will give them the desire to be one, United people. They will have one goal—to worship Me all their lives. (Jeremiah 32:39a ERV)

Unstained by Sin, Undefiled

> He is, therefore, exactly the kind of High Priest we need; for He is holy and blameless, Unstained by Sin, Undefiled by sinners, and to Him has been given the place of honor in heaven. (Hebrews 7:26 TLB)

Perfect Unity, United in One Love, Unbounded Joy

> So, I'm asking you, my friends, that you be joined together in Perfect Unity—with one heart, one passion, and United in One Love. Walk together with one harmonious purpose and You will fill My heart with Unbounded Joy. (Philippians 2:2 TPT)

Unapproachable Light of Divine Glory, Universe

> He alone is the immortal God, living in the Unapproachable Light of Divine Glory! No one has

ever seen His fullness, nor can they, for all the glory and endless authority of the Universe belongs to Him, forever and ever. Amen! (1 Timothy 6:16 TPT)

Universe, Keep It Up

Let all the Universe praise Him! The high heavens and everyone on earth, praise Him! Let the oceans deep, with everything in them, Keep it Up! (Psalm 69:34 TPT)

Universe

Faith empowers us to see that the Universe was created and beautifully coordinated by the power of God's words! He spoke and the invisible realm gave birth to all that is seen. (Hebrews 11:3 TPT)

For then you will be seen as innocent, faultless, and pure children of God, even though you live in the midst of a brutal and perverse culture. For you will appear among them as shining lights in the Universe. (Philippians 2:15 TPT)

Because of this my praises rise to the King of all the Universe who is indestructible, invisible, and full of glory, the only God who is worthy of the highest honors throughout all of time and throughout the eternity of eternities! Amen! (1 Timothy 1:17 TPT)

Then Jesus came close to them and said, "All authority of the Universe has been given to Me." (Matthew 28:18 TPT)

Universe, Us

The Son is the dazzling radiance of God's splendor, the exact expression of God's true nature—His mirror image! He holds the Universe together and expands it by the mighty power of His spoken word. He accomplished for

Us the complete cleansing of sins, and then took His seat on the highest throne at the right hand of the majestic One. (Hebrews 1:3 TPT)

Entire Universe

Let the Entire Universe erupt with praise to God. He spoke and created it all—from nothing to something. (Psalm 148:5 TPT)

Overflows within Us, Universe

And our own completeness is now found in Him. We are completely filled with God as Christ's fullness Overflows Within Us. He is the Head of every kingdom and authority in the Universe! (Colossians 2:10 TPT)

Universe, Unseen

For in Him was created the Universe of things, both in the heavenly realm and on the earth, all that is seen and all that is Unseen. Every seat of power, realm of government, principality, and authority—it all exists through Him and for His purpose! (Colossians 1:16 TPT)

He Chose Us, Universe, Unstained Innocence

And in love He Chose Us before He laid the foundation of the Universe! Because of His great love, He ordained Us, so that we would be seen as holy in His eyes with an Unstained Innocence. (Ephesians 1:4 TPT)

Universe, Unable, Us

Who could ever divorce us from the endless love of God's Anointed One? Absolutely no one! For nothing in the Universe has the power to diminish His love toward us. Troubles, pressures, and problems are Unable to come between Us and heaven's love. What about persecutions, deprivations, dangers, and death threats? No, for they are all impotent to hinder omnipotent love. (Romans 8:35 TPT)

Unlimited Power, Entire Universe

He does what He pleases with Unlimited Power and authority, extending His greatness throughout the Entire Universe! (Psalm 135:6 TPT)

Spoken to Us, Made the Universe

In these last days, He has Spoken to Us by His Son. God has appointed Him heir of all things and Made the Universe through Him. (Hebrews 1:2 CSB)

Unconditional Love

May the Unconditional Love of the Lord Jesus, the Anointed One, be with your spirit! (Philemon 1:25 TPT)

Strong Hand Upholds Me

My whole being clings to You; Your Strong Hand Upholds Me. (Psalm 63:8 CEB)

Uphold Me

Restore to me the joy of Your salvation, and Uphold Me with a willing spirit. (Psalm 51:12 AMPC)

Unseen

So, we do not focus on what is seen, but on what is Unseen. For what is seen is temporary, but what is Unseen is eternal. (2 Corinthians 4:18 CSB)

Unceasingly, Unwavering Hope

Recalling Unceasingly before our God and Father your work energized by faith, and your service motivated by love and Unwavering Hope in [the return of] our Lord Jesus Christ. (1 Thessalonians 1:3 AMP)

Purpose Is Unchangeable, Hope Set Before Us

> In the same way God, desiring even more to demonstrate to the heirs of the promise the fact that His Purpose Is Unchangeable, confirmed it with an oath, so that by two Unchangeable things in which it is impossible for God to lie, we who have taken refuge would have strong encouragement to hold firmly to the Hope Set Before Us. (Hebrews 6:17–18 NASB)

Unique, Unchangeable

> But He is Unique and Unchangeable, and who can turn Him? And what His soul desires, that He does. (Job 23:13 AMP)

Unite My Heart

> Teach me Thy way, O Lord, I will walk in Thy truth; Unite My Heart to fear Thy name. (Psalm 86:11 KJ21)

PRAYERS (USING U WORDS)

We praise You for being the King of the ***universe***. We are in awe of Your beautiful creation of the ***universe***. Lord, You are ***unchangeable***. Your ***unfailing*** love is the same yesterday, today, and forever! We are ***united*** in perfect ***unity*** with You, Lord Jesus. Our faith is trusting the ***unseen*** throughout eternity. We are blessed to receive Your ***unconditional*** love, and Your strong right hand ***upholds*** us. This gives us ***unwavering*** hope in Your ***unlimited*** power. Jesus, we know that You are holy and blameless and ***unstained*** by sin. Thank You, God, for making forgiveness possible for us through Your ***unfailing*** love.

We praise You, Father God, for being such an ***understanding*** God! In Your holy name, we pray.

Amen.

V

Victorious

To the One who is Victorious, I will give the right to sit with me on My throne, just as I was Victorious and sat down with My Father on His throne. (Revelation 3:21 EHV)

If you can hear, listen to what the Spirit is saying to the churches. I will allow those who emerge Victorious to eat from the tree of life, which is in God's paradise. (Revelation 2:7 CEB)

And yet, from long ago God has been my King, the one who has been Victorious throughout the earth. (Psalm 74:12 GW)

My faithfulness and mercy will be with Him, and in My name, He will be Victorious. (Psalm 89:24 GW)

Don't be afraid, because I am with you. Don't be intimidated; I am your God. I will strengthen you. I will help you. I will support you with my Victorious right hand. (Isaiah 41:10 GW)

Those who are Victorious will come from Mount Zion to rule Esau's Mountain. The kingdom will belong to the Lord. (Obadiah 1:21 GW)

Rejoice with all your heart, people of Zion! Shout in triumph, people of Jerusalem! Look! Your King is coming to you: He is righteous and Victorious. He is humble and rides on a donkey, on a colt, a young pack animal. (Zechariah 9:9 GW)

You will be Victorious over your enemies. (Leviticus 26:7 GNT)

The Lord's enemies will be destroyed; He will thunder against them from heaven. The Lord will judge the whole world; He will give power to His King; He will make His chosen King Victorious. (1 Samuel 2:10 GNT)

Who is this great King? He is the Lord, strong and mighty, the Lord, Victorious in battle. (Psalm 24:8 GNT)

The king will drink from the stream by the road, and strengthened, He will stand Victorious. (Psalm 110:7 GNT)

The king is glad, O Lord, because You gave him strength; He rejoices because You made him Victorious. (Psalm 21:1 GNT)

Victorious, Victory

Look! Here comes Lord Yahweh as a Victorious warrior; He triumphs with His awesome power. Watch as He brings with Him His reward and the spoils of Victory to give to His people. (Isaiah 40:10 TPT)

Victory, Victories

Now I know that the Lord gives Victory to His chosen king; He answers Him from His holy heaven and by His power gives Him great Victories. (Psalm 20:6 GNT)

Victory

Because every child of God is able to defeat the world. And we win the Victory over the world by means of our faith. (1 John 5:4 GNT)

And in your majesty Go on to Victory, Defending truth, humility, and justice. Go forth to awe-inspiring deeds! (Psalm 45:4 TLB)

I wait quietly before God, for my Victory comes from Him. (Psalm 62:1 NLT)

He will swallow up death in Victory; and the Lord GOD will wipe away tears from off all faces; and the rebuke of his people shall He take away from off all the earth: for the Lord hath spoken it. (Isaiah 25:8 KJ21)

Everyone who wins the Victory will wear white clothes. Their names will not be erased from the book of life, and I will tell my Father and his angels that they are my followers. (Revelation 3:5 CEV)

All who win the Victory will be given these blessings. I will be their God, and they will be my people. (Revelation 21:7 CEV)

But thanks be to God, who giveth us the Victory through our Lord Jesus Christ. (1 Corinthians 15:57 KJ21)

You answer us by giving us Victory, and You do wonderful things to save us. People all over the world and across the distant seas trust in You. (Psalm 65:5 GNT)

Shield of Victory

You have given me your Shield of Victory. Your right hand supports me; Your help has made me great. (Psalm 18:35 NLT)

Virtue

A person's insight gives him patience, and his Virtue is to overlook an offense. (Proverbs 19:11 CSB)

Glory and Virtue

Because of His divine power having granted us all things pertaining to life and godliness through the knowledge of the One having called us by His own Glory And Virtue, through which qualities He has granted us the precious and greatest things-promised in order that through these you might become sharers of the divine nature, having escaped-from the corruption in the world by evil desire; and indeed for this very reason you having applied all diligence in your faith supply Virtue; and in your Virtue, knowledge. (2 Peter 1:3–5 DLNT)

Virtues

And over all these Virtues put on love, which binds them all together in perfect unity. (Colossians 3:14 NIV)

The Virtues of God's lovers shine brightly in the darkness, but the flickering lamp of the ungodly will be extinguished. (Proverbs 13:9 TPT)

Starry Vault, Voice

God's splendor is a tale that is told, written in the stars. Space itself speaks His story through the marvels of the heavens. His truth is on tour in the Starry Vault of the sky, showing His skill in creation's craftsmanship. Each day gushes out its message to the next, night by night whispering its knowledge to all—without a sound, without a word, without a Voice being heard. (Psalm 19:1–3 TPT)

Voice

I heard your Voice in my heart say, "Come, seek my face;" my inner being responded, "Yahweh, I'm seeking your face with all my heart." (Psalm 27:8 TPT)

The Voice of the Lord echoes through the skies and seas. The Glory-God reigns as he thunders in the clouds. So powerful is His Voice, so brilliant and bright—how majestic as He thunders over the great waters! (Psalm 29:3–4 TPT)

Now he moves Zion's mountains by the might of his Voice, shaking the snowy peaks with his earsplitting sound! (Psalm 29:6 TPT)

Speaking His Voice, Mighty Voice, Thunderbolt Voice

God reveals Himself when He makes the fault lines quake, shaking deserts, Speaking His Voice. God's Mighty Voice makes the deer to give birth. His Thunderbolt Voice lays the forest bare. In His temple all fall before Him with each one shouting, "Glory, glory, the God of glory!" (Psalm 29:8–9 TPT)

Now I'll listen carefully for your Voice and wait to hear whatever you say. Let me hear your promise of peace— the message every one of your godly lovers' longs to hear. Don't let us in our ignorance turn back from following You. (Psalm 85:8 TPT)

Lord, you have reigned as King from the very beginning of time. Eternity is Your home. Chaos once challenged you. The raging waves lifted themselves over and over, high above the ocean's depths, letting out their mighty roar! Yet at the sound of Your Voice, they were all stilled by Your might. What a majestic King, filled with power! (Psalm 93:2–4 TPT)

Come, let us worship and bow down. Let us kneel before the Lord our maker, for He is our God. We are the people He watches over, the flock under His care. If only you would listen to His Voice today! (Psalm 95:6–7 NLT)

Bless the Lord, you His angels, You mighty ones who do His commandments, Obeying the Voice of His Word! (Psalm 103:20 AMP)

I thank You, Lord, and with all the passion of my heart I worship You in the presence of angels! Heaven's mighty ones will hear my Voice as I sing my loving praise to You. (Psalm 138:1 TPT)

O Lord, You are my God and my saving strength! My Hero- God, You wrap Yourself around me to protect me. For I'm surrounded by Your presence in my day of battle. Lord Yahweh, hear my cry. May my Voice move your heart to show me mercy. (Psalm 140:6–7 TPT)

Stick with wisdom and she will stick to you, protecting you throughout your days. She will rescue all those who passionately listen to her Voice. (Proverbs 4:6 TPT)

And then finally you'll admit that you were wrong and say, "If only I had listened to wisdom's Voice and not stubbornly demanded my own way, because my heart hated to be told what to do!" (Proverbs 5:12 TPT)

The remnant lifts up its Voice with a joyful shout. From the west they praise the majesty of the Lord Yahweh. (Isaiah 24:14 TPT)

Hear My Voice, listen to My words, and pay close attention to My parable. (Isaiah 28:23 TPT)

Yes, the people of Zion who live in Jerusalem will weep no more. How compassionate He will be when He hears your cries for help! He will answer you when He hears your Voice! (Isaiah 30:19 TPT)

Even though the Lord may allow you to go through a season of hardship and difficulty, He Himself will be there with you. He will not hide Himself from you, for your eyes will constantly see him as your Teacher. When you turn to the right or turn to the left, you will hear His Voice behind you to guide you, saying, "This is the right path; follow it." (Isaiah 30:20–21 TPT)

A thunderous Voice cries out in the wilderness: "Prepare the way for Yahweh's arrival! Make a highway straight through the desert for our God!" (Isaiah 40:3 TPT)

Go up on a high mountain, you joyful messengers of Zion, and lift up your Voices with power. You who proclaim joyous news to Jerusalem, shout it out and don't be afraid. Say to the cities of Judah, "Here is your God!" (Isaiah 40:9 TPT)

Then suddenly the Voice of the Father shouted from the sky, saying, "This is my Son—the Beloved! My greatest delight is in Him." (Matthew 3:17 TPT)

And He will send His messengers with the loud blast of the trumpet, and with a great Voice they will gather His beloved chosen ones from the four winds, from one end of heaven to the other! (Matthew 24:31 TPT)

My own sheep will hear My Voice and I know each one, and they will follow Me. (John 10:27 TPT)

Can it be that Israel hasn't heard the message? No, they have heard it, for: The Voice has been heard throughout the world, and its message has gone to the ends of the earth! (Romans 10:18 TPT)

And because the gatekeeper knows who He is, He opens the gate to let Him in. And the sheep recognize the Voice of the true Shepherd, for He calls His own by name and leads them out, for they belong to Him. And when He has brought out all His sheep, He walks ahead of them and they will follow Him, for they are familiar with His Voice. But they will run away from strangers and never follow them because they know it's the Voice of a stranger. (John 10:3–5 TPT)

He is a thunderous Voice of one who shouts in the wilderness: "Prepare your hearts for the coming of the Lord Yahweh, and clear a straight path inside your hearts for Him!" (Mark 1:3 TPT)

"So, Father, bring glory to Your name!" Then suddenly a booming Voice was heard from the sky, "I have glorified My name! And I will glorify it through you again!" (John 12:28 TPT)

While He was still speaking, suddenly a bright cloud overshadowed them, and a Voice from the cloud said, "This is My beloved Son, with whom I am well pleased. Listen to Him." (Matthew 17:5 MEV)

So now the case is closed. There remains no accusing Voice of condemnation against those who are joined in life-union with Jesus, the Anointed One. (Romans 8:1 TPT)

Then, with a unanimous rush of passion, you will with one Voice glorify God, the Father of our Lord Jesus Christ. (Romans 15:6 TPT)

This is why the Holy Spirit says, "If only you would listen to His Voice this day!" (Hebrews 3:7 TPT)

The earth was rocked at the sound of His Voice from the mountain, but now He has promised, "Once and for all I will not only shake the systems of the world, but also the unseen powers in the heavenly realm!" (Hebrews 12:26 TPT)

Yes, Father God lavished upon Him radiant glory and honor when His distinct Voice spoke out of the realm of majestic glory, endorsing Him with these words: This is My cherished Son, marked by My love. All My delight is found in Him! (2 Peter 1:17 TPT)

When I saw Him, I fell down at His feet as good as dead, but He laid His right hand on me and I heard His reassuring Voice saying: Don't yield to fear. I am the Beginning and I am the End. (Revelation 1:17 TPT)

Thunderous Voices

And as I watched, all of them were singing with Thunderous Voices: "Worthy is Christ the Lamb who was slaughtered to receive great power and might, wealth and wisdom, and honor, glory, and praise!" Then every living being joined the angelic choir. Every creature in heaven and on earth, under the earth, in the sea, and everything in them, were worshiping with one Voice, saying: "Praise, honor, glory, and dominion be to God-Enthroned and to Christ the Lamb forever and ever!" (Revelation 5:12–13 TPT)

Voice, Villages

Let the wilderness and the cities thereof lift up their Voice, the Villages that Kedar doth inhabit: let the inhabitants of the rock sing, let them shout from the top of the mountains. (Isaiah 42:11 KJ21)

Vows

Then I will sing praises to Your name forever as I fulfill my Vows each day. (Psalm 61:8 NLT)

Again, your ancestors were taught, "Never swear an oath that you don't intend to keep," but keep your Vows to the Lord God. (Matthew 5:33 TPT)

Very Present Help in Trouble

God is our refuge and strength, a Very Present Help in Trouble. (Psalm 46:1 KJ21)

True Vine, Vinedresser

I am the True Vine, and My Father is the Vinedresser. Every branch in Me that bears no fruit, He takes away. And every branch that bears fruit, He prunes, that it may bear more fruit. You are already clean through the word which I have spoken to you. Remain in Me, as I also remain in you. As the branch cannot bear fruit by itself, unless it remains in the Vine, neither can you, unless you remain in Me. I am the Vine; you are the branches. He who remains in Me, and I in Him, bears much fruit. For without Me you can do nothing. (John 15:1–5 MEV)

Veil

> For He has dedicated a new, life-giving way for us to approach God. For just as the Veil was torn in two, Jesus' body was torn open to give us free and fresh access to Him! (Hebrews 10:20 TPT)

Very Great

> Bless the Lord, O my soul! O Lord my God, you are Very Great! You are clothed with honor and majesty. (Psalm 104:1 MEV)

Very God of Peace

> May the Very God of Peace sanctify you completely. And I pray to God that your whole spirit, soul, and body be preserved blameless unto the coming of our Lord Jesus Christ. (1 Thessalonians 5:23 MEV)

Voice, Vast

> His Voice scooped out the seas. The ocean depths He poured into Vast reservoirs. (Psalm 33:7 TPT)

Vast

> And then there is the sea! So Vast! So wide and deep—swarming with countless forms of sea life, both small and great. (Psalm 104:25 TPT)

> One day Jesus saw a Vast crowd of people gathering to hear Him, so He went up the slope of a hill and sat down. With His followers and disciples spread over the hillside, (Matthew 5:1 TPT)

> When He saw the Vast crowds of people, Jesus' heart was deeply moved with compassion, because they seemed weary and helpless, like wandering sheep without a shepherd. (Matthew 9:36 TPT)

Vast, Very Armies of Heaven

> Then all at once in the night sky, a Vast number of glorious angels appeared, the Very Armies Of heaven! And they all praised God, singing: "Glory to God in the highest realms of heaven! For there is peace and a good hope given to the sons of men." (Luke 2:13–14 TPT)

> For He knew all about us before we were born and He destined us from the beginning to share the likeness of His Son. This means the Son is the oldest among a Vast family of brothers and sisters who will become just like Him. (Romans 8:29 TPT)

Vast, Victorious

> After this I looked, and behold, right in front of me I saw a Vast multitude of people—an enormous multitude so huge that no one could count—made up of Victorious ones from every nation, tribe, people group, and language. They were all in glistening white robes, standing before the throne and before the Lamb with palm branches in their hands. (Revelation 7:9 TPT)

Virgin Birth

> Therefore, the Lord Himself shall give you a sign: The Virgin shall conceive, and bear a son, and shall call His name Immanuel. (Isaiah 7:14 MEV)

Valuable

> Consider the birds—do you think they worry about their existence? They don't plant or reap or store up food, yet your Heavenly Father provides them each with food. Aren't you much more Valuable to your Father than they? (Matthew 6:26 TPT)

> Your instructions are more Valuable to me than millions in gold and silver. (Psalm 119:72 NLT)

Value, Valuable

What is the Value of your soul to God? Could your worth be defined by any amount of money? God doesn't abandon or forget even the small sparrow He has made. How then could He forget or abandon you? What about the seemingly minor issues of your life? Do they matter to God? Of course, they do! So, you never need to worry, for you are more Valuable to God than anything else in this world. (Luke 12:6–7 TPT)

Valuable

And what could be more Valuable to you than your own soul? (Mark 8:37 TPT)

For wisdom is far more Valuable than rubies. Nothing you desire can compare with it. (Proverbs 8:11 NLT)

So don't be afraid; you are more Valuable to God than a whole flock of sparrows. (Matthew 10:31 NLT)

I once thought these things were Valuable, but now I consider them worthless because of what Christ has done. (Philippians 3:7 NLT)

Value, Vanish

All the enemies of God will perish. For the wicked have only a momentary Value, a fading glory. Then one day they Vanish! Here today, gone tomorrow. (Psalm 37:20 TPT)

Values

Dedicate your children to God and point them in the way that they should go, and the Values they've learned from you will be with them for life. (Proverbs 22:6 TPT)

If you were to give your allegiance to the world, they would love and welcome you as one of their own. But because you won't align yourself with the Values of this world, they will hate you. I have chosen you and taken you out of the world to be mine. (John 15:19 TPT)

Value

So, let's be clear. To have the Lord's approval and commendation is of greater Value than bragging about oneself. (2 Corinthians 10:18 TPT)

Your calling is to fulfill the royal law of love as given to us in this Scripture: "You must love and Value your neighbor as you love and Value yourself!" For keeping this law is the noble way to live. (James 2:8 TPT)

Recognize the Value of every person and continually show love to every believer. Live your lives with great reverence and in holy awe of God. Honor your rulers. (1 Peter 2:17 TPT)

Valleys

The Valleys will be filled, and the mountains and hills made level. The curves will be straightened, and the rough places made smooth. And then all people will see the salvation sent from God. (Luke 3:5–6 NLT)

Even when I walk through the darkest Valley, I will not be afraid, for You are close beside me. Your rod and Your staff protect and comfort me. (Psalm 23:4 NLT)

The grazing meadows are covered with flocks, and the fertile Valleys are clothed with grain, each one dancing and shouting for joy, creation's celebration! They're all singing their songs of praise to You! (Psalm 65:13 TPT)

Vessels

Nevertheless, the firm foundation of God stands, having this seal: "The Lord knows those who are His," and, "Let everyone who names the name of the Lord keep away from unrighteousness." Now in a great house, there are not only Vessels of gold and silver, but also of wood and clay—some for honor and some for common use. Therefore, if anyone cleanses himself from these, He will be a Vessel for honor—sanctified, useful to the Master, prepared for every good work. (2 Timothy 2:19–21 TLV)

PRAYERS (Using V Words)

Thank You, God, for the *Virgin* birth of Your Son who came into the world because You *valued* us so much so we can have a Savior. We are in awe because we can have amazing *victory* through You. You are the *Vine*, and we are the branches. We know that we can do nothing without You. You are our true Shepherd, and we are your sheep. We follow You and are familiar with Your *voice*, which guides us on the right path in life. We praise You for being a *very* present help in times of trouble. You are a *very* great God of peace. We are grateful to have spiritual *vision* to see You transforming us to be more like Jesus. We rejoice because You have made us *victorious* through Your awesome power. Thank You for making us *valuable* in Your sight. Lord, we are grateful for all the wonderful *verses* You have revealed to us in Your Word.

When we go through the *valley*, we praise You that You are there! In Jesus's *victorious* and *vibrant* name,

Amen.

A VIRTUE A DAY

BIBLICAL PRAYERS

Salvation

Lord, let salvation spring up in me so that I may obtain the salvation that is in Christ Jesus with eternal glory.

> And so, I am willing to put up with anything. Then God's special people will be saved and given eternal glory because they belong to Christ Jesus. (2 Timothy 2:10 CEV)

Growth in Grace

I pray that I may "grow in the grace and knowledge of our Lord and Savior Jesus Christ."

> But continue to grow and increase in God's grace and intimacy with our Lord and Savior, Jesus Christ. May He receive all the glory both now and until the day eternity begins. Amen! (2 Peter 3:18 TPT)

Love

Grant, Lord, that I may learn to live a life of love through the Spirit who dwells in me.

> And walk in love, just as Christ loved us and gave Himself for us, as a fragrant offering and sacrifice to God. (Ephesians 5:2 EHV)

Honesty and Integrity

May integrity and honesty be my virtue and my protection.

> Your perfection and faithfulness are my bodyguards, for
> You are my hope and I trust in You as my only protection.
> (Psalm 25:21 TPT)

Self-Control

Father, help me not be like many others around me. Instead, let me be alert and self-controlled in all that I do.

> So, we should not be like other people. We should not be
> sleeping, but we should be awake and have self-control.
> (1 Thessalonians 5:6 ERV)

A Love for God's Word

May I grow to find Your Word more precious than gold and sweeter than honey from the honeycomb.

> The rarest treasures of life are found in His truth. That's
> why God's Word is prized like others prize the finest gold.
> Sweeter also, than honey are his living words—sweet
> words dripping from the honeycomb! (Psalm 19:10 TPT)

Justice

God, help me love justice as You do and act justly in all that I do.

> He has told you, human one, what is good and what the
> Lord requires from you: to do justice, embrace faithful
> love, and walk humbly with your God. (Micah 6:8 CEB)

Mercy

May I always "be merciful, just as my Father also is merciful."

> Overflow with mercy and compassion for others, just
> as your Heavenly Father overflows with mercy and
> compassion for all. (Luke 6:36 TPT)

Respect for Self, Others, and Authority

Father, grant that I may show proper respect to everyone—as Your Word commands.

> Recognize the value of every person and continually show love to every believer. Live your lives with great reverence and in holy awe of God. Honor your rulers. (1 Peter 2:17 TPT)

Strong, Biblical Self-Esteem

Help me develop strong self-esteem that is rooted in the realization that I am God's workmanship, created in Christ Jesus.

> For we are His workmanship, created in Christ Jesus for good works, which God prepared beforehand so that we should walk in them. (Ephesians 2:10 MEV)

Faithfulness

Never let loyalty and faithfulness leave me. Instead, bind these twin virtues around my neck and write them on the tablet of my heart.

> Hold on to loyal love and don't let go, and be faithful to all that you've been taught. Let your life be shaped by integrity, with truth written upon your heart. (Proverbs 3:3 TPT)

Courage

May I always be strong and courageous in my character and actions.

> Be strong and of a good courage. Fear not, nor be afraid of them, for the Lord your God, it is He who goes with you. He will not fail you, nor forsake you. (Deuteronomy 31:6 MEV)

Purity

God, create in me a clean heart and let your purity of heart be shown in my actions.

Keep creating in me a clean heart. Fill me with pure thoughts and holy desires, ready to please you. (Psalm 51:10 TPT)

Kindness

Lord, may I always try to be kind to everyone.

Instead, be kind to each other, tenderhearted, forgiving one another, just as God through Christ has forgiven you. (Ephesians 4:32 NLT)

Generosity

Grant that I may be generous and willing to share, storing up treasures for myself as a good foundation for the coming age, so that I may take hold of what is truly life.

Tell them to use their money to do good. They should be rich in good works and should give happily to those in need, always being ready to share with others whatever God has given them. By doing this they will be storing up real treasure for themselves in heaven—it is the only safe investment for eternity! And they will be living a fruitful Christian life down here as well. (1 Timothy 6:18–19 TLB)

Peace, Peaceability

Father, let me pursue what promotes peace and what builds up others.

So then, make it your top priority to live a life of peace with harmony in your relationships, eagerly seeking to strengthen and encourage one another. (Romans 14:19 TPT)

Grace, Knowledge

Father, I pray that I may grow in the grace and knowledge of our Lord and Savior Jesus Christ.

But continue to grow in the grace and knowledge of our Lord and Savior Jesus Christ. To Him be the glory, now and forever! Amen. (2 Peter 3:18 GNT)

Joy

May I be filled with joy from the Holy Spirit.

> And you became like us and like the Lord. You suffered much, but still you accepted the teaching with joy. The Holy Spirit gave you that joy. (1 Thessalonians 1:6 ERV)

Perseverance

Lord, teach me perseverance in all I do—and help me especially to run with endurance the race that lies before me.

> Since we have such a huge crowd of men of faith watching us from the grandstands, let us strip off anything that slows us down or holds us back, and especially those sins that wrap themselves so tightly around our feet and trip us up; and let us run with patience the particular race that God has set before us. (Hebrews 12:1 TLB)

Humility

God, please cultivate in me the ability to do nothing out of selfish ambition or conceit and—in humility—consider others as more important than myself.

> Do nothing out of selfishness or conceit, but with humility consider others as more important than yourselves. (Philippians 2:3 TLV)

Compassion

Lord, please clothe me with the virtue of compassion.

> Therefore, as God's chosen people, holy and dearly loved, clothe yourselves in tender compassion, kindness, humility, gentleness, and patience. (Colossians 3:12 TLV)

Responsibility

Grant that I may learn responsibility because each person will have to carry their own load.

> For each person will have to carry his own load. (Galatians 6:5 CSB)

Contentment

Father, teach me "in any and all circumstances … the secret of being content so that I am 'able to do all things through You who strengthens me.'"

> I know how to live on almost nothing or with everything. I have learned the secret of contentment in every situation, whether it be a full stomach or hunger, plenty or want; for I can do everything God asks me to with the help of Christ who gives me the strength and power. (Philippians 4:12–13 TLB)

Faith

I pray that faith will find root and grow in my heart so that, in my life, faith is the reality of what is hoped for, the proof of what is not seen.

> Now faith is the confidence of things hoped for, and the evidence of things not seen. (Hebrews 11:1 RGT)

A Servant Heart

God, please help me develop a servant's heart, that I may serve wholeheartedly—as to the Lord and not to people.

> Do your work, and be happy to do it. Work as though it is the Lord you are serving, not just an earthly master. (Ephesians 6:7 ERV)

Hope

May the God of hope fill me so that I may overflow with hope by the power of the Holy Spirit.

I pray that the God who gives hope will fill you with much joy and peace as you trust in Him. Then you will have more and more hope, and it will flow out of you by the power of the Holy Spirit. (Romans 15:13 ERV)

The Willingness and Ability to Work Hard

Teach me, Lord, to value work and to work hard at everything I do, as something done for the Lord.

Whatever work you do, do it with all your heart. Do it for the Lord and not for men. (Colossians 3:23 NLV)

A Passion for God

Lord, please instill in me a soul that clings passionately to You.

I hold on to you tightly. Your powerful right hand takes good care of me. (Psalm 63:8 NIRV)

Self-Discipline

Father, I pray that I may develop self-discipline and prudent behavior, doing what is right and just and honest.

Their purpose is to teach people to live disciplined and successful lives, to help them do what is right, just, and fair. (Proverbs 1:3 NLT)

Prayerfulness

Grant, Lord, that my life may be marked by prayerfulness so that I may learn to pray at all times in the Spirit with every prayer and request.

You must pray at all times as the Holy Spirit leads you to pray. Pray for the things that are needed. You must watch and keep on praying. Remember to pray for all Christians. (Ephesians 6:18 NLV)

Gratitude

Help me live a life that is always overflowing with gratitude so that I give thanks always for everything to God the Father in the name of our Lord Jesus Christ.

> Always give thanks to God the Father for everything in the name of our Lord Jesus Christ. (Ephesians 5:20 CEB)

A Heart for Missions

Lord, please help me to develop a heart for missions and a desire to see Your glory declared among the nations, Your marvelous deeds among all peoples.

> Don't stop! Keep on singing! Make His name famous! Tell everyone every day how wonderful He is. Give them the good news of our great Savior. Take the message of His glory and miracles to every nation. Tell them about all the amazing things He has done. (Psalm 96:3 TPT)

W

Worship Wonderful Yahweh

Be in awe before His majesty. Be in awe before such power and might! Come Worship Wonderful Yahweh, arrayed in all His splendor, bowing in Worship as He appears in the beauty of holiness. Give Him the honor due His name. Worship Him wearing the glory-garments of your holy, priestly calling! (Psalm 29:2 TPT)

Worship

Then the sovereignty, power and greatness of all the kingdoms under heaven will be handed over to the holy people of the Most High. His kingdom will be an everlasting kingdom, and all rulers will Worship and obey Him. (Daniel 7:27 NIV)

Where is He that is born King of the Jews? For we have seen His Star in the East and have come to Worship Him. (Matthew 2:2 KJ21)

Instead, you must Worship Christ as Lord of your life. And if someone asks about your hope as a believer, always be ready to explain it. (1 Peter 3:15 NLT)

Just think how much more the blood of Christ will purify our consciences from sinful deeds so that we can Worship the living God. For by the power of the eternal Spirit, Christ offered Himself to God as a perfect sacrifice for our sins. (Hebrews 9:14 NLT)

Then all the disciples bowed down before Him and Worshiped Jesus. They said in adoration, "You are truly the Son of God!" (Matthew 14:33 TPT)

And I will give them one heart and one purpose: to Worship Me forever, for their own good and for the good of all their descendants. (Jeremiah 32:39 NLT)

Honor the Lord for the glory of His name. Worship the Lord in the splendor of His holiness. (Psalm 29:2 NLT)

Everything on earth will Worship You; they will sing Your praises, shouting Your name in glorious songs. (Psalm 66:4 NLT)

Lord, We Worship You, so show Your great love for us. (Psalm 33:22 ERV)

Come, let us Worship and bow down. Let us kneel before the Lord our maker. (Psalm 95:6 NLT)

You must follow the Lord Your God and fear Him. You must keep His commands and listen to Him; you must Worship Him and remain faithful to Him. (Deuteronomy 13:4 CSB)

Those who Worship the Lord on a special day do it to honor Him. Those who eat any kind of food do so to honor the Lord, since they give thanks to God before eating. And those who refuse to eat certain foods also want to please the Lord and give thanks to God. (Romans 14:6 NLT)

For we have already experienced "heart-circumcision," and we Worship God in the power and freedom of the Holy Spirit, not in laws and religious duties. We are those who boast in what Jesus Christ has done, and not in what we can accomplish in our own strength. (Philippians 3:3 TPT)

You alone are the Lord. You made the skies and the heavens and all the stars. You made the earth and the seas and everything in them. You preserve them all, and the angels of heaven Worship You. (Nehemiah 9:6 NLT)

Beloved friends, what should be our proper response to God's Marvelous mercies? To surrender yourselves to God to be His sacred, living sacrifices. And live in holiness, experiencing all that delights His heart. For this becomes your genuine expression of Worship. (Romans 12:1 TPT)

Worship, Walk

Happy are those who hear the joyful call to Worship, for they will Walk in the light of Your presence, Lord. (Psalm 89:15 NLT)

Welcome, Worship

But I know that You will Welcome me into your house, for I am covered by Your covenant of mercy and love. So, I come to Your sanctuary with deepest awe to bow in Worship and adore You. (Psalm 5:7 TPT)

Written, Worship

And Jesus answered and said unto him, "Get thee behind Me, Satan! For it is Written: 'Thou shalt Worship the Lord thy God, and Him only shalt thou serve.'" (Luke 4:8 KJ21)

Worship Him and Do His Will

But He is ready to hear those who Worship Him and Do His Will. (John 9:31b NLT)

Worship, Word

I bow down before Your divine presence and bring You my deepest Worship as I experience Your tender love and

Your living truth. For Your Word and the fame of Your name have been magnified above all else! (Psalm 138:2 TPT)

Worshippers Will Worship

But a time is coming and now is here when the real Worshippers Will Worship the Father in spirit and in truth, for those are the kind of Worshippers the Father seeks. (John 4:23 EHV)

Please God by Worshipping Him

Since we are receiving a Kingdom that is unshakable, let us be thankful and Please God by Worshiping Him with holy fear and awe. (Hebrews 12:28 NLT)

Whole World Worship You

Let the Whole World Worship You. Let everyone sing praises to Your name. (Psalm 66:4 ERV)

World, Angels Worship Him

And when He brought His supreme Son into the World, God said, "Let all of God's Angels Worship Him." (Hebrews 1:6 NLT)

Worship, Walk

Happy are those who hear the joyful call to Worship, for they will Walk in the light of Your presence, Lord. (Psalm 89:15 NLT)

Worship Him, Wonders

Go ahead and give God thanks for all the glorious things He has done! Go ahead and Worship Him! Tell everyone about His Wonders! (Psalm 105:1 TPT)

Wait, Who

> So, the Lord must Wait for you to come to Him so He can show you His love and compassion. For the Lord is a faithful God. Blessed are those Who Wait for His help. (Isaiah 30:18 NLT)

Wait

> I Wait quietly before God, for my victory comes from Him. (Psalm 62:1 NLT)

Wait, Watch

> My strength is found when I Wait upon You. Watch over me, God, for You are my mountain fortress; You set me on high! (Psalm 59:9 TPT)

With God, We Wait

> But We have the true hope that comes from being made right With God, and by the Spirit We Wait eagerly for this hope. (Galatians 5:5 TPT)

Written, We Wait

> Such things were Written in the Scriptures long ago to teach us. And the Scriptures give us hope and encouragement as We Wait patiently for God's promises to be fulfilled. (Romans 15:4 NLT)

Waiting, Sins Washed Away

> What are you Waiting for? Get up and be baptized. Have your Sins Washed Away by calling on the name of the Lord. (Acts 22:16 NLT)

With the Lord, Waiting

> Here's what I've learned through it all: Don't give up; don't be impatient; be entwined as one With the Lord.

Be brave and courageous, and never lose hope. Yes, keep on Waiting—for He will never disappoint you! (Psalm 27:14 TPT)

Eagerly Waiting

But our citizenship is in heaven. We are Eagerly Waiting for a Savior from there, the Lord Jesus Christ. (Philippians 3:20 EHV)

Waited, God Would

I Waited and Waited and Waited some more, patiently, knowing God Would come through for me. Then, at last, He bent down and listened to my cry. (Psalm 40:1 TPT)

When some Believers Came, Walk in Truth

It gave me great joy When some believers Came and testified about your faithfulness to the Truth, telling how you continue to Walk in it. (3 John 1:3 NIV)

Walk, Wise

So, pay close attention to how you Walk, not as unwise people but as Wise. Make the most of your time because the days are evil. (Ephesians 5:15–16 TLV)

Walking in His Ways, Written, Wherever

And keep the charge of the Lord Your God, Walking in His Ways, keeping His statutes, His commandments, His judgments, and His testimonies, as it is Written in the Law of Moses, that you may prosper in all that you do and Wherever you turn. (1 Kings 2:3 MEV)

God's Ways, Won't Walk with the Wicked

What delight comes to the one who follows God's Ways! He Won't Walk in step With the Wicked, nor share the sinner's way, nor be found sitting in the scorner's seat. (Psalm 1:1 TPT)

Walk with Me, What is Right, Salvation Will Unfold

> The life that pleases Me is a life lived in the gratitude of grace, always choosing to Walk With Me in What is Right. This is the sacrifice I desire from you. If you do this, more of my Salvation Will Unfold for you. (Psalm 50:23 TPT)

Walked with, Worked with

> But it was You, my intimate friend—one like a brother to me. It was You, my adviser, the companion I Walked With and Worked With! (Psalm 55:13 TPT)

Walk

> For You have saved my soul from death and my feet from stumbling so that I can Walk before the Lord bathed in His life-giving light. (Psalm 56:13 TPT)

Will Live Enthroned with You Forever, Walking

> I Will Live Enthroned With You Forever! Guard me, God, With Your unending, unfailing love. Let me live my days Walking in grace and truth before You. (Psalm 61:7 TPT)

Walk Faithfully, Following My Ways

> O that my people would once and for all listen to Me and Walk Faithfully in My footsteps, following My Ways. (Psalm 81:13 TPT)

Wrapping Himself around Me, Walk along His Paths with Integrity

> For the Lord God is brighter than the brilliance of a sunrise! Wrapping Himself around Me like a shield, He is so generous with His gifts of grace and glory. Those who Walk along His Paths With Integrity Will never lack one thing they need, for He provides it all! (Psalm 84:11 TPT)

Work, Walk Onward in Your Truth, Within

> Teach me more about You, how You Work and how You move, so that I can Walk Onward in Your Truth until everything Within me brings honor to Your name. (Psalm 86:11 TPT)

Who Know the Triumphant Shout, Walk in the Radiance

> O Lord, how blessed are the people Who Know the Triumphant Shout, for they Walk in the Radiance of Your presence. (Psalm 89:15 TPT)

Never Walk Away, Nor Would He Forsake

> For the Lord will Never Walk Away from His cherished ones, Nor Would He Forsake His chosen ones who belong to Him. (Psalm 94:14 TPT)

When You Walk, Walking in the Light of God's Word

> You're only truly happy When You Walk in total integrity, Walking in the Light of God's Word. (Psalm 119:1 TPT)

Word of God, Walking in Its Truth

> How can a young man stay pure? Only by living in the Word of God and Walking in its Truth. (Psalm 119:9 TPT)

Walk

> I've chosen to obey Your truth and Walk in the splendor-light of all that You teach me. (Psalm 119:30 TPT)

Will Walk with You

> I Will Walk With You in complete freedom, for I seek to follow Your every command. (Psalm 119:45 TPT)

Walking

> See if there is any path of pain I'm Walking on, and lead me back to Your glorious, everlasting way—the path that brings me back to You. (Psalm 139:24 TPT)

Walk on the Highway of Light, Way Shines

> But the lovers of God Walk on the Highway of Light, and their Way Shines brighter and brighter until the perfect day. (Proverbs 4:18 TPT)

Walking in Righteousness

> Abundant life is discovered by Walking in Righteousness. (Proverbs 12:28a TPT)

With You, You Will Not Drown, Walk through Persecution, Will Not Burn

> When you pass through the deep, stormy sea, you can count on Me to be there With You. When you pass through raging rivers, You Will Not Drown. When you Walk through Persecution like fiery flames, you Will Not be Burned; the flames Will not harm you. (Isaiah 43:2 TPT)

World, Those Who Embrace Me Will Never Walk in Darkness

> Then Jesus said, "I am light to the World, and Those Who Embrace Me Will experience life-giving light, and they Will Never Walk in Darkness." (John 8:12 TPT)

Work Hard, There Will Be Peace

> Work Hard to live together as one by the help of the Holy Spirit. Then There Will Be Peace. (Ephesians 4:3 NLV)

Work, Working for the Lord

> In all the Work you are given, do the best you can. Work as though you are Working for the Lord, not any earthly master. (Colossians 3:23 ERV)

Worked, Welfare

> He Worked enthusiastically for the good of His people and was an advocate for the Welfare of all His descendants. (Esther 10:3b NET)

Work Together for Good, Those Who Love God, Who Are Called

> And We know that God causes all things to Work Together for Good to those Who Love God, to those Who Are Called according to His purpose. (Romans 8:28 NASB)

Miracle-Working God

> Give thanks to the only Miracle-Working God! His tender love for us continues on forever! (Psalm 136:4 TPT)

Fearfully and Wonderfully Made, Works Are Wonderful, Full Well

> I Praise You because I am Fearfully and Wonderfully Made; Your Works Are Wonderful; I know that full Well. (Psalm 139:14 NIV)

We Are His Workmanship, Good Works, We should Walk

> For We Are His Workmanship, created in Christ Jesus for Good Works, which God prepared beforehand, that We should Walk in them. (Ephesians 2:10 ESV)

Always Will Be My King, Working Wonders all over the World

> You have always been, and Always Will Be My King. You are the mighty conqueror, Working Wonders all over the World. (Psalm 74:12 TPT)

Work, Starts with Believing

> Jesus answered, "The Work you can do for God Starts with Believing in the One He has sent." (John 6:29 TPT)

We Want, Your Wonderful Works

> God, our hearts spill over with praise to You! We overflow with thanks, for Your name is the "Near One." All We Want to talk about is Your Wonderful Works! (Psalm 75:1a TPT)

Whole Heart, His Works, Wherever

> I will bless and praise the Lord with my Whole Heart! Let all His Works throughout the earth, Wherever His dominion stretches—let everything bless the Lord! (Psalm 103:22 TPT)

Artistic Work

> Yet still, Yahweh, You are our Father. We are like clay and You are our Potter. Each one of us is the creative, Artistic Work of Your hands. (Isaiah 64:8 TPT)

Those Who Love, Will Come, Light Will Reveal, it Was God, Fruitful Works

> But Those Who Love the truth Will Come into the Light, for the Light Will Reveal that it Was God Who produced their Fruitful Works. (John 3:21 TPT)

Who Leads us, Works through us all

> And He is the perfect Father Who Leads us all, Works through us all, and lives in us all! (Ephesians 4:6 TPT)

Want You Who Believe in God Will Do Good Works

> How true and faithful is this message! I Want You to especially emphasize these truths, so that those Who

Believe in God Will be careful to devote themselves to Doing Good Works. It is always beautiful and profitable for believers to do Good Works. (Titus 3:8 TPT)

The Word, Word Was With God, Word Was God

In the beginning was the Word, and the Word Was With God, and the Word Was God. (John 1:1 KJ21)

Written, Word

But He replied, "It is Written, 'Man shall not live by bread alone, but by every Word that comes from the mouth of God.'" (Matthew 4:4 ESV)

Withers, Word of Our God

But even though grass Withers and the flower fades, the Word of Our God stands strong forever! (Isaiah 40:8 TPT)

Words

The Spirit of the Lord speaks through me; His Words are upon my tongue. (2 Samuel 23:2 NLT)

Word of God Discerns the Thoughts and Intents of the Heart

For the Word of God is living, and active, and sharper than any two-edged sword, and piercing even to the dividing of soul and spirit, of both joints and marrow, and quick to Discern the Thoughts and Intents of The Heart. (Hebrews 4:12 ASV)

Word of the Lord

All people are like grass. Their greatness is like the flowers. The grass dries up and the flowers fall off. But the Word of the Lord will last forever. (1 Peter 1:24–25a NLV)

Words, Worth, Wealth, Whole World

> The Words you speak to Me are Worth more than all the riches and Wealth in the Whole World! (Psalm 119:72 TPT)

Word of God

> I trust in the Lord. And I praise Him! I trust in the Word of God. And I praise Him! (Psalm 56:10 TPT)

Will, Your Living Words, Written

> I delight to fulfill Your Will, my God, for Your Living Words are Written upon the pages of my heart. (Psalm 40:8 TPT)

Word of God

> Standing firm in the heavens and fastened to eternity is the Word of God. (Psalm 119:89 TPT)

God Will Bless, Who Listen, Word of God

> "Yes," said Jesus, "but God Will Bless all Who Listen to the Word of God and carefully obey everything they hear." (Luke 11:28 TPT)

Eternal and Living Word of God, Seed Planted Within You, Will Live

> For through the Eternal and Living Word of God you have been born again. And this "Seed" that He Planted Within You can never be destroyed but Will Live and grow inside of you forever. (1 Peter 1:23 TPT)

World, I Have Defeated the World

> I have told you this, so that you might have peace in your hearts because of Me. While you are in the World, you will have to suffer. But cheer up! I have Defeated the World. (John 16:33 CEV)

Wisdom

> By Wisdom the Lord founded the earth; by understanding He created the heavens. (Proverbs 3:19 NLT)

> Teach us to number each of our days so that We may grow in Wisdom. (Psalm 90:12 GW)

> Let the message about Christ, in all its richness, fill your lives. Teach and counsel each other With all the Wisdom He gives. Sing psalms and hymns and spiritual songs to God with thankful hearts. (Colossians 3:16 NLT)

> But if any of you lack Wisdom, you should pray to God, Who Will give it to you; because God gives generously and graciously to all. (James 1:5 GNT)

> But the Wisdom from above is always pure, filled with peace, considerate and teachable. It is filled with love and never displays prejudice or hypocrisy in any form. (James 3:17 TPT)

> Lord, You created so many things! With Your Wisdom, You made them all. The earth is full of the living things You made. (Psalm 104:24 ERV)

> Praise the one who used Wisdom to make the skies! His faithful love will last forever. (Psalm 136:5 ERV)

> He said to mankind, "The fear of the Lord—that is Wisdom. And to turn from evil is understanding." (Job 28:28 CSB)

> But all Wisdom and knowledge are hidden away in Him. (Colossians 2:3 CEV)

True Wisdom, He Knows What We Should Do

> But True Wisdom and power are God's. He alone Knows What We Should Do; He understands. (Job 12:13 TLB)

Who, Wonderful, Wisdom

> This also comes from the Lord of Hosts, Who has made His counsel Wonderful and His Wisdom great. (Isaiah 28:29 AMP)

Lamb Who Was Worthy, Wealth, Wisdom

> And sang in a loud voice: "The Lamb Who Was killed is Worthy to receive power, Wealth, Wisdom, and strength, honor, glory, and praise!" (Revelation 5:12 GNT)

Want, Wisdom, Wise

> If you Want to grow in Wisdom, spend time with the Wise. (Proverbs 13:20a TPT)

Be Wise, Who Understands Ways of God, Wisdom's

> If you consider yourself to be Wise and one Who Understands the Ways of God, advertise it with a beautiful, fruitful life guided by Wisdom's gentleness. (James 3:13a TPT)

Walk in Wisdom

> My child, never drift off course from these two goals for your life: to Walk in Wisdom and to discover your purpose. Don't ever forget how they empower you. (Proverbs 3:21 TPT)

Wisdom, Word, Within

> Wisdom is a gift from a generous God, and every Word He speaks is full of revelation and becomes a fountain of understanding Within you. (Proverbs 2:6 TPT)

Wisdom, Cannot Be Purchased with Jewels, Worthless

> Wisdom is more valuable than gold and crystal. It Cannot Be Purchased With Jewels mounted in fine gold. Coral and jasper are Worthless in trying to get it. The price of Wisdom is far above rubies. (Job 28:17–18 NLT)

Way to Wisdom, Where It Can Be Found, Whole Earth, Winds

> God alone understands the Way to Wisdom; He knows Where It Can Be Found, for He looks throughout the Whole Earth and sees everything under the heavens. He decided how hard the Winds should blow and how much rain should fall. (Job 28:23–25 NLT)

Wisdom, Wise, Praise Will Be Sung

> Wisdom begins with fear and respect for the Lord. Those who obey Him are very Wise. Praises Will Be Sung to Him forever. (Psalm 111:10 ERV)

Free from Worry

> My people will live Free from Worry in secure, quiet homes of peace. (Isaiah 32:18 TPT)

Never Worry

> Jesus taught His disciples, saying, "Listen to me. Never let anxiety enter your hearts. Never Worry about any of your needs, such as food or clothing." (Luke 12:22 TPT)

Worth More, Whole Flock of Birds

> God even knows how many hairs are on your head. So don't be afraid. You are Worth More than a Whole Flock of Birds. (Matthew 10:30–31 ERV)

Will Be a Sign, Baby Wrapped

> And this Will Be a Sign for you; you will find a Baby Wrapped in swaddling cloths and lying in a manger. (Luke 2:12 ESV)

Weapons We Fight With, World

> The Weapons We Fight With are not the Weapons of the World. On the contrary, they have divine power to demolish strongholds. (2 Corinthians 10:4 NIV)

Wonderful Day, Will Sing, What He Has Done

> In that Wonderful Day you Will Sing: "Thank the Lord! Praise His name! Tell the nations What He Has Done. Let them know how mighty He is! (Isaiah 12:4 NLT)

Wonderful Counselor

> For to us a child is born, to us a Son is given, and the government will be on His shoulders. And He will be called Wonderful Counselor, Mighty God, Everlasting Father, Prince of Peace. (Isaiah 9:6 NIV)

Your Will Be Done

> Your kingdom come. Your Will Be Done On earth as it is in heaven. (Matthew 6:10 AMP)

Whosoever Drinketh of the Water, Well of Water

> But Whosoever Drinketh of the Water that I shall give him shall never thirst; but the Water that I shall give him shall be in him a Well of Water springing up into everlasting life. (John 4:14 KJ21)

With Water and With Blood

> Jesus Christ is the one who came. He came With Water and With Blood. He did not come by Water only. No, Jesus came by both Water and blood. And the Spirit tells us that this is true. The Spirit is the truth. (1 John 5:6 ERV)

Washed With Pure Water

> Sprinkled with the blood of Christ, our hearts have been made free from a guilty conscience, and our bodies have been Washed With Pure Water. So come near to God with a sincere heart, full of confidence because of our faith in Christ. (Hebrews 10:22 ERV)

Whoever Believes, Living Water

> Whoever Believes in me, as the Scripture has said, "Out of his heart will flow rivers of Living Water." (John 7:38 ESV)

Who Is Worthy to Be Praised

> I will call upon the Lord, Who Is Worthy to Be Praised; And I am saved from my enemies. (Psalm 18:3 AMP)

Worthy of Praise

> Great is the Lord! He is most Worthy of Praise! No one can measure His greatness. (Psalm 145:3 NLT)

I Am the Way

> Jesus told him, "I Am the Way, the truth, and the life. No one can come to the Father except through me." (John 14:6 NLT)

Willing, Will Obey Me, You Will Feast

> If you have a Willing heart to let Me help you, and if you Will Obey Me, You Will Feast on the blessings of an abundant harvest. (Isaiah 1:19 TPT)

Wondrous Works of God

> Hear this, O Job; stop and consider the Wondrous Works of God. (Job 37:14 NRSVA)

All His Wondrous Works

> Sing to Him, sing praise to Him; tell about All His Wondrous Works! (1 Chronicles 16:9 CSB)

All His Wonderful Acts

> Sing to Him, sing praises to Him; Speak of All His Wonderful Acts and devoutly praise them. (Psalm 105:2 AMP)

Behold Wondrous Things

> Open my eyes, that I may Behold Wondrous Things out of Your law. (Psalm 119:18 AMPC)

Your Love is Wonderful

> Your Love is Wonderful. By Your power You save from their enemies those who trust you. (Psalm 17:7 ICB)

Who Alone Does Wonderful Things

> Blessed be the Lord God, the God of Israel, Who Alone Does Wonderful Things! (Psalm 72:18 AMP)

PRAYERS (USING W WORDS)

We **worship** You, Lord, because You are most **worthy** of praise! We know, Jesus, that You are the only **way** to God. We are in awe because of Your **willingness** to forgive and love us. We have been **washed** by the blood of the lamb. We are grateful for Your **Living Water**. May Your **will** be done on earth as it is in heaven. You are our **wonderful** Prince of Peace. We don't need to **worry** because Your **Word** says You care for us. Thank You for creating the **wonders** of the **whole world**. Your **wisdom** has helped us become **wise**. We are Your **workmanship**, and You continue to **work** in us and through us. You are **worthy**, Lord, and You are **worth** so much to us as we **worship** You. We praise You, God, for Your beautiful **Word**.

We pray this in Your **wonderful** Son's name.

Amen.

X

Example

> For you were called to this, because Christ also suffered for you, leaving you an eXample, that you should follow in His steps. (1 Peter 2:21 CSB)

> Don't let anyone look down on you because you are young, but set an eXample for the believers in speech, in conduct, in love, in faith and in purity. (1 Timothy 4:12 NIV)

> So don't allow your hearts to grow dull or lose your enthusiasm, but follow the eXample of those who fully received what God has promised because of their strong faith and patient endurance. (Hebrews 6:12 TPT)

Examples

> The lovers of God will walk in integrity, and their children are fortunate to have godly parents as their eXamples. (Proverbs 20:7 TPT)

Example, Experiencing

> We point to you as an eXample of unwavering faith for all the churches of God. We boast about how you continue to demonstrate unflinching endurance through all the persecutions and painful trials you are eXperiencing. (2 Thessalonians 1:4 TPT)

Experience

> Like newborn babies, you must crave pure spiritual milk so that you will grow into a full eXperience of salvation. Cry out for this nourishment. (1 Peter 2:2 NLT)

> And patient endurance will refine our character, and proven character leads us back to hope. And this hope is not a disappointing fantasy, because we can now eXperience the endless love of God cascading into our hearts through the Holy Spirit who lives in us! (Romans 5:4–5 TPT)

> Because of You, I know the path of life, as I taste the fullness of joy in Your presence. At Your right side I eXperience divine pleasures forevermore! (Psalm 16:11 TPT)

> Drink deeply of the pleasures of this God. eXperience for yourself the joyous mercies He gives to all who turn to hide themselves in Him. (Psalm 34:8 TPT)

> So, I've learned from my eXperience that God protects the vulnerable. For I was broken and brought low, but He answered me and came to my rescue! (Psalm 116:6 TPT)

> I bow down before Your divine presence and bring You my deepest worship as I eXperience Your tender love and Your living truth. For Your Word and the fame of Your name have been magnified above all else! (Psalm 138:2 TPT)

> I speak to you this eternal truth: whoever cherishes my words and keeps them will never eXperience death. (John 8:51 TPT)

Bring Me everyone who is called by My name, the ones I created to eXperience My glory. I Myself formed them to be who they are and made them for My glory. (Isaiah 43:7 TPT)

I am the Gateway. To enter through Me is to eXperience life, freedom, and satisfaction. (John 10:9 TPT)

My purpose for telling you these things is so that the joy that I eXperience will fill your hearts with overflowing gladness! (John 15:11 TPT)

Eternal life means to know and eXperience You as the only True God, and to know and eXperience Jesus Christ, as the Son whom You have sent. (John 17:3 TPT)

For those living in constant goodness and doing what pleases Him, seeking an unfading glory and honor and imperishable virtue, will eXperience eternal life. (Romans 2:7 TPT)

And it's true: "Everyone who calls on the Lord's name will eXperience new life." (Romans 10:13 TPT)

We are among those who have faith and eXperience true life! (Hebrews 10:39b TPT)

Expectation

My soul, wait thou only upon God; for my eXpectation is from Him. (Psalm 62:5 KJV)

All praise to God, the Father of our Lord Jesus Christ. It is by His great Mercy that we have been born again, because God raised Jesus Christ from the dead. Now we live with great eXpectation. (1 Peter 1:3 NLT)

Praise Yahweh forever, the God of Israel! He is the one and only God of wonders, surpassing every eXpectation. (Psalm 72:18 TPT)

Shout in celebration of praise to the Lord! Everyone who loves the Lord and delights in Him will cherish His words and be blessed beyond eXpectation. (Psalm 112:1 TPT)

Living within you is the Christ who floods you with the eXpectation of glory! This mystery of Christ, embedded within us, becomes a heavenly treasure chest of hope filled with the riches of glory for His people, and God wants everyone to know it! (Colossians 1:27 TPT)

Exalted

The eXalted God is my shield, the one who delivers the morally upright. (Psalm 7:10 NET)

The fear of man brings a snare, but whoever trusts in and puts his confidence in the Lord will be eXalted and safe. (Proverbs 29:25 AMP)

I will be glad and shout in triumph. I will sing praise to Your eXalted name, O Most High. (Psalm 9:2 TPT)

Lord God, be eXalted as You soar throughout the heavens. May Your shining glory be seen in the skies! Let it be seen high above over all the earth! (Psalm 57:5 TPT)

We can do nothing but leap for joy all day long, for we know who You are and what You do, and You've eXalted us on high. (Psalm 89:16 TPT)

It's so enjoyable to come before You with uncontainable praises spilling from our hearts! How we love to sing our praises over and over to You, to the matchless God, high and eXalted over all! (Psalm 92:1 TPT)

But You, O Lord, are eXalted forever in the highest place of endless glory. (Psalm 92:8 TPT)

For you are King-God, the Most High God over all the earth. You are eXalted above every supernatural power! (Psalm 97:9 TPT)

Lord God, be eXalted as you soar throughout the heavens. May Your shining glory be seen high above all the earth! (Psalm 108:5 TPT)

The character of God is a tower of strength, for the lovers of God delight to run into His heart and be eXalted on high. (Proverbs 18:10 TPT)

Exclaim

My whole being will eXclaim, "Who is like you, Lord? You rescue the poor from those too strong for them, the poor and needy from those who rob them." (Psalm 35:10 NIV)

Extinguish

Do not eXtinguish the Spirit. (1 Thessalonians 5:19 EHV)

Explain

Teach me, and I will be silent; eXplain to me how I have been wrong. (Job 6:24 TLV)

Exercise

So, prepare your minds for action and eXercise self-control. Put all your hope in the gracious salvation that will come to you when Jesus Christ is revealed to the world. (1 Peter 1:13 NLT)

Expressions of Love, Exceeding, Expectations

O Lord, our God, no one can compare with You. Such wonderful works and miracles are all found with You! And You think of us all the time with Your countless eXpressions Of Love—far eXceeding our eXpectations! (Psalm 40:5 TPT)

PERSONAL REFLECTIONS IN PRAISING GOD

Expectation, Example, Exalted

> We look away from the natural realm and we focus our
> attention and eXpectation onto Jesus who birthed faith
> within us and who leads us forward into faith's perfection.
> His eXample is this: Because His heart was focused on
> the joy of knowing that you would be His, He endured
> the agony of the cross and conquered its humiliation,
> and now sits eXalted at the right hand of the throne of
> God! (Hebrews 12:2 TPT)

Excuses

> Obviously, the law applies to those to whom it was given,
> for its purpose is to keep people from having eXcuses,
> and to show that the entire world is guilty before God.
> (Romans 3:19 NLT)

<u>PRAYERS</u> (USING X WORDS)

Thank You, God, for letting us *eXperience* the hope we have in You.
We hope we can *eXperience* eternal life someday. You have *eXplained*
so many revelations to us in Your Word. It has been more than we
could have ever *eXpected*. We do not want to *eXtinguish* the power
of the Holy Spirit who lives in us. We praise You for Your *eXpressions*
of love and faithfulness to us. As we look back, we can see Your hand
providing us with many godly *eXamples*. These are wonderful believers,
and we have been blessed beyond *eXpectations*. You are our shield,
and we delight in You because You surpassed all of our *eXpectations*.
We worship and *eXalt* You on high.

We worship our *eXcellent* Savior, Jesus. In Your *eXalted* name, we
pray.

Amen.

Y

You, Yahweh, Your

> But I'll keep coming closer and closer to You, Lord Yahweh, for Your name is good to me. I'll keep telling the world of Your awesome works, my faithful and glorious God! (Psalm 73:28 TPT)

> I am Yahweh, the only God there is, and You'll never find another. I will strengthen You for victory, even though You do not intimately know who I am. (Isaiah 45:5 TPT)

> Yahweh has established His throne in heaven; His kingdom rules the entire universe. (Psalm 103:19 TPT)

> For this reason, the Lord is still waiting to show His favor to You so He can show You His marvelous love. He waits to be gracious to You. He sits on His throne ready to show mercy to You. For Yahweh is the Lord of justice, faithful to keep His promises. Overwhelmed with bliss are all who will entwine their hearts in Him, waiting for Him to help them. (Isaiah 30:18 TPT)

> I know Yahweh gives me all that I ask for and brings victory to His anointed King. My deliverance cry will be heard in His holy heaven. By His mighty hand miracles will manifest through His saving strength. Some find their strength in their weapons and wisdom, but my

miracle-deliverance can never be won by men. Our boast is in Yahweh our God, who makes us strong and gives us victory! (Psalm 20:6–7 TPT)

Look! Yahweh now reigns as King! He has covered Himself with majesty and strength, wearing them as His splendor-garments. Regal power surrounds Him as he sits securely on His throne. He's in charge of it all, the entire world, and He knows what He's doing! (Psalm 93:1 TPT)

The Lord Yahweh will reveal to them who He really is, and the Egyptians will know Him intimately. They will worship Him with sacrifices and burnt offerings. They will make vows to the Lord Yahweh, and they will keep them. (Isaiah 19:21 TPT)

Because I set You, Yahweh, always close to me, my confidence will never be weakened, for I experience Your wraparound presence every moment. (Psalm 16:8 TPT)

Direct me, Yahweh, throughout my journey so I can experience Your plans for my life. Reveal the life-paths that are pleasing to You. (Psalm 25:4 TPT)

So, they will know that You, and You alone, are Yahweh, the only Most High God exalted over all the earth! (Psalm 83:18 TPT)

And God said to Moses, 'I am Yahweh—the Lord.' (Exodus 6:2 NLT)

The Lord is a warrior; Yahweh is His name! (Exodus 15:3 NLT)

The Lord passed in front of Moses, calling out, "Yahweh! The Lord! The God of compassion and mercy! I am slow to anger and filled with unfailing love and faithfulness." (Exodus 34:6 NLT)

Then they will know that Your name is Yahweh—that You alone are the Lord. They will know that You are God Most High, ruler over all the earth! (Psalm 83:18 ERV)

He is the one who made the mountains. He created the wind. He lets people know His thoughts. He changes the darkness into dawn. He walks over the mountains of the earth. His name is Yahweh, Lord God All-Powerful. (Amos 4:13 ERV)

He built his upper rooms above the skies. He put His skies over the earth. He calls for the waters of the sea and pours them out as rain on the land. Yahweh is His name. (Amos 9:6 ERV)

I will thank the Lord for His righteousness; I will sing about the name of Yahweh the Most High. (Psalm 7:17 HCSB)

Yahweh, our Lord, how magnificent is Your name throughout the earth! You have covered the heavens with Your majesty. (Psalm 8:1 HCSB)

I will worship You, Yahweh, with extended hands as my whole heart erupts with praise! I will tell everyone everywhere about Your wonderful works! (Psalm 9:1 TPT)

Could there be any other God like Yahweh? For there is not a more secure foundation than You. (Psalm 18:31 TPT)

So, I thank You, Yahweh, with my praises! I will sing my song to the highest God, so all among the nations will hear me. (Psalm 18:49 TPT)

Be in awe before His majesty. Be in awe before such power and might! Come worship wonderful Yahweh, arrayed in all His splendor, bowing in worship as He appears in the beauty of holiness. Give Him the honor due His name. Worship Him wearing the glory-garments of Your holy, priestly calling! (Psalm 29:2 TPT)

Sing to God! Sing praises to His name. Exalt Him who rides on the clouds—His name is Yahweh—and rejoice before Him. (Psalm 68:4 HCSB)

Sing to Yahweh, praise His name; proclaim His salvation from day to day. (Psalm 96:2 HCSB)

My soul, praise Yahweh, and all that is within me, praise His holy name. (Psalm 103:1 HCSB)

Hallelujah! Give praise, servants of Yahweh; praise the name of Yahweh. Let the name of Yahweh be praised both now and forever. (Psalm 113:1–2 HCSB)

From the rising of the sun to its setting, let the name of Yahweh be praised. Yahweh is exalted above all the nations, His glory above the heavens. Who is like Yahweh our God—the One enthroned on high. (Psalm 113:3–5 HCSB)

Our help is in the name of Yahweh, the Maker of heaven and earth. (Psalm 124:8 HCSB)

Yahweh is great and is highly praised; His greatness is unsearchable. (Psalm 145:3 HCSB)

My mouth will declare Yahweh's praise; let every living thing praise His holy name forever and ever. (Psalm 145:21 HCSB)

They each held the harps of God and they were singing the song of Moses, God's servant, and the song of the Lamb: "Mighty and marvelous are Your miracles, Lord Yahweh, God Almighty! Righteous and true are Your ways, O Sovereign King of the ages!" (Revelation 15:3 TPT)

Yahweh, You

> But the Lord Yahweh is always faithful to place You on a firm foundation and guard You from the Evil One. (2 Thessalonians 3:3 TPT)

> "I will be a true Father to You, and You will be my beloved sons and daughters," says the Lord Yahweh Almighty. (2 Corinthians 6:18 TPT)

You, Yahweh, Your

> You are to love the Lord Yahweh, Your God, with a passionate heart, from the depths of Your soul, with Your every thought, and with all Your strength. This is the great and supreme commandment. (Mark 12:30 TPT)

Yahweh

> With justice the Lord Yahweh, Commander of Angel Armies, displays His greatness, and righteousness sets Him apart as the holy God. (Isaiah 5:16 TPT)

Yields

> Sweet friendships refresh the soul and awaken our hearts with joy, for good friends are like the anointing oil that Yields the fragrant incense of God's presence. (Proverbs 27:9 TPT)

Yield, Your, You

> But the angel reassured her, saying, "Do not Yield to Your fear, Mary, for the Lord has found delight in You and has chosen to surprise You with a wonderful gift." (Luke 1:30 TPT)

> Do not Yield to fear, for I am always near. Never turn Your gaze from me, for I am Your faithful God. I will infuse You with my strength and help You in every situation. I will hold You firmly with my victorious right hand. (Isaiah 41:10 TPT)

Let me emphasize this: As You Yield to the dynamic life and power of the Holy Spirit, You will abandon the cravings of Your self-life. (Galatians 5:16 TPT)

I am with You now, even close to You, so never Yield to fear. I will bring Your children from the east; from the west I will gather You. (Isaiah 43:5 TPT)

I leave the gift of peace with You—my peace. Not the kind of fragile peace given by the world, but my perfect peace. Don't Yield to fear or be troubled in Your hearts—instead, be courageous! (John 14:27 TPT)

You, You'll, Yielding

We pray that You would walk in the ways of true righteousness, pleasing God in every good thing You do. Then You'll become fruit-bearing branches, Yielding to His life, and maturing in the rich experience of knowing God in His fullness! (Colossians 1:10 TPT)

Your, Yield

Then I will give You rain in due season, and the land shall Yield her increase, and the trees of the field shall Yield their fruit. (Leviticus 26:4 KJ21)

Yield

And don't let us Yield to temptation, but rescue us from the evil one. (Matthew 6:13 NLT)

Then the earth will Yield its harvests, and God, our God, will richly bless us. (Psalm 67:6 NLT)

But the wisdom from above is first of all pure. It is also peace loving, gentle at all times, and willing to Yield to others. It is full of mercy and the fruit of good deeds. It shows no favoritism and is always sincere. (James 3:17 NLT)

When I saw Him, I fell down at His feet as good as dead, but He laid His right hand on me and I heard His reassuring voice saying: Don't Yield to fear. I am the Beginning and I am the End. (Revelation 1:17 TPT)

Yields

Sweet friendships refresh the soul and awaken our hearts with joy, for good friends are like the anointing oil that Yields the fragrant incense of God's presence. (Proverbs 27:9 TPT)

Yielded

God always makes His grace visible in Christ, who includes us as partners of His endless triumph Through our Yielded lives He spreads the fragrance of the knowledge of God everywhere we go. (2 Corinthians 2:14 TPT)

Yearning, You

O God of my life, I'm lovesick for You in this weary wilderness. I thirst with the deepest longings to love You more, with cravings in my heart that can't be described. Such Yearning grips my soul for You, my God! (Psalm 63:1 TPT)

Yearnings, Your

I'm lovesick with Yearnings for more of Your salvation, for my heart is entwined with Your Word. (Psalm 119:81 TPT)

Yearn, You

At night I Yearn for You with all my heart; in the morning my spirit reaches out to You. When You display Your judgments on the earth, people learn the ways of righteousness. (Isaiah 26:9 TPT)

Yearn, You, Your

> I Yearn to come and be face-to-face with You and get to know You. For I long to impart to You some spiritual gift that will empower You to stand strong in Your faith. (Romans 1:11 TPT)

Your, Yearn

> Christ's resurrection is Your resurrection too. This is why we are to Yearn for all that is above, for that's where Christ sits enthroned at the place of all power, honor, and authority! (Colossians 3:1 TPT)

Yearning

> The entire universe is standing on tiptoe, Yearning to see the unveiling of God's glorious sons and daughters! (Romans 8:19 TPT)

Year

> From one Sabbath to the next, one month to the next, one Year to the next, all humanity will come to worship Me! (Isaiah 66:23 TPT)

Your, Year

> Wisdom will extend Your life, making every Year more fruitful than the one before. (Proverbs 9:11 TPT)

> Does worry add anything to Your life? Can it add one more Year, or even one day? (Luke 12:25 TPT)

Years

> Then God said, "Let lights appear in the sky to separate the day from the night. Let them be signs to mark the seasons, days, and Years." (Genesis 1:14 NLT)

> I consider the days of old, and remember the Years of long ago. (Psalm 77:5 NRSVA)

But do not overlook this one fact, beloved, that with the Lord one day is as a thousand Years, and a thousand Years as one day. (2 Peter 3:8 ESV)

You, Years

Living in the worship and awe of God will bring You many Years of contented living. So how could the wicked ever expect to have a long, happy life? (Proverbs 10:27 TPT)

You, Your, Years

And He called Him Lord, saying, "Lord, You formed the earth in the beginning and with Your own hands You crafted the cosmos. They will both one day disappear, but You will remain forever! They will all fade like a worn-out garment, And they will be changed like clothes, and You will fold them up and put them away. But You are 'I AM.' You never change, Years without end!" (Hebrews 1:10–12 TPT)

My child, never forget the things I have taught you. Store my commands in Your heart. If You do this, you will live many Years, and Your life will be satisfying. (Proverbs 3:1–2 NLT)

Yelled

"Away with Him," they Yelled. "Away with Him—crucify Him!" "What? Crucify Your king?" Pilate asked. "We have no king but Caesar," the chief priests shouted back. (John 19:15 NLT)

You, Yoke, Your

Come to Me, all who are weary and burdened, and I will give You rest. Take My Yoke upon You and learn from Me, for I am gentle and humble in heart, and You will find rest for Your souls. For My Yoke is easy and My burden is light. (Matthew 11:28–30 NIV)

Yoke, Young

> It is good for a man to bear the Yoke while he is Young. (Lamentations 3:27 NIV)

Yoked

> Do not be Yoked together with unbelievers. For what do righteousness and wickedness have in common? Or what fellowship can light have with darkness? (2 Corinthians 6:14 NIV)

Yesterday

> Jesus Christ is the same Yesterday, and today, and forever. (Hebrews 13:8 NIV)

Yesterday, Young

> It seems as though we were born Yesterday. We are too Young to know anything. Our days on earth are very short, like a shadow. (Job 8:9 ERV)

Ye, Yonder

> Then cometh Jesus with them unto a place called Gethsemane, and saith unto the disciples, Sit Ye here, while I go Yonder and pray. (Matthew 26:36 ASV)

<u>PRAYERS</u> (Using Y Words)

We are in awe of *You*, God, and we *yield* our lives to *You*. We exalt *You*, King *Yahweh*. Thank *You* for the *years* of *yesterday* that we have grown in *You*, Lord. We continue to *yearn* for more of *You*, Jesus, in our lives. Thank *You* for *Your yoke* upon us. We want to *yield* to *You* and all *Your* ways. We are grateful, Jesus, that *You* are the same *yesterday*, today, and forever. We trust *You*, dear Lord, and we know that *You* will never change. *You* are the Lord *Yahweh* Almighty, and we know *You* are the true God. We will love *You*, worship *You*, and praise *You* forever. Thank *You*, Father God, for keeping us in our *youth*.

We pray this in *Your* glorious name, *Yahweh!*

Amen.

Z

Zion

Listen! The watchmen are shouting in triumph! Lifting their voices together, they are singing for joy! For right before their eyes, they can see Yahweh returning to Zion! (Isaiah 52:8 TPT)

It is high and magnificent; the whole earth rejoices to see it! Mount Zion, the holy mountain, is the city of the great King! (Psalm 48:2 NLT)

From Mount Zion, the perfection of beauty, God shines in glorious radiance. (Psalm 50:2 NLT)

Why do you look with envy, O rugged mountains, at Mount Zion, where God has chosen to live, where the Lord Himself will live forever? (Psalm 68:16 NLT)

Those who trust in the Lord are as secure as Mount Zion; they will not be defeated but will endure forever. (Psalm 125:1 NLT)

Harmony is as refreshing as the dew from Mount Hermon that falls on the mountains of Zion. And there the Lord has pronounced His blessing, even life everlasting. (Psalm 133:3 NLT)

Glorify the Lord, O Jerusalem! Praise your God, O Zion! (Psalm 147:12 NLT)

Zion will be restored by justice; those who repent will be revived by righteousness. (Isaiah 1:27 NLT)

People from many nations will come and say, "Come, let us go up to the mountain of the Lord, to the house of Jacob's God. There He will teach us His ways, and we will walk in His paths." For the Lord's teaching will go out from Zion; His word will go out from Jerusalem. (Isaiah 2:3 NLT)

But everyone who calls on the name of the Lord will be saved, for some on Mount Zion in Jerusalem will escape, just as the Lord has said. These will be among the survivors whom the Lord has called. (Joel 2:32 NLT)

The Lord's voice will roar from Zion and thunder from Jerusalem, and the heavens and the earth will shake. But the Lord will be a refuge for His people, a strong fortress for the people of Israel. "Then you will know that I, the Lord Your God, live in Zion, my holy mountain. Jerusalem will be holy forever, and foreign armies will never conquer her again." (Joel 3:16–17 NLT)

Rejoice, O people of Zion! Shout in triumph, O people of Jerusalem! Look, your King is coming to you. He is righteous and victorious, yet He is humble, riding on a donkey—riding on a donkey's colt. (Zechariah 9:9 NLT)

Zion Realm

God's glory-light shines out of the Zion-Realm with the radiance of perfect beauty. (Psalm 50:2 TPT)

Zealously

Elijah replied, "I have Zealously served the Lord God Almighty." (1 Kings 19:10a NLT)

Zealously, God, we ask You to come save Israel from all her troubles, for You provide the ransom price for Your people! (Psalm 25:22 TPT)

In fact, that is why the twelve tribes of Israel Zealously worship God night and day, and they share the same hope I have. (Acts 26:7a NLT)

Zealous

I became very Zealous to honor God in everything I did, just like all of you today. (Acts 22:3b NLT)

Zeal

Yahweh goes out to battle like a hero and stirs up His passion and Zeal like a mighty warrior. Yes, His God-shout is a mighty battle cry; He will triumph heroically over all his foes. (Isaiah 42:13 TPT)

My Zeal and passion for the doctrines of Judaism distinguished me among my people, for I was far more advanced in my religious instruction than others my age. But then God called me by His grace, and chose me from my birth to be His. (Galatians 1:14–15 TPT)

Zechariah

Then the Spirit of God came upon Zechariah son of Jehoiada the priest. He stood before the people and said, "This is what God says: Why do you disobey the Lord's commands and keep yourselves from prospering? You have abandoned the Lord, and now He has abandoned you!" (2 Chronicles 24:20 NLT)

Uzziah sought God during the days of Zechariah, who taught him to fear God. And as long as the king sought guidance from the Lord, God gave him success. (2 Chronicles 26:5 NLT)

Then this message came to Zechariah from the Lord: "This is what the Lord of Heaven's Armies says: Judge fairly, and show mercy and kindness to one another." (Zechariah 7:8–9 NLT)

Zechariah and Elizabeth were righteous in God's eyes, careful to obey all of the Lord's commandments and regulations. (Luke 1:6 NLT)

And when Zacharias saw him, he was troubled, and fear fell upon him. But the angel said unto him, Fear not, Zacharias: for thy prayer is heard; and thy wife Elizabeth shall bear thee a son, and thou shalt call his name John. (Luke 1:12–13 KJ21)

Instantly Zacharias could speak again, and he began praising God. (Luke 1:64 TLB)

Then his father, Zechariah, was filled with the Holy Spirit and gave this prophecy: "Praise the Lord, the God of Israel, because He has visited and redeemed His people. He has sent us a mighty Savior from the royal line of His servant David, just as He promised through His holy prophets long ago." (Luke 1:67–70 NLT)

Annas and Caiaphas were the high priests. At this time a message from God came to John son of Zechariah, who was living in the wilderness. Then John went from place to place on both sides of the Jordan River, preaching that people should be baptized to show that they had repented of their sins and turned to God to be forgiven. (Luke 3:2–3 NLT)

Zebulun

Nevertheless, that time of darkness and despair will not go on forever. The land of Zebulun and Naphtali will be humbled, but there will be a time in the future when Galilee of the Gentiles, which lies along the road that runs between the Jordan and the sea, will be filled with glory. The people who walk in darkness will see a great light. For those who live in a land of deep darkness, a light will shine. (Isaiah 9:1–2 NLT)

Zephaniah

> The Lord Your God is with you as a hero who will save you. He takes great delight in you; He will quiet you with His love. He will rejoice over you with singing. (Zephaniah 3:17 EHV)

Zacchaeus

> When Jesus came by, he looked up at Zacchaeus and called him by name. "Zacchaeus!" he said. "Quick, come down! I must be a guest in your home today." Zacchaeus quickly climbed down and took Jesus to his house in great excitement and joy. Meanwhile, Zacchaeus stood before the Lord and said, "I will give half my wealth to the poor, Lord, and if I have cheated people on their taxes, I will give them back four times as much!" Jesus responded, "Salvation has come to this home today, for this man has shown himself to be a true son of Abraham. For the Son of Man came to seek and save those who are lost." (Luke 19:5, 6, 8, 9, 10 NLT)

Zebedee

> When Simon Peter realized what had happened, he fell to his knees before Jesus and said, "Oh, sir, please leave us—I'm too much of a sinner for you to have around." For he was awestruck by the size of their catch, as were the others with him, and his partners too—James and John, the sons of Zebedee. Jesus replied, "Don't be afraid! From now on you'll be fishing for the souls of men!" (Luke 5:8–10 TLB)

PRAYERS (USING Z WORDS)

Thank You for teaching us about Mount ***Zion***. We can lift our voices and sing for joy. You shine in glorious radiance, and You are the perfection of beauty. We love the story of ***Zacchaeus***, and we are grateful that You came to save those who are lost. We are very ***zealous*** in honoring You, God, in everything we do. We are blessed with the verse in ***Zephaniah*** that You take great delight in us and rejoice over us with singing. This is so beautiful. We praise You for filling ***Zechariah*** with the Holy Spirit and sending us a mighty Savior to redeem Your people. In ***Zebulun***, You provided a great light to shine for those who lived in deep darkness and despair. We praise You for the brilliant ***dazzling*** light that You provide for all of us.

Thank You, Jesus, for the ***zeal*** in our lives, and we pray in Your name.

Amen.

These beautiful psalms are wonderful for praising and worshipping God:

PSALM 91 (NIV)

Whoever dwells in the shelter of the Most High will rest in the shadow of the Almighty. I will say of the Lord, "He is my refuge and my fortress, my God, in whom I trust." Surely, He will save you from the fowler's snare and from the deadly pestilence. He will cover you with his feathers, and under His wings you will find refuge; His faithfulness will be your shield and rampart. You will not fear the terror of night, nor the arrow that flies by day, nor the pestilence that stalks in the darkness, nor the plague that destroys at midday. A thousand may fall at your side, ten thousand at your right hand, but it will not come near you. You will only observe with your eyes and see the punishment of the wicked. If you say, "The Lord is my refuge," and you make the Most High your dwelling, no harm will overtake you, no disaster will come near your tent. For he will command his angels concerning you to guard you in all your ways; they will lift you up in their hands, so that you will not strike your foot against a stone. You will tread on the lion and the cobra; you will trample the great lion and the serpent. "Because he loves me," says the Lord, "I will rescue him; I will protect him, for he acknowledges my name. He will call on me, and I will answer him; I will be with him in trouble, I will deliver him and honor him. With long life I will satisfy him and show him my salvation."

PSALM 96 (NLT)

Sing a new song to the Lord! Let the whole earth sing to the Lord! Sing to the Lord; praise His name. Each day proclaim the good news that He saves. Publish His glorious deeds among the nations. Tell everyone about the amazing things He does. Great is the Lord! He is most worthy of praise! He is to be feared above all gods. The gods of other nations are mere idols, but the Lord made the heavens! Honor and majesty surround him; strength and beauty fill his sanctuary.

O nations of the world, recognize the Lord; recognize that the Lord is glorious and strong. Give to the Lord the glory he deserves! Bring your offering and come into his courts. Worship the Lord in all His holy splendor. Let all the earth tremble before him. Tell all the nations, "The Lord reigns!" The world stands firm and cannot be shaken. He will judge all peoples fairly.

Let the heavens be glad, and the earth rejoice! Let the sea and everything in it shout His praise! Let the fields and their crops burst out with joy! Let the trees of the forest sing for joy before the Lord, for He is coming! He is coming to judge the earth. He will judge the world with justice, and the nations with His truth.

PSALM 97 (NIV)

The Lord reigns, let the earth be glad; let the distant shores rejoice. Clouds and thick darkness surround Him; righteousness and justice are the foundation of His throne. Fire goes before Him and consumes his foes on every side. His lightning lights up the world; the earth sees and trembles. The mountains melt like wax before the Lord, before the Lord of all the earth. The heavens proclaim His righteousness, and all peoples see His glory. All who worship images are put to shame, those who boast in idols— worship him, all you gods!

Zion hears and rejoices and the villages of Judah are glad because of your judgments, Lord. For you, Lord, are the Most High over all the earth; you are exalted far above all gods. Let those who love the Lord hate evil, for He guards the lives of his faithful ones and delivers them from the hand of the wicked. Light shine on the righteous and joy on the upright in heart. Rejoice in the Lord, you who are righteous, and praise His Holy Name.

CONCLUSION

I choose to believe.

I am chosen and appointed by Christ to go and bear fruit:

> You did not choose Me, but I chose you, and appointed you, that you should go and bear fruit, and that your fruit should remain, that the Father may give you whatever you ask Him in My name. (John 15:16 MEV)

I am chosen by God:

> God always does what He plans, and this is why He appointed Christ to choose us. (Ephesians 1:11 CEV)

I am sealed by God with the Holy Spirit.

> The truth is the Good News. When you heard the truth, you put your trust in Christ. Then God marked you by giving you His Holy Spirit as a promise. (Ephesians 1:13 NLV)

Thank You, Jesus, for choosing me before I was born. I am in awe!

I choose You above anything else!

I choose You, Father God.

I choose You, Lord Jesus.

I choose You, Holy Spirit.

I choose to believe You created the heavens and the earth and all living things.

I choose to believe in Your virgin birth, crucifixion, resurrection, and ascension.

I choose to believe You shed Your precious blood on the cross for me.

I choose to believe You died for me.

I choose to believe You rose from the dead and defeated death, hell, and the enemy.

I choose to believe You are seated at the right hand of the Father.

I choose to believe You are the Son of the living God.

I choose to believe You sent Your Holy Spirit to live in me.

I choose to believe You are the only way to eternal life.

I choose to believe You are the way, the truth, and the life—and no one comes to the Father except through You, Jesus.

I choose to believe that every knee shall bow and every tongue will confess that Jesus Christ is Lord.

I choose to believe You love me.

I choose to believe You created me.

I choose to believe I can confess and repent of my sins and that You will forgive me.

I choose to believe that You have a plan for my life.

I choose to believe in Your Word.

I choose to believe Your Word is the truth.

I choose to believe in Your life-changing, transforming power.

I choose to believe in the hope I have in You.

I choose to believe in forgiving others so that I can be forgiven.

NOTES FOR YOUR FAVORITE VERSES

www.ingramcontent.com/pod-product-compliance
Lightning Source LLC
Chambersburg PA
CBHW021659120626
46545CB00004B/1309